LIFE INSURANCE
in
ASIA

Winning
in the
Next Decade

LIFE
INSURANCE
in
ASIA

Winning
in the
Next Decade

STEPHAN BINDER
and
JOSEPH LUC NGAI

John Wiley & Sons (Asia) Pte. Ltd.

This publication is designed to provide accurate and authoritative information in regard to the subject matter covered. It is sold with the understanding that the publisher is not engaged in rendering professional services. If professional advice or other expert assistance is required, the services of a competent professional person should be sought.

Other Wiley Editorial Offices

John Wiley & Sons Inc., 111 River Street, Hoboken, NJ 07030, USA

John Wiley & Sons Ltd., The Atrium, Southern Gate, Chichester, West Sussex P019 8SQ, United Kingdom

John Wiley & Sons (Canada) Ltd., 5353 Dundas Street West, Suite 400, Toronto, Ontario M9B 6H8, Canada

John Wiley & Sons Australia Ltd., 42 McDougall Street, Milton, Queensland 4064, Australia

Wiley-VCH, Boschstrasse 12, D-69469 Weinheim, Germany

Library of Congress Cataloging-in-Publication Data

ISBN 978-0-470-82440-5

Typeset in 11/13.5 point, AGaramond by diacriTech, India.
Printed in Singapore by SNP Security Printing Pte. Ltd.
10 9 8 7 6 5 4 3 2 1

Contents

Acknowledgments

This book has drawn upon the collective experience of McKinsey & Company's Insurance Practice, accumulated over more than a decade. Needless to say, its authorship has been a tremendous team effort. Numerous people have contributed to the knowledge we have created in the life insurance industry in the region and we cannot possibly list them all here. However, there are a few people that we wish to specifically mention because this book could not have been written without them.

First of all, we would like to thank all of our friends in the industry who have contributed. In particular, we would like to thank **Dominic Leung**, Executive Vice President and Chief Insurance Business Officer of Ping An Insurance (Group) Company of China for sharing his experience from his long career in Asian life insurance. **Simon Swanson**, Managing Director of CommInsure, was especially generous with his time and contributed significantly to the Australian chapter. We would also like to thank **Winston Yung**, CFO of Shin Kong Financial Holding Company, for his valuable insights into the Taiwan market.

Of all our internal supporters, we would first like to thank **Bonnie Leung**, an outstanding engagement manager in McKinsey's Insurance Practice. We could not have done this without her. She tirelessly supported this project from the beginning, helping write and edit the various chapters, challenging the logic and flow of the arguments, and maintaining the momentum with exceptional calmness and dedication.

We are also indebted to the leadership of **Tab Bowers** who heads our Financial Institutions Practice in Asia. He was a strong supporter and driver of the creation this book and supported us along the way, tirelessly going through every chapter and contributing terrific insights.

Our thanks also go to our colleagues—**Angus Sullivan**, **Rae Chen**, **Ziqi Zhang**, and **Samuel Wills**—for their contributions to key parts of the book. We would also like to specially thank our partner colleagues in the region for their invaluable comments on the country-specific chapters. In particular, we would like to thank **Daisuke Aranami** in Japan, **Yongah Kim** and **Jungin Kim** in South Korea, **Anu Magdavkar**, **Joydeep Sengupta**, and **Tilman Ehrbeck** in India, **Jessica Tan** and **Nigel Andrade** in Singapore, and **Robin Loh** and **Arjay Gavankar** on *takaful* insurance.

Our colleagues from our research and information department have been superb for being so relentless in pulling together, and constantly updating, the data used in this book. Special mention goes to **Grace Li**, **Jackey Yu**, **Karen Hsu**, **Kun Zhao**, **Nayoung Park**, **Shiomi Sato**, and **Suneet Jain**. Both throughout the process and during the final stretch, **Anuradha Sekar** gave us tremendous support in pulling everything together.

Our thanks also go to **Steve Vines**, a writer from Hong Kong, who helped a great deal in putting the first draft of the manuscript together, and to **Lili Lim**, for sharing her experience as an insurance agent in Indonesia.

We are grateful to our publisher and editor, **Nick Wallwork** and his team at John Wiley & Sons (Asia) Pte. Ltd., who gave us a lot of encouragement and supported the creation of this book.

Lastly, this book could not have been written without the understanding and support of our families. Stephan's family has been remarkably patient in dealing with this extra burden. Our thanks also go to **Angela** and the **Ngai boys**, **Matthew** and **Michael**, as well as **Joe's parents** and **sister Grace** who had to put up with his typing during weekends and their vacations.

Stephan Binder and Joe Ngai

Preface

The year 2008 will be long remembered in the financial services industry globally. In Asia, coming off the enormous growth period of the past several years, the 2008 financial crisis quickly reminded everyone how vulnerable the industry is. Insurers around Asia have been severely hit by this crisis. From the bankruptcy of Yamato Life in Japan and the bailout of AIG by the US government, to the severe losses in the investment portfolios of Chinese and Taiwanese insurers, Asian life insurers are facing extremely challenging times that would have been unthinkable just a year ago.

Against the onslaught of the financial crisis, the near-term priorities of Asian life insurers have changed drastically. Growth, which we have taken for granted for so long, has taken a back seat to more immediate measures such as fixing investment and risk management, raising capital, cutting costs, and for some players, opportunistic acquisitions. In particular, the financial crisis has brought to the forefront again the evergreen issue of asset-liability mismatches and the vulnerability of Asian life insurers who take undue risk on their investment portfolios. Furthermore, the crisis has led to unprecedented acquisition opportunities. AIG's divestiture of its Asian assets will be a particularly closely watched auction across most Asian markets. Meanwhile, Fubon's acquisition of ING's Taiwan life business has created another giant in the Taiwan market.

We must remind ourselves, in the midst of all this gloom, that the long-term prospects in Asian life insurance have never looked brighter. Macro-economic factors are overwhelmingly positive for most Asian countries, including the emergence of the middle class, high savings rates, and the growing need to save and invest for retirement. These macroeconomic drivers will enable life insurance to grow rapidly over the next decade, with most countries growing at high single digits or low double digits. In fact, as we explore the implications of the financial crisis, we are more optimistic than ever that the ten-year outlook for Asian life insurance remains extremely robust.

Over the next five years, we predict that 40 percent of the growth in global life insurance will come from Asia. Moreover, there is huge growth potential for the next decade and beyond, driven mainly by China and India. Markets in the US and Europe, with their high life insurance penetration, slowing population growth, and mature economies, will no doubt continue to decelerate and Asia will thus rise to become the most attractive region in the global life insurance arena. While many leading global life insurers are seeking to capture this growth opportunity, Asia has also bred its own class of globally large and valuable life companies. We believe some of these may become dominant players across Asia and beyond.

Life insurance in Asia: Winning in the Next Decade is about an industry facing significant challenges, but also entering a period of tremendous growth and massive changes. The attractiveness of the opportunity has led to unprecedented levels of competition, which will only become more intense in the decade to come. Local incumbents and attackers—Asian or multinationals—will compete to be among the winners.

Known for its conservatism, the Asian life insurance market is now being invaded by fast-growing attackers who aggressively recruit new agents, develop new channels, and sell new products. Markets such as China and India are approaching the size and scale which make them extremely relevant in the global life insurance landscape. Top indigenous players in these markets are now ranked among the most valuable life insurers in the world, and are expanding their geographic footprint overseas. Meanwhile, a handful of multinationals who have created a sizeable position in Asia are now reaping the benefits of these investments; Asia represents an increasing portion of their global revenue, and accounts for an even larger portion of their market valuation.

Battle lines are being drawn between local incumbents, attackers, and foreign players. While local incumbents have significant advantages in massive armies of agents and recurring premium income from in-force policies, the attackers are gearing up their multi-channel approach, and selling far more innovative products on the market. The war for talent is heating up as well, with fierce poaching wars happening across markets, where salaries of top managers and agents have increased dramatically.

In this book, we will describe the nature of this opportunity, the key challenges that market participants are facing, and what we believe it will take to win.

We have deliberately taken a pan-Asian perspective. We fully acknowledge the many differences between the individual markets within Asia; our theme, though, is the emergence of some players that will eventually dominate in multiple markets across the region. Some of these will come from Asia, while many others will be multinationals.

The endgame is far from certain. The winners in the next decade will have to overcome significant challenges in distribution, product innovation, investments, and operations. We are sure of one thing though: the winners of tomorrow will likely be a different set of players than the leaders of the past.

Why We Wrote *Life Insurance in Asia: Winning in the Next Decade*

Life Insurance in Asia: Winning in the Next Decade is written from a practitioner's perspective. As the two leaders in McKinsey & Company's Asia Insurance Practice, we have witnessed the challenges and opportunities described in this book firsthand. After moving to Shanghai from Germany, in 2004, to lead McKinsey's Asia Insurance Practice, Stephan Binder, a director in our Shanghai office, has advised insurers in virtually every country described in this book. He has focused on the insurance industry for most of his 12 years at McKinsey. As a Hong Kong native, Joe Ngai, a partner in our Hong Kong office, has spent a significant part of his time in the past several years advising insurance companies all across Asia on topics such as sales force transformation, investment management, call center management, and operations centers. His work has taken him all over the region, from India to South Korea to mainland China, working with some of the fastest-growing local companies as well as with multinationals.

We conceived this book after coming to the realization that there is no published material, to date, that covers the industry across Asia. This is a shame, since this is an industry that employs millions in Asia, with hundreds of millions of customers. What's more important—there is a revolution happening out there that will likely change the landscape of this industry significantly over the next decade.

As we started writing, many of the experiences and lessons we learned over the past several years flowed rapidly onto the pages. This strengthened our belief that this is a story that clearly needs to be told.

Who Needs to Read *Life Insurance in Asia: Winning in the Next Decade*

We believe that there are several categories of readers who would find this book interesting.

First, **CEOs and senior executives of life insurers in the region** should read it. Most executives will find not only their own country chapters relevant, but will find stories and examples from other markets equally interesting. As we work across the region, we observe many fascinating experiments happening today across Asia. We hope that our readers will also be able to draw inspiration from many of these examples. The last chapter also considers the challenges and priorities of the future—for life insurers to drive value in their organizations, many of these challenges and priorities will need to be addressed with determination and persistence.

Second, **global life insurers with an interest in the region** will need to read this book. In many ways, Asia represents the future of the industry. Surely, the challenges of building a business in Asia are multifold; but for those who succeed, the rewards are also immense. We believe that part of this success lies in a willingness to understand the differences in Asia and respond to them by doing things differently; this book will highlight many of these differences and should give the Western reader a good sense of the day-to-day challenges in these markets.

Third, **banking executives who see bancassurance/insurance products as one of the most important growth areas** will have an interest in seeing the story from the perspective of their partners and, potentially, their competitors. Today, life insurance is already one of the key products sold in many bank branches. To serve the emerging-middle-class customers across Asia, banks will have to further develop their retail and wealth management offerings, and insurance products will likely remain one of the key priorities. This book describes the challenges as seen from the life insurer's perspective, including the challenging economics, the need to establish more value-added partnerships, and the upcoming, inevitable convergence between the banking wealth management offerings and the insurance industry's financial advisory proposition

Fourth, **investors in life insurers with an Asian presence** should find this book helpful in understanding the value drivers of the industry. With deregulation in many markets as well as the listing of domestic players, access to investments in Asian life insurers is plentiful. The question for investors is where to find value. These pages should reveal the key opportunities across the markets, and also what to look for in Asian insurers.

Fifth, **life insurance regulators** across Asia should read this publication. While not written specifically from a regulatory perspective, we highlight many of the challenges and risks of the industry in each country. By anticipating future developments, both within their own countries and across the region, regulators can play a more effective role in safeguarding their industries.

Sixth, **media organizations, as well as other professional services organizations serving the industry,** can rely on this book as an industry reference. With data, research, and a wide coverage of markets, we believe that it will become one of the most handy reference tools for industry professionals.

Lastly, **academics and students of the life insurance industry** will find this book a valuable addition to their libraries. To date, *Life Insurance in Asia: Winning in the Next Decade* is the only, and most comprehensive, volume describing the life insurance industry's historic and forward-looking perspective across Asia.

Asia consists of complex life insurance markets in transition—*Life Insurance in Asia: Winning in the Next Decade* provides a useful interpretation of all the action occurring in the markets today. The industry we see is the result of the interplay of multiple forces, many of them based on regulatory and legacy reasons. Most of today's incumbents and market leaders reached their current standing through historically privileged positions. While we acknowledge that many industry leaders did create solid franchises, the journey ahead will be nothing like the past. Winning is a deliberate act, and one that will require companies to outperform others in an increasingly transparent and competitive world. Winning in the next decade, in Asia's life insurance industry, is not going to be easy.

Life Insurance in Asia: Winning in the Next Decade   1

This first chapter is a series of executive summaries of the subsequent chapters, designed as an orientation to the rest of the book, or—for the time-constrained executive—a quick way to scan the key messages. The structure starts with our observations on key trends across the region. Following our pan-Asian perspective, we then look at some of the markets in more detail. We have grouped together those markets that we believe show important commonalities in terms of the types of opportunities and challenges that market participants are facing.

These groups are: (i) China and India, (ii) Japan, (iii) Asian Tigers— Hong Kong, Taiwan, South Korea, and Singapore, (iv) Southeast Asia—Indonesia, Malaysia, the Philippines, Thailand, and Vietnam, and (v) Australia.

Despite the diversity and complexities across Asia, these clusters made a lot of sense to us in providing a pan-Asian perspective on the life insurance opportunities for the next decade. China and India share many of the same characteristics and are the "can't miss" markets for most players with serious Asian ambitions. Japan can never be logically grouped with any other market and, truly, is unique in almost all aspects. The Asian Tigers— while there are significant differences between Hong Kong, Taiwan, South Korea, and Singapore—represent the more mature but still growing parts of Asia. The Southeast Asian markets, represented for our purpose by Indonesia, Malaysia, the Philippines, Thailand, and Vietnam, were all badly damaged during the 1997 Asian financial crisis but are re-emerging as high-growth countries. Australia, "the Western part of Asia," is another unique market, having few commonalities with the rest of the region.

However, it is an interesting market and we strongly believe it should be in the interest of Australian life companies to have more of an Asian perspective so as not to miss out on the emerging opportunities in the region.

Finally, in the last chapter, we look at what we believe it will take for life insurers to win in Asia in the next decade.

Chapter 2—Emerging Themes in Asia

Asia is a region of immense diversity, with at least as many differences as there are similarities among the various markets. This chapter attempts to synthesize some of the emerging themes in Asia, and highlight various perspectives on how industry players can think about the region as a whole. While generalization will always be problematic and exceptions can always be found, we believe that many of these themes ring true across most of these markets, and will help form a framework to discuss each of the different markets later in the book. The one exception is Australia, whose differences caused us to exclude it from the discussion in this chapter.

We have identified five pan-Asian themes. They include continued rapid growth of the market, an emerging middle class, the rise of multinational players, the evolution of distribution, and changing product mix due to the new needs of Asian consumers.

First, the Asian life insurance markets will see continued rapid growth. Asia ex-Japan[1] delivered only 12 percent of global life premiums in 2007, but accounted for 25 percent of growth between 2002 and 2007. More importantly, Asia is expected to deliver around 40 percent of global life insurance premium growth over the next five years. Across the region, we anticipate that most markets will be growing at high single digits to low double digits. Some of the less-developed markets will continue to play "catch up" with close to 20 percent annual growth. Of course, growth will not come in a straight line. Asia is notorious for volatility—but for those willing to take the risks and adopt a long-term perspective, Asia will drive much of global growth in the next decade.

Second, the emergence of the Asian middle class is truly one of the most important phenomenon across the region. There are 110 million households earning over US$10,000 per annum[2] in the 12 countries we studied; by 2012, there will be over 200 million.[3] This massive increase in the middle-class population is a fundamental force in shaping the life insurance industry. Increasingly, these middle-class customers are found in second and third tier cities, and even in rural areas, as well as in the established large cities in Asia. As such, the build-out of distribution channels to get to these new customers is paramount; the traditional approach of focusing only on the top cities to get to the market will not tap into this growth area. Moreover, because these emerging-middle-class customers are forming increasingly distinct segments (for example, white-collar workers, SME business owners), more diversity of channels and products will be needed to effectively target these customers.

Third, multinational insurers are already present in all of the key markets in Asia, and will continue to thrive as they take share from their local competitors. Although only a handful of foreign players have a true pan-Asian footprint (most have a presence in a few selected markets), we believe that the next decade will be one where operational excellence and product/channel innovation will be critical—and this will play to the strengths of most foreign players. In 2007, foreign players took less than a quarter of gross written premium (GWP) share in the 12 Asian markets we observed—this certainly has room to grow over the next decade: we predict the share of foreign players to increase to 30–35 percent. This is not to say that domestic players will be a walkover. In fact, we anticipate that the next decade will witness the emergence of some dominant Asian players that will both be able to defend their own markets and grow beyond. However, in general, we do anticipate foreign players to be able to take share away from local players in most markets; this is especially evident in markets with large local incumbents who are saddled with legacy issues.

Fourth, the face of distribution in Asia will change, with major changes coming for the long-dominant, tied-agency sales force and bancassurance. While one of the hallmarks of Asia life insurance has been the massive, tied-agent forces, this will be the channel under the most pressure over the next decade. Already, in markets such as Japan and South Korea, the traditional "housewives" model has lost share rapidly to other channels, as well as to the more professional, and younger, sales forces. Even in markets like China, where the sales force is still growing rapidly, there are signs that this channel will soon reach its limits for expansion. The revamping of this traditional distribution channel will be one of the key trends to observe—for traditional players unable to make the transition, this could be fatal.

In addition to the more evolutionary change in the agent channel, bancassurance has created a real discontinuity in Asia's life insurance markets. From virtually nowhere, banks have captured 30–50 percent of new business in most markets. While we believe that the rapid increase in market share will level off, this channel is here to stay. Banks have been able to convert parts of their huge deposit base of retail customers in Asia into simple investment products, fueling massive growth in life insurance. But in many markets, banks have also been able to capture most of the upside from this additional growth in the form of commissions that leave little value with the life insurers. Going forward, we believe that a "next generation model" is needed in bancassurance where a much tighter cooperation between insurers and banks enables them to sell more value-added policies—with more attractive margins.

At the same time, we are witnessing the emergence of alternative distribution channels such as brokers, direct selling, retail stores, etc. While these will remain small for quite some time, they are consistently outgrowing the rest of the market across the region.

Fifth, we are seeing an increasing complexity in the product offerings of life insurers. Asian consumers are growing more sophisticated in financial products and increasingly distinct customer segments are emerging: from advice-seeking, white-collar, middle-class workers, to (soon-to-be) pensioners, to small entrepreneurs, to better-off rural customers. These customer segments are requiring targeted product offerings, and life insurers with a one-size-fits-all product offering will increasingly come under pressure. For example, as the markets mature, traditional products will no longer be sufficient to satisfy the rapidly diversifying customer needs. Asians are heavy savers, with some of the highest savings rates in the world (in many markets, household savings rates are well over 20 percent). As the market moves from a traditional product-push model to a customer-centric, advice model, insurers cannot afford to get caught on the wrong side of the equation. Investment-linked products have already captured much of the growth in the past few years; although the long, bull-market run that has certainly helped fuel that growth has come to a rapid end, this trend is here to stay. Furthermore, products such as accident and health, annuities, and even Islamic insurance, will open significant additional opportunities across the region.

Chapter 3—China and India: Yes, Size Does Matter

Arguably, the two most important growth markets in the world for all life insurers—global and Asian—to focus on over the next decade will be in Asia—China and India. With 37 percent of the world's population and gross domestic product (GDP) growing at 8–10 percent per annum, these markets will surely rise to global prominence over the next decade.

The greatest attraction of China and India in life insurance is obviously their enormous growth potential. The general economic growth is propelling more and more people—beyond the large urban centers of today—into income levels where, for the first time, they can afford to buy financial products such as life insurance. This emergence of a new middle class will fuel double-digit growth rates in life insurance well beyond the next decade.

However, while these growth prospects have benefited many local companies and are reflected in valuations that have elevated some of the Chinese life insurers, such as China Life and Ping An, to become among the most valuable life companies by market cap in the world, foreign players have had to contend with much more humble beginnings. The key reason for this is regulation that prevents them from competing on a level playing field.

The situation is unlikely to become any easier going forward. We are already seeing rapidly increasing competition and we believe this trend is going to accelerate even further. In addition, market participants will have to deal with the enormous operational challenges of running organizations in markets that look more like continents than countries. In particular, building distribution is the top challenge. Today, this is mostly centered around building a sustainable tied-agent model, but it is rapidly expanding into finding a value-creating model in bancassurance and exploring the rapidly growing alternative channels. Finally, the need to serve increasingly distinctive customer segments, from white-collar workers in large cities to affluent customers in rural areas, dramatically increases the complexity, not only in distribution but also in the product portfolio.

Winning in China and India will not be easy for anyone. The next decade will see an increasing separation of those winning players that are able to overcome the enormous operational challenges from the rest of the pack. We believe that among the winners will be some of the leading domestic companies of today—but also some newcomers and foreign players.

Like so many other markets in Asia, taking a long-term perspective is important. In particular, for foreign players there will not be immediate rewards from these two markets in the short term. Breakeven will surely take at least several years and up to a decade. Nonetheless, the rewards can be large—players serious about staking a foothold in the global insurance landscape can ill-afford not to play in this high-stakes game.

Chapter 4—Japan: New Tricks in an Old Market

In the 1980s, almost all of the largest life insurance companies of the world were Japanese. Today, only one of them is in the top 10. This is symptomatic of a Japanese life insurance market that has declined over the last decade. While the massive Japan market used to account for three-quarters of the total Asian life market in the early 2000s, forecasts indicate that it will be just one-quarter by the mid-2010s. This decline, plus its fiercely domestic characteristics, has made Japan one of the most frustrating markets for many new players.

However, there are some highly interesting market segments hidden under the surface. While the traditional life market is declining and looks increasingly unattractive, new opportunities are popping up in the retirement area, health insurance, investment-related products, and other nontraditional channels, including bancassurance. Given the size of the Japanese market, each one of these niche areas (if they can even be called niche) is worth more than most Asian countries in their entirety. More importantly, in recent years, some foreign players have succeeded in capturing some of these opportunities. Most notably, The Hartford created a 23 percent market position in variable annuities with over US$5.9 billion in premium income from Japan in 2007. Prudential (US) created a consultative financial advisory sales force over two decades ago and is now reaping US$3–4 billion a year in premium income from Japan.

If we fast forward to the late 2010s, it is likely that the life insurance market in Japan will look quite different from today. First, most of the domestic, incumbent life insurers are likely to fall victim to their own traditions that have become legacy issues. Retirement, medical, and investment products will dominate growth, and new, more sophisticated sales channels will surely emerge to serve customers in these new areas. With this shift in market dynamics, some of the attackers will continue to take share from the domestic incumbents. These new players are likely to be a mixture of foreign and domestic players.

Given the impressive size of this opportunity and the rapidly changing landscape, we believe developing a position in Japan life insurance has a significant upside. This is not to say that the market is any easier to enter today; most of the historic challenges remain. It will take highly ambitious life insurers to invest in this market; however, for those who succeed, this could create a sustainable advantage that will be almost impossible to replicate by competitors.

Chapter 5—Asian Tigers: Maturing Markets Still Going Strong

Taiwan, Singapore, Hong Kong, and South Korea have historically been the most profitable markets for life insurers in the region. These fast-growing economies, with their high savings rates and some of the highest GDPs per capita in Asia, have created significant growth and profit pools. With no major restrictions for foreign players to enter, some foreign insurers have staked out significant positions very early on and have reaped the rewards of these investments.

Relative to most Western markets, these markets still have very attractive margins today. Since products are still relatively opaque in structure, pricing pressure has not driven margins down quite as severely yet. Moreover, given that most policies are sold through tied-agency forces, players that have developed a loyal agency force through the years are sitting on a well-oiled cash cow.

The four Asian Tigers are among the highest-penetrated markets globally, have a long history of foreign insurers' participation, and are highly competitive market environments. These markets are certainly not easy to enter—formidable challenges remain—but the challenges are quite different from high-growth markets like China and India.

Hong Kong has been one of the oldest insurance markets to open up in Asia, and as such, many multinational insurers have been in the market for decades. Today, the top insurers are all foreign, with AIG, Manulife, and Prudential (UK) leading the pack. Potentially, the Hong Kong market can demonstrate how many Asian markets may end up. In Hong Kong, the key challenge is to professionalize the agency force—which means transforming agents from product-pushing, insurance salespeople to professional financial advisors. Also, Hong Kong has been one of the prime breeding grounds for management talent; many of the current top executives in mainland China are either Hong Kong natives or were originally trained in Hong Kong.

Singapore has many similarities with the Hong Kong life insurance market—with the exception of a much more interventionist regulator, and also a few local incumbents like NTUC Income and Great Eastern. For many years, Singapore adopted a "closed-door policy" that prevented new entrants into the market, but that was revised in 2000 due to a stagnating industry. Since then, the industry has flourished and grown rapidly. Much of the insurance market today is driven by supporting government policies such as the contribution to the mandatory Central Provident Fund (CPF).

In South Korea, a battle is brewing between the local incumbents, with their massive "housewife" sales forces, and the smaller foreign and local attackers who are selling more investment-linked products with younger and more professional sales forces. Market statistics indicate that the attackers are rapidly eating away market share from the incumbents. Furthermore, attackers are innovating on channels and several interesting distribution experiments can be found in South Korea today. Despite recent attempts to transform their business models, the incumbents will most likely continue to lose market share for a while—but the stage is set for the battle for future market dominance.

In many ways Taiwan resembles the market in South Korea, with a few large local incumbents dominating the traditional market, except that the gap between the local incumbents and the attackers is much smaller. Given the small and inwardly focused domestic market, there is not a lot of room for innovation. Any innovation is rapidly copied by competitors—Taiwan is probably one of the least differentiated markets in Asia, not only in life insurance but also for any kind of financial services.

As such, market share has not changed much between the players over the past several years, with the exception of acquisitions and, more recently, players who have sold aggressive bancassurance policies over often captive banking channels. In recent years, the top challenge for Taiwanese insurers has been a difficult investment environment—the financial crisis of 2008 has left some of the top insurers in vulnerable positions.

For any player from outside this region, it will be very challenging to enter organically given the maturity of these markets. Acquisitions may be a possibility, but targets are few and transactions will most likely be done at high premiums—although the recent financial crisis might create some opportunities. For players already in the market, these markets remain great value contributors—growth may slow down from the earlier rapid growth period but given the high savings rates and economic upside, these markets still have more potential growth than most Western markets. We expect growth to range from high single digits to low teens over the next several years. With a decent market size, and attractive prospects, these markets will continue to be a "sweet spot" for many multinational insurers.

Chapter 6—Southeast Asia: Back on a Growth Trajectory

Although severely affected by the Asian financial crisis of 1997, and recently overshadowed by the rapid ascent of China and India, the potential of Southeast Asia remains large. Size alone is on its side: the combined markets of Indonesia, Malaysia, the Philippines, Thailand, and Vietnam have a population of some 486 million, equivalent to 43 percent of India or 37 percent of China. Currently very small as individual markets, we expect these markets to grow on average at roughly 15 percent over the next several years.

Clearly there are many differences between markets in this region. Thailand, the Philippines, and Malaysia are relatively more mature and penetrated markets, whereas Indonesia and Vietnam seem to offer more rapid growth potential due to the sizes of their populations, low penetration, and GDP growth expectations. In particular, Vietnam has captured the imagination of many in the last few years, although by 2008 its economic growth trajectory seemed to start hitting significant challenges.

In each of these markets, the competition between foreign insurers and local companies is fierce. Although foreign ownership restrictions exist in some markets, the regulatory barriers to entering the life insurance industry in this region are far less stringent when compared to those in China and India. As such, it is common to find high market share of foreign insurers in these markets. For example, AIG received over US$3.7 billion in gross premium from these five markets in 2006, equivalent to over 5 percent of AIG's global GWP for that year. It has dominant positions in these markets—most prominently with close to 40 percent market share in Thailand.

Going forward, these markets offer a unique opportunity in Asia. While individually they are not large today, they are very accessible and have ample room for further penetration and growth. Taking a mid-term (5–8 years) time horizon, it is possible to imagine an organic entry that will capture a meaningful, say 5 percent, market position in some of these countries. Of course, competition in each market is still extremely challenging, and the lack of managerial talent will be a constant headache for market entrants. However, as we will stress throughout this book, none of the markets in Asia are "easy" any more—the first mover advantage, if there ever was any, expired many years ago.

Chapter 7—Australia: Light at the End of the Tunnel?

Australia is often characterized as "the Western market in Asia." In life insurance it is certainly a market unlike any in the rest of the region. Well-established, mature, and low growth, it is in fact an antithesis of the themes in Asia. The market structure of Australia is also different—the introduction of the superannuation scheme has dominated the market for investments and savings, relegating the insurance industry to three distinct, and relatively very small, segments: risk products, annuities, and investment-linked products. The creation of the superannuation scheme, along with the deregulation of the banking industry and the demutualization of life insurers, has resulted in market consolidation and a dramatic shrinkage in the upside of the industry. Moreover, distribution and product manufacturing have disaggregated in this market, so that the large, tied-agency forces—so powerful in other Asian markets—are not an asset that life insurers in Australia can depend on.

Nonetheless, there are fundamental factors that support the continued growth of the industry, even if this growth pales by comparison to the rest of Asia. Australians are notorious for being extremely underinsured—many studies and surveys have indicated that Australians are somewhat unrealistically optimistic and believe that they are less likely to experience a negative event. Today, Australians are outliving their life expectancies, spending more on health, and facing longer retirement periods. Factor in the shift in the responsibility of managing the risk of retirement from the government to individuals and it is clear that Australians are more vulnerable than ever before. Two-thirds of Australians admit that their level of coverage is inadequate or nonexistent. This gives rise to product opportunities that play to insurers' strengths and that are also not available in other forms in the market—including long-term, guaranteed products, longevity risk products, and morbidity and old-age products (including health products).

Given these market circumstances, there should be some upside for insurers already in Australia. To capture these opportunities, insurers will need to succeed in product development, distribution innovation, and cost management. Product innovation around annuities and hybrid products will be particularly important. In addition, market participants should lobby the government to support the industry in rejuvenating the growth of the Australian life insurance market.

Given the mature state of the market, for life insurers not yet in the market, organic entry is unlikely to provide sufficient return on investment, especially if compared with other market entry options in the rest of Asia—unless, of course, that entry is based on a disruptive business model that can unsettle the current status quo.

Chapter 8—The Next Decade: What it Takes to Win in Asia

Life insurance in Asia is undeniably reaching a turning point. The growth trajectory remains extremely strong, but the key success factors are definitely changing. Traditional models are under stress, new customer segments with diverging needs are emerging, and foreign players and local attackers are threatening to take market share from local incumbents. To win in the next decade, we believe that insurers must focus on five key factors. These include building a sustainable agent force, creating value in bancassurance and alternative channels, upgrading the business model to combat intensifying competition, capturing the pan-Asian opportunity, and sustaining margin pressure.

First, building a sustainable agent force is probably the number one priority for most players. Life insurance is still very much a distribution game, and in Asia, tied agents will likely retain their importance despite challenges from other channels. Therefore, restructuring the current sales force and developing a more sustainable agent model will be a key success factor.

Second, insurers will need to find value in the fast-expanding bancassurance channel as well as develop alternative channels. Today's bancassurance model does not work well for insurers; the fast premium growth is generally not matched with equal value creation—that is to say, profits. Developing the next generation bancassurance model, where insurers can add more value and achieve better margins, will be critical. In addition, insurers who can capture the rapid growth in alternative channels, such as brokerage and direct sales, will find themselves in an attractive, albeit small, niche.

Third, upgrading the business model from a "landgrab" to an "outcompete" model will be important. This requires much more emphasis on product innovation, IT, and operations excellence, as well as professionalization in investment and risk management.

Fourth, only large insurers who have the right management bench will be able to capture the pan-Asian opportunity. This includes foreign players as well as large, well-run, domestic giants. Creating a pan-Asian presence will be highly rewarded by the market, and the next decade will be a critical period for this undertaking.

Finally, insurers will need to shift from a growth to a value mindset, as margins start to come down in the region. Optimizing product portfolios, managing costs more efficiently, and balancing risks and returns in investment management are some of the critical elements in this value paradigm.

For the different types of players, large local incumbents, smaller local attackers, and multinational corporations (MNCs), the next decade presents a much more demanding set of opportunities with some unique challenges. The large incumbents will be spending much of their time transforming the core of their operations, namely, the large, tied-agent sales force. This legacy is still a key strength, but a successful transformation will cement the incumbents' success for the future. This will be a long, painful, but necessary process. These incumbents will also need to create new growth horizons in parallel, whether this means creating new distribution channels, entering new geographies, or diversifying into related financial services businesses. For many of them, simply relying on the traditional models will lead them closer to losing their dominant market position.

For the smaller foreign and local attackers, who are chasing the incumbents, the priorities will be to deepen their niche in distribution and product differentiation. In particular, those smaller players who are successful in creating differentiated sales forces, usually much higher in quality and with better infrastructure, are likely to get ahead. Better usage of alternative channels will also be a major theme for these players over the next decade, as we expect these channels to grow exponentially from today's small base. Product innovation will continue to be important—although it is usually not only the new product itself but also the superior ability of the distribution channels to sell it that will be the critical differentiating factor. In markets where the attackers are rapidly catching up merely by participating in market growth (the most obvious examples are the smaller local players in China and India), the limitations of the "me-too" strategy will soon become obvious, and points of differentiation will be needed, whether in distribution, products, or simply better execution.

For the well-established, foreign, pan-Asian players, the future has never looked brighter. With their formidable positions in many markets across Asia, the contributions from Asia will only go up as a percentage of global revenues and, even more, as a percentage of value creation. For these players, the particular priority will be to ensure that they capture the massive opportunities in China and India. Over the next decade, missing the boat on these two markets would be disastrous, especially coming from their position of strength in Asia. In addition to landgrabbing in China and India, capturing emerging niches in markets such as South Korea and Japan will also be fundamental, since these markets represent major market dislocations and will continue to be some of the most sizeable and profitable markets in Asia. Finally, capturing synergies across Asia, from operations to product development, will also be increasingly important, given the inevitable margin pressure.

For latecomers to the region, Asia presents a dilemma. None of the markets present first-mover advantages anymore, and every market has its own unique challenges and is fiercely competitive. Breaking even in many of these markets will require a 6–8 year time horizon, especially when building a proprietary sales force. Without taking a long-term view, Asia will simply not be worth the trouble—and just "following the crowd" will not take a new player far. We believe that Asia still represents a very good opportunity for foreign latecomers with a long-term horizon. Many Asian markets are still at the beginning of their development curve, and many more will be going through disruptive stages where new players with determination and distinctive skills will be able to grab disproportionate share. Moreover, these markets generate a large part of the growth of the global insurance industry—so the opportunity cost of not participating in this growth opportunity will continue to rise. For that consideration, we believe that the opportunities in this region are still hard to beat. To enter, latecomers will need to choose their entry models and local partners carefully, and look for acquisition opportunities along the way.

A decade from now, the Asian life insurance landscape will be very different from what it is today. If the 1990s, for most of Asia, can be characterized as a "gold rush" or a "landgrab," this coming decade will likely be characterized as one of "outperformance." The need to reinvent old models and to capture new growth areas has never been more critical. For those who have the foresight and determination and are willing make the investments, the prize will be well worth the effort.

Emerging Themes in Asia

Joining an insurance company in the 1960s in Hong Kong was not an obvious choice. In fact, the industry was poorly understood, and only a few multinationals were active in the market at the time. Insurance agents had a difficult time explaining to customers what the product was about, and many viewed such agents with suspicion. It was in such an environment that Dominic Leung joined AIA (a subsidiary of AIG) as an IT analyst. He remembered that "AIA was essentially run by locals—besides a few expats from the US, most of the management team consisted of Hong Kong executives." Over the years, the industry blossomed as life insurance became one of the first financial products that most middle-class people purchased. As AIG expanded its presence across Asia, Dominic moved to Taiwan in 1989 to become the country head. There, AIG was known by its Chinese name, Nanshan (a company AIA acquired some years before). Over the years, many multinational insurers followed the lead of AIG in entering Asia, including AXA, Manulife, Prudential (UK), and ING. By the mid-1990s, as more multinational companies aggressively entered the Asian markets, Dominic was headhunted away to be the CEO of Prudential (UK)'s greater China operations, overseeing the three markets of China, Hong Kong, and Taiwan.

In January 2004, Dominic made his latest career move (and he claims it will be his last)—he moved to Ping An, the fast-growing, second-largest life insurer in China, and became the chairman of its life insurance subsidiary (which contributes the vast majority of the value of the group). In 2006, Dominic took over responsibility for all of Ping An's insurance activities, including life, property and casualty, pensions, and health insurance.

During his tenure, Ping An grew to US$10.8 billion in life insurance premiums by 2007. It went public in 2004, and boasted a market capitalization of US$53.4 billion by June 2008. As he reflected on his career move in Ping An's internal newsletter in 2004, "I wanted to use my 30-plus years in the insurance industry to contribute to the development of the mainland China market. This is a once-in-a-lifetime, unique opportunity."

From the international finance center of Hong Kong to the fast-growing Taiwan market and then to the huge domestic economy of China—in many ways Dominic's career reflects the development of the Asian life insurance market. From a global life insurance perspective, opportunities in the industry developed quickly in the more accessible markets like Hong Kong, before growing rapidly in the next wave of developing markets such as Taiwan and South Korea, and finally reaching the massive markets of China and India.

As can be seen from the various phases of development, the Asian life insurance market is no more a single market than any other financial market in Asia, spanning a region far too diverse to allow such a simplistic view of its complexity. Nobody, for example, is going to seriously suggest an intense commonality between say Japan and India, where in the former, per capita gross domestic product (GDP) stood at around US$36,000 in 2007, while India's was a little over US$1,000.

And there are many other differences, such as levels of market penetration and regulation of foreign players, not forgetting the rather more obvious differences in culture and outlook in a region that sweeps eastward from the borders of Europe and Africa to the shores of the Indian and Pacific Oceans.

Although generalization is always problematic, we have identified five pan-Asian themes, which are evident in most, if not all, of these markets. These are important themes that provide a key to understanding the life insurance market in Asia, including continued rapid growth of the market, an emerging-middle-class of 110 million new households, the rise of multinational players, the changing face of distribution and the rapid growth of bancassurance, and a changing product mix due to the new needs of Asian consumers. Because the Australian market differs significantly in its characteristics to the rest of Asia, it is not included in the discussion for this chapter. All references to Asia in this book exclude Australia and the rest of Oceania, unless otherwise noted.

Continued Rapid Growth

The big story of the last decade was about the growth of the life insurance market in the Asian region exceeding all other regions in the world. Asia ex-Japan, accounted for 12 percent of global life premiums in 2007 (see Figure 2.1), but, perhaps more significantly, it accounted for almost 25 percent of the growth in the global market from 2002 to 2007, and is expected to deliver around 40 percent of life insurance premium growth over the next five years. Moreover, the profitability of Asian markets is higher than that of mature markets. Thus, from a value creation perspective, Asia looks even more attractive.

The majority of Asian markets outperformed the world average on surplus return[1] in the period between 2001 and 2006 and they enjoyed

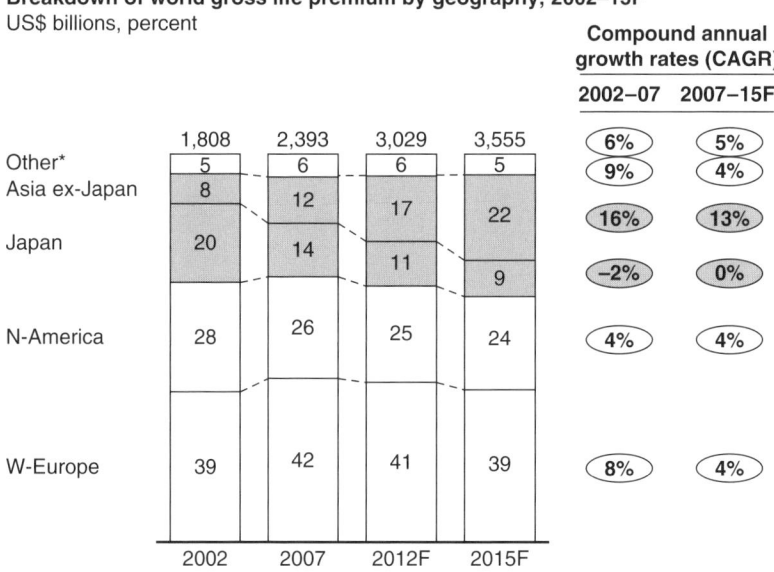

Figure 2.1 Asia is a major driver of global life insurance

Source: Sigma; various regulatory authorities; McKinsey

higher profit margins than their US and European peers in 2006. Figure 2.2 details these market's 2007 premiums and provides indications of future growth prospects.

Double-digit growth is likely to be a hallmark of many Asian markets for the next decade. This is thanks to a growing but aging population, steadily increasing wealth levels, changing attitudes about personal finances, high savings rates, and an extension of geographic scope, mainly seen in the penetration into new markets outside the biggest urban areas.

The United Nations' Population Database shows that projected demographics are staggeringly in favor of Asia. The combined population of the countries under review in this book is expected to grow from 3.2 billion in 2005 to 3.7 billion in 2020, adding another 500 million potential customers. In the same time frame, the United States population will grow by a mere 40 million and that of Europe will

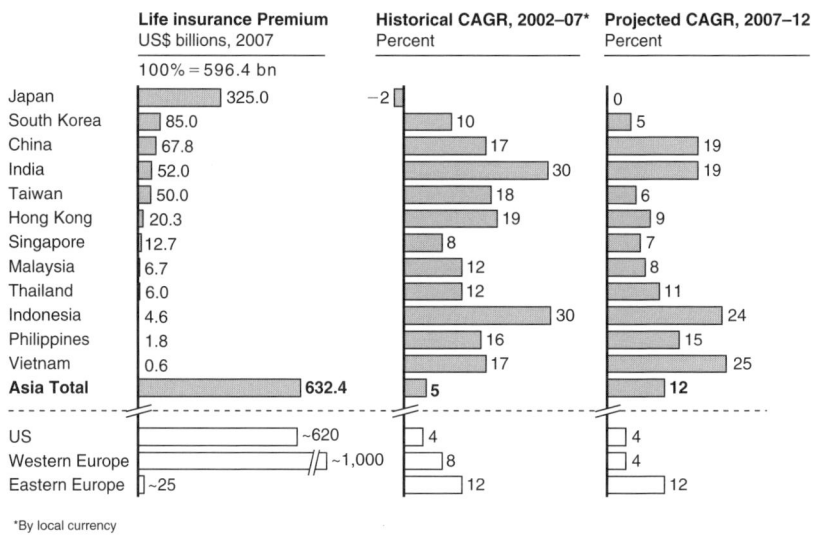

*By local currency
**2003–2006, or most recent available data

Figure 2.2 Asian life insurance markets are growing quickly

Source: Swiss Re Sigma; regulatory reports; CIRC; China Insurance Yearbook, IRDA; FSS; McKinsey analysis

decline by almost 10 million. That means that Asia will have more than 15 times the total population growth of the US and Europe combined, or in absolute terms, Asia will grow by almost double the United States' current population.

This growth will be unevenly distributed; Indian, Malaysian, and Filipino populations will increase by 7–8 percent; the north Asian countries such as China, Taiwan, and South Korea growing by 2–4 percent; and Japan will experience a slight decrease in population.

At the same time, some of these countries, such as South Korea and Japan—like many in the Western world—will see the emergence of a large aging population due to the baby-boom bulge. The proportion of the population over the age of 65 is expected to increase significantly until 2020.

As a result, the number of working adults supporting each retiree will decrease from 10 in 2005 to eight in 2020 and four by 2050, dramatically altering the shape of the age pyramid. This phenomenon is expected to drive growth in the retirement market, as aging Asians look to retirement planning. This, in turn, gives rise to a growing demand for life insurance products such as health insurance, annuities, and endowment policies.

It is a well-known fact that economic growth in Asia is currently much higher than elsewhere in the world but it is worth reminding ourselves just how significant this trend is. The projected real gross domestic product (GDP) growth rate for these countries falls in the range of 5–9 percent per annum between 2007 and 2012. In contrast, the US economy is only expected to grow by less than 3 percent during the same period. In total, the 12 Asian countries accounted for 19 percent of world GDP growth between 2002 and 2007 and 40 percent of projected growth between 2007 and 2012. As Figure 2.3 shows, even nations projecting rather more modest levels of growth are still expected to almost double the estimated pace of growth in the US economy.

With fast-growing GDP levels, the personal financial assets of the population will grow over proportionally. For example, personal financial assets in China and India grew at annual rates of 16 percent and 23 percent respectively during 2001–06, whereas the volume grew 5 percent in the US and 8 percent in the UK over the same period.

While the increase in personal financial assets will naturally drive growth for life insurance products, it can be argued that a changing attitude on

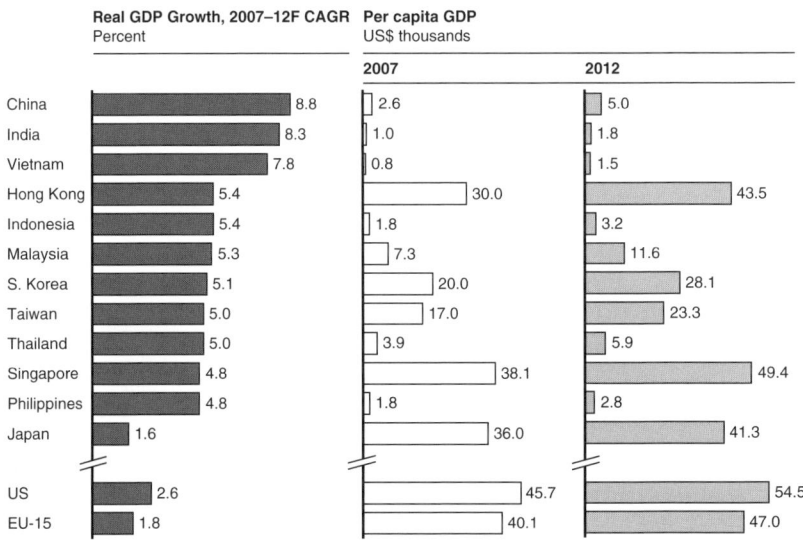

Figure 2.3 The strong growth of Asian economies
Source: Global Insight; EIU

investments and personal finances is accelerating this opportunity even beyond these absolute growth numbers.

Traditionally, Asians are more prone to leaving personal financial assets in deposits or cash. In 2002, Chinese consumers put 84 percent of their personal financial assets in cash or bank deposits, India 74 percent, and Thailand 72 percent. There has already been a considerable shift away from savings through bank deposits into investments. Between 2002 and 2006, without exception, consumers from these Asian nations shifted their cash into investment products. By 2006, the Chinese put only 79 percent of their financial assets in cash, India 65 percent, and Thailand 58 percent. There is much more room for development—in mature markets such as the UK and the US, the cash holdings as a percentage of personal financial assets are at 22 percent and 13 percent respectively.

As Asians move from "savers" to "investors," a great deal more money will become available for investment in mutual funds, equities, and life insurance. Will the Asian consumer choose to invest this cash in life insurance rather than other investment products? In markets where life insurance ownership is very low, the answer is a resounding yes. In markets such as China, India, Vietnam, and Indonesia, market penetration of life insurance is very low, currently at less than 5 percent of GDP. For many customers in these markets, life insurance is the first financial product that they purchase, with the life insurance agent often being the only source of financial know-how.

In the more highly penetrated markets, such as Taiwan and Hong Kong, life insurance faces more competition from other forms of financial products. Even so, it is still likely that growth will continue. We believe that it is likely that one day life insurance penetration in Asia will exceed levels seen in the West. The reasons for this assertion are threefold.

First, premium density per capita, on an absolute scale, is still lower than that of some Western markets. Figure 2.4 demonstrates that even in Taiwan and Hong Kong, which enjoy Asia's highest levels of life insurance market penetration, density has yet to equal those of the UK and Switzerland.

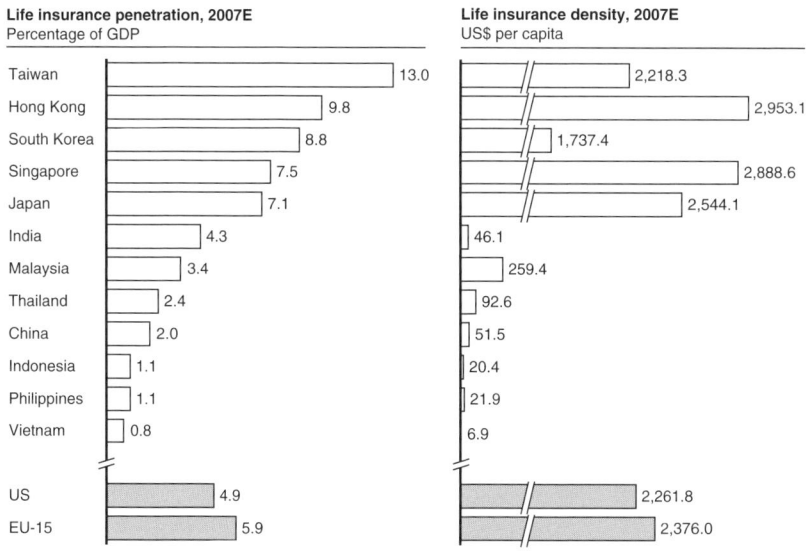

Figure 2.4 Life insurance penetration and density for select Asia markets
Source: Various insurance regulatory bodies, Global Insight, Swiss Re Sigma

Second, despite a high premium level, a large proportion of this was savings products, and the level of protection as indicated by mortality sum assured is lower, relatively, than in more developed countries. For example, Singapore and Hong Kong's 2007 per capita mortality sum assured[2] was about US$45,000 and US$49,000 respectively, whereas it was US$63,000 in the US in 2006. Therefore, despite the high level of ownership, there is still a lot of room to grow in traditional protection products.

Thirdly, Asian consumers have significantly higher savings rates than those in Western markets. Asians are notorious for their penchant for savings—the 2007 personal savings rates in China and India were 14 percent and 27 percent respectively, compared to –1.0 percent for the UK and 4.4 percent for the US. These significantly higher savings rates translate into a higher level of personal financial assets at any given level of economic development (see Figure 2.5). Given this level of personal savings, it is not inconceivable that Asia will one day surpass the Western markets in many of the penetration benchmarks we observe today.

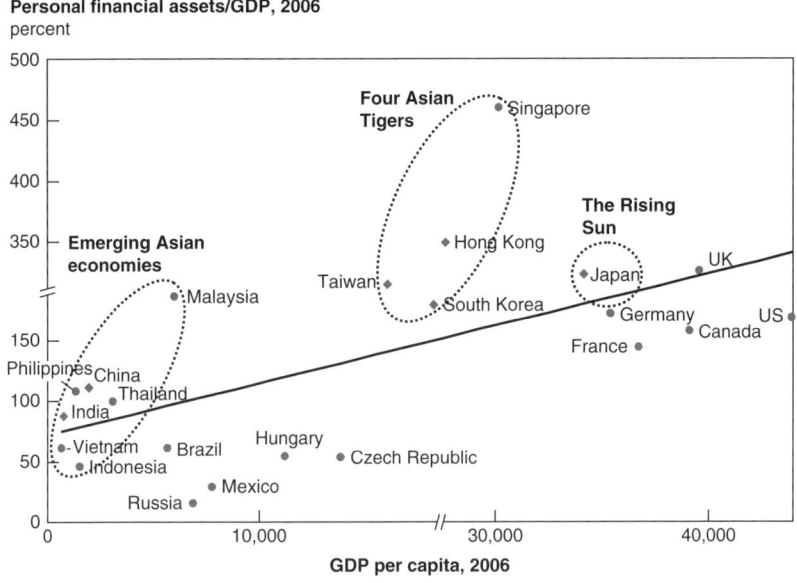

Figure 2.5 Asians are generally strong savers

Source: Global Insight; various regulatory bodies, central banks, monetary authorities; McKinsey

Hence, growth is undeniably one of the greatest hallmarks of the Asian markets. Of course, growth will not be uniform across these countries. Major growth markets will include China, India, Indonesia, and Vietnam with forecast growth rates in the region of 15–25 percent. The four Asian Tigers will likely grow at a slower but still healthy pace, probably in the high single digits. The exception is Japan, where there has been no growth between 2002 and 2007 and this is unlikely to change in the future. While Asian players take this growth for granted, these growth rates represent one of the most exciting opportunities for global insurers, as they contrast this growth scenario with their often lackluster home markets. In many boardrooms of global insurers today, Asia, rightfully so, is becoming a crucial part of the overall strategic plan.

The Emerging Middle Class: 200 Million New Customers!

The second trend across Asia is the rapidly changing complexion of life insurance customers. This is a trend that is more prevalent in the nascent markets of China, India, Indonesia, and Vietnam, and describes the expansion of the insurance market into previously untapped territory. The numbers are staggering: There are 110 million households earning US$10,000 per annum in the 12 countries we studied; by 2012 there will be over 200 million. In the US there were 107 million households with the same income level in 2007 and is expected to increase to 113 million in 2012 the same year, there will be slightly more than 110 million US households with that same income level. This translates to an influx of approximately 200 million new customers into the Asian market over the next five years.[3]

Where do these new customers come from? As Asian countries become wealthier at their breakneck pace of growth, a large middle class is emerging in many of these markets. In China, for example, where 99 percent of urban households were considered "poor"[4] in 1985, by 2005, 22 percent of urban households were considered "middle class," and it is projected that by 2025, about 80 percent of urban households will be in that category. In absolute terms, that means an additional 250 million middle-class households in China! Similarly, in India, the middle class currently only constitutes 5 percent of the population but is expected to be more than 40 percent of the population by 2025.[5]

It is important to note that middle class in Asia does not connote the same absolute wealth levels as in the developed countries. For reference, a household that makes between US$3,500 and US$14,000 a year is already considered middle class in China. The United States Department of Health and Human Services set the 2008 poverty guideline for a four person family at US$21,200.[6] That is to say, all households who fell into the "middle-class" definition in China would be considered poor in US. However, when accounting for purchasing-power parity, a household income of US$14,000 would buy a Chinese family the same lifestyle as that of a household earning US$40,000 in the United States. For these consumers—Chinese, Indians, and Vietnamese—this growth in wealth means they will, for the first time, have money to spare for items beyond the basic necessities. We are already seeing spending patterns shifting towards discretionary items in both India and China.

Continued urbanization is a key factor driving the creation of this new middle class. In China, the McKinsey Global Institute estimates that by 2025, there will be over 200 cities with over one million inhabitants, com-pared to around 120 today; in Europe today, there are only 35 cities of that size. Consequently, China's urban population will grow by more than 350 million within 20 years, which is roughly the same population size as the United States today. By 2025, it is estimated that two-thirds of China's citizens, or nearly one billion people, will live in cities. Even with conservative assumptions, urban GDP will more than quadruple between 2005 and 2025, reaching around US$8,200–9,600 per capita from today's figure of less than US$3,000.

What is the impact of this rapid urbanization and emerging-middle-class customers on life insurers? We believe there are two main implications.

The first implication is access—how can insurers get to these customers before everyone else? Since many of these new middle-class households will be first-time buyers of insurance products, a large sales force with a strong focus on consumer education will be needed. Our proprietary survey results showed that many consumers are seeking financial advice and are not receiv-ing it. In Indonesia, for example, agents reported to us that explaining the features of insurance products is a big part of their selling process. At the same time, a large sales force will be required to capture market share, given that many of these customers will have relatively small policy amounts. Building these large sales forces is no easy task—with an 80–90 percent turnover rate in many instances, scaling up quickly is a massive endeavor and probably one of the most critical issues facing many insurers today. This is further complicated by the fact that much of this growth will come from second- and third-tier cities. Simply building sales forces in a few major cities won't be sufficient to capture the growth of the middle class.

Second, our market research shows the increasing complexity within the middle class is creating several distinct segments of customers. For example, the growing number of professionals and white-collar workers, the small-business owners, and the aging savers, are all categories that will fit into the middle-class definition but have very different needs. Increasingly, life insurers will need to understand the various segments of the middle class in order to serve them better. While this is at an early stage, there are already a few insurers that are creating products and channels catering to the increasingly divergent segments. For example, some insurers have found success with remote, direct channels such as outbound call centers for customers who are comfortable with such methods. Others have focused on investment products with sophisticated investment structures for those who seek more adventurous returns. In any case, insurers will need to improve their game and find their competitive edge in order to compete for the subsegments within the middle class.

The Rise of the Multinational Insurers in Asia

Multinational insurance companies (MNCs) are not new in Asia. The best known example is AIG, which has its roots in Shanghai, and a large presence across most of the region (see Box 2A). However, the recent bailout of AIG by the US government in late 2008 will likely change the ending of this story. Apart from AIG and a few other large MNCs that have a true pan-Asia business, most MNCs have a much smaller footprint across Asia, and are mostly active in the financial centers of Hong Kong and Singapore.

In the last decade though, we have seen a strong rise in the foreign presence in Asian insurance markets. Across all markets, foreign players have increased their market share substantially, often at the expense of local incumbents. Several changes in the marketplace fostered this growth of foreign participation in Asia markets: deregulation, economic conditions conducive for entry, and superior capabilities which allow foreign insurers to grow once they have arrived in the market.

2A—AIG: A pioneer in Asia

At the time of writing this book, there is high uncertainty or whether AIG's Asia business will survive in its current form. However, with its long history in Asia and extensive coverage of its markets, AIG has historically been the multinational insurer most committed to the region and serves as an interesting example.

American International Assurance Company (AIA), the founder company of the AIG group, was established in Shanghai, China in 1919. In 1992, after a hiatus of more than 40 years, AIG re-entered the market, becoming the first licensed foreign insurer in China. Despite being headquartered in the US, AIG's life insurance business is highly concentrated abroad. In 2007, a mere 20 percent of its life insurance revenue was generated in the US. During the same period, total Asia, excluding Japan, life insurance revenue was 47 percent of AIG's total.[7] AIG enjoys a dominant position in many of the Asian markets: in the 12 markets we studied, AIG ranked in the top five for nine of these countries in 2007.

The American insurer built this position by being in the vanguard of Asia insurance. Long before other foreign insurers ventured to Asia, AIG was already the first mover in many of the markets. The company has had a constant presence in Tokyo since 1946, and was the first foreign company to sell life insurance in the almost closed Japanese market in 1973. It was in Thailand, Malaysia, and the Philippines before 1950. During the 1960s, it was instrumental in creating the life insurance industry in Hong Kong. In 1992, it was the first foreign insurer to re-enter the Chinese market.

Aside from its early-mover position, AIG's success is largely attributable to a long and winding road in building relationships and commitment to Asia. For 30 years, former chairman, Maurice R. "Hank" Greenberg, cultivated the business by hobnobbing with Asian leaders, from serving on the Hong Kong Chief Executive's Council of International Advisers to offering advice on China's entry into the World Trade Organization (WTO). In China for example, AIG received the first and only foreign, wholly-owned, life and non-life insurance license through its subsidiary AIA (other foreign companies have to comply with a 50 percent limit on ownership), but it took some 18 years to get there. During 1975–92, Hank Greenberg paid dozens of visits to China, establishing long-term personal relationships with senior Chinese officials, including Jiang Zemin and Zhu Rongji,

(continued)

2A (continued)

both mayors of Shanghai during this period, and later to become China's President and Premier, respectively. Greenberg himself sat on the Advisory Committee to Shanghai. Throughout the 1990s, AIG demonstrated its commitment to China in multiple dimensions. It contributed to the drafting of China's first insurance law that was passed in 1995, helped People's Bank of China (PBOC) establish its branch offices in New York, actively lobbied the US. Congress to allow China into the WTO, and even bought Chinese historic antiques from Paris and donated them to China! AIG's efforts paid off. Today, AIA is the undisputed leader among foreign insurers in China. In 2007, it held a 1.8 percent share of the Chinese market, diminutive in absolute terms, but two and a half times greater than the nearest competitor.

AIG's legacy, however, will be put under the test by the financial crisis. As this book goes to press, the US government has offered US$150 billion to AIG to save it from bankruptcy. Many pieces of the AIG empire will likely be sold, including part (or all) of the Asian portfolio.

Of all the factors driving the increasing market share of MNCs, deregulation was the most critical. In some markets, deregulation created access where there was none; in other cases, deregulation allowed foreign players to exploit new channels or market niches and enter markets that were technically open but *de facto* monopolized by local incumbents. Figure 2.6 shows the spectrum of regulations across the Asian markets.

As Figure 2.6 shows, India was the slowest nation in allowing the entry of foreign players. The insurance sector was deregulated in 2000 after over 40 years of market domination by a single government entity—Life Insurance Corporation (LIC). Since deregulation, over 20 private life players have entered the market, most of them joint ventures with MNCs such as Allianz, Prudential (UK), and New York Life. It is important to note that while the deregulation happened very late, once deregulated, there were very few handicaps preventing the foreign joint ventures from expanding across the country. This is in contrast to China, where expansion into new cities requires regulator approval on a case-by-case basis, which is the single largest deterrent to growth in China for foreign insurers.

Country	Year first foreign insurer entered	Year bancassurance allowed	Year investment-linked allowed	▢ Within 10 years
China	1992	2000	1999	
India	2000	2003	2000	
Japan	1954	2001	1986	
Korea	1986	2002	2001	
Taiwan	1987	2000	2000	
Hong Kong	1897	1990s	NR	
Singapore	1931	2001	1992	
Indonesia	1975	1999	1998	
Thailand	1938	NR	2005	
Malaysia	1924	1993	1997	
Philippines	1895	NR	2002	
Vietnam	1999	n/a	2007	

NR: Never restricted
n/a: Not applicable

Figure 2.6 Deregulation in Asia has opened markets
Source: Country regulators; literature search

At another end of the spectrum is South Korea where foreign players had been permitted to operate but the market was so locked up by the domestic "Big 3" players—Samsung Life, Kyobo, and Korea Life—that foreign insurers could make little headway. However, the competitive landscape shifted with the introduction of variable (investment-linked) products in 2001 and bancassurance the following year. Once these products and channels were opened, MNCs took advantage of their superior know how and experience from other markets, which helped them grow market share significantly.

This phenomenal growth in Asia for MNCs happened at a time when growth in their home markets was slowing down. Coupled with higher profitability in Asia compared to their home markets, Asia has quickly become a high priority for many MNCs. For example, Prudential (UK)'s new business profit from Asia is already at more than half of the company's total and is rising in line with the region's rapid growth. "It is an Asian story," says Barry Stowe, the chief executive of Prudential's Asia business. "And it is happening at a phenomenal pace."[8]

There are operational factors that also make MNCs competitive in Asia. MNCs can leverage their product knowledge across markets, often coming up with the more innovative product features compared to the locals. Another important skill is sales force management. A survey of insurance agents showed that across six markets—South Korea, China, Taiwan, Hong Kong, Singapore, and Indonesia—agents overwhelmingly preferred to work for MNCs, with better training and sales force management being the most frequently cited reasons.

In addition, MNCs also tend to recruit higher quality agents capable of selling more sophisticated products. In South Korea, for example, MNCs revolutionized the agency channel by moving away from the "housewife" model, where insurers employed housewives to sell insurance during their free time—often to friends and family. In contrast, MNCs targeted college-educated candidates who were dedicated to the job full-time, and were savvier in selling more sophisticated products such as investment-linked insurance. Similar approaches were also observed in Japan and Taiwan.

An interesting question is whether MNCs who operate across several Asian countries have advantages over those who only have operations in a few select countries. The diversity of the Asian markets with the myriad of languages and local regulations may suggest that synergies across markets are limited, and therefore operating across more countries does not give MNCs additional advantages. However, this narrow view misses a very important point: executive talent. One of the key success factors in Asia is the quality and depth of the top executive bench. MNCs without scale across Asia have generally found it tough to attract a high-caliber executive team. Without a strong team at the top, it is very difficult to redeploy resources, leverage high value-added activities across countries (for example, investments and risk management), and develop a truly pan-Asian business for the long term. The difference between those who have critical mass and accelerating growth in the region and those who have a few operations and are barely keeping up with the market, stands in stark contrast. This is not to say that the large players are always performing better or always attract the top performers, but without scale ambitions, it is difficult to see the smaller MNCs consistently attracting the right talent across the board to bring them to the next level.

The entry options for MNCs are greenfield setups, joint ventures, and acquisitions. While most MNCs have entered Asia as greenfield operations, there has been a handful of acquisitions over the years. For example, Prudential (UK) bought Chinfon in 1999 as a way of gaining access to Taiwan.

Allianz bought First Life in South Korea in 1999. But given the scarcity of deals and the complexity involved in dealing with local insurers' legacy issues (for example, high guaranteed policies and aging sales forces), acquisitions remain difficult, if not impossible, as an entry method. Forming joint ventures, on the other hand, is a common strategy, especially in markets where it is mandated by regulations (such as China and India). Since opening its market to foreign participation in 1992, China has only granted AIA a license to operate independently. The other 24 companies entering after AIG all operate on a joint-venture basis. Under China's WTO commitment, foreign insurers can hold up to 50 percent stakes in the joint ventures. Meanwhile, the Indian government has banned outright wholly-owned foreign insurers. Foreign players must tie up with a local enterprise, with the requirement that foreign investment should not exceed more than 26 percent of the joint venture's equity. The industry has been pushing for an increased proportion of 49 percent but it is unclear when this will be allowed.

As of December 2007, among the top 10 largest non-Asian insurers—life, non-life, and reinsurance—in the world measured by market capitalization,[9] eight were already present in Asia, with six operating in more than five markets. The two exceptions are Berkshire Hathaway and State Farm. As Asia life insurance enters an era where outperformers will dominate—the future has never looked brighter for those MNCs who are able to find their competitive edge in these markets.

The Changing Face of Distribution

Life insurance distribution in Asia has long been dominated by the tied-agent model. While we are convinced that this will remain an important channel for the future, we have already seen bancassurance capturing shares of up to 50 percent in some markets. Furthermore, we will continue to see alternative and broker channels grow faster than the market—although from a still very small base.

Revamping the Agency Force

Asian insurers have typically built up large "tied" agency sales forces that rely heavily on relationship-based selling. These agents are often managed in a multilevel marketing, or pyramid, sales-force model. At the bottom of the pyramid are the new agents who have just entered the sales force. As these agents recruit others to join the sales force and attain some stated standards (usually a minimum number of recruits as well as some level of personal sales), they get promoted to the next level. At this level, their compensation will depend on the sales of their recruited agents, which are often called the override commissions, as well as their own sales. These pyramids can continue to grow up to several layers, with the agency manager at the top of the pyramid managing a sales force of a few hundred agents.

Due to the strong relationships in these sales forces (that is to say, most of the agents are in some way linked to one another), each of these pyramid agencies can take on unique characteristics that are highly dependent on the philosophy and charisma of the agency manager. For example, in a large insurer in China, one of the largest agencies has over 800 agents, occupies a few floors in its own location, has its own internal rules, and even has its own chauffeured vehicles!

These sales forces have been extremely effective in these fast-growing markets, as the local networks of these agents can penetrate all levels of society and geography. However, as one can imagine, the quality of these sales forces varies greatly. Ranging from part-timers to neighborhood housewives to more professional financial advisers, insurance agents come in all sorts and forms. Many of these agents are high-school dropouts, most do not come with a strong financial background, and many have not done sales-related jobs before. As such, trial-and-error is the *modus operandi* for recruiting agents. For example, in rapidly growing sales forces like those in China and India, it is not uncommon to see agent turnover rate of up to 70–80 percent per year, with up to one-third of the agents selling less than one policy per month.

Most of the traditional insurers have begun to revamp their sales forces in one way or another. One of the main themes is the ongoing standardization and upgrading of the agents, and the elimination of part-timers. For example, in Taiwan, the total number of agents dropped from nearly 250,000 in 2001 to 190,000 in 2006. At the same time, the proportion of part-time agents decreased by 4 percent, translating into an increase in first-year premium sales per agent of 3.85 times. In South Korea, the largest domestic insurers have been slowly adjusting their housewives model through a process of elimination and upgrading in order to be more competitive with the foreign insurers' younger agents. In Japan, the traditional insurers have been shrinking the size of their sales forces every year over the past seven years.

However, given the size and the history of these sales forces, this revamping process will be long and painful. For many of these large insurers, this upgrading of their sales forces will be their main challenge for the next several years. While those that can adapt quicker will be able to participate in the market growth, there will be many that will see their competitiveness and market share erode as the legacy issues prove too much to overcome. While these large sales forces are still very valuable assets for local insurers, it is imperative that they understand the urgency to revamp this model.

Growth of Alternative Channels and Brokers

Compared to Western markets, independent financial advisers have not made much of a dent in Asia despite having gradually increased their presence in most markets from a low base. We do not expect this channel to become as significant as it is in many Western markets, where regulation encourages this form of selling. In the more mature Asia markets, such as Japan and Singapore, this channel has been growing fast, but it will take many more years for this channel to have any meaningful share of the overall market.

Other forms of alternative channels, such as direct sales, are also being experimented with. Insurers in South Korea and Japan have been quite innovative in this area, trying out new distribution channels such as home shopping channels. In the Philippines, players have tried selling micro-insurance policies via text message since 2006. In China, companies such as MetLife and Ping An have set up direct outbound call centers, which, although small in size, have had encouraging results. While all these experiments make up interesting case studies, it is unlikely that any of these channels will challenge tied-agency distribution any time soon. They do, however, represent a rapidly growing part of the market.

The Bancassurance Revolution

The one channel that has captured a very significant share from tied agents across Asia is bancassurance, meaning sales of life products by banks. Bancassurance is emerging as a strong distribution channel across all Asian markets after regulators opened this channel for banks to get involved in life insurance. This has been a recent phenomenon: China, Taiwan, and India opened up bancassurance in 2000. Between 2001 and 2007, bancassurance activity increased across all 12 countries studied. In five of these countries bancassurance sales accounted for 30–50 percent of new life premiums sold in 2007. In South Korea, for example, bancassurance sales accounted for 40 percent of new life premiums in 2007.

The success of bancassurance can be attributed to the following factors: i) strong credibility of banking institutions; ii) extensive branch networks with long customer relationships; and iii) products that cater to deposit-centric, Asian customers. Consumers appear to be quite willing to accept a bank as a credible channel for buying insurance. For example, 33 percent of Asia ex-Japan survey respondents indicated that they "prefer to buy life insurance from the bank."[10] Banks are seen as the bedrock of the financial system, and, even in countries like China, where banks were under stress in the early 2000s due to nonperforming loans, consumers never doubted that the banks would always be backed by the government. Compared to the product-oriented agency channel whose agent turnover are extremely high in many Asian markets, the banking channels are perceived to be a more stable and trustworthy channel. Furthermore, in most Asian urban areas, bank branches are plentiful. For example, in Taipei, one of the most heavily branched geographies, there are 3.2 bank branches for every 10,000 people, compared to two bank branches per 10,000 Londoners and 0.3 bank branches per 10,000 Sydney residents. The extensive coverage of the bank branches in Asia makes bancassurance a particularly convenient channel. Finally, many bancassurance products were designed as deposit substitutes that could be easily sold over the bank counters. As interest rates went down during the initial years of bancassurance deregulation, these products became quite popular with banking customers looking for a slightly better return on their large deposit holdings.

The rapid growth of bancassurance warrants the question "Will banks eventually crowd out the agent sales forces?" Globally, there are some examples of markets where bancassurance has become the dominant channel, such as Italy and France. At least in the initial phase, this has mainly been driven by tax incentives making simple, single-premium investment products with little or no protection cover more attractive than alternative investments. Banks sell these products as a key component of customers' investment portfolios to optimize from a tax perspective. Consumers have a limit of tax-exempt funds they can contribute on their insurance products, and they usually purchase up to the limit in quite an automatic fashion. This has created enormous growth in the life insurance market and led to the dominant position of banks as the largest channel in the life industry. However, a closer look reveals that even in these markets agents have continued to grow. Bancassurance has virtually created a new market within life insurance—but agents, especially the better qualified ones, keep growing their traditional business which is more focused on protection and recurring premium products. In other global markets, where life products are more on a level playing field with other investment products, such as Germany or the UK, bancassurance has also grown but agents—or independent financial advisers in the UK—have very much defended their space, especially the better qualified and independent ones.

Likewise in Asia, while bancassurance took a significant proportion of total market share, the agent channel kept growing (see Figure 2.7). Tax incentives for life products in this part of the world are scarce and the fast growth in bancassurance has been driven primarily by simple investment products. This has effectively been a kind of deposit conversion—fuelled by

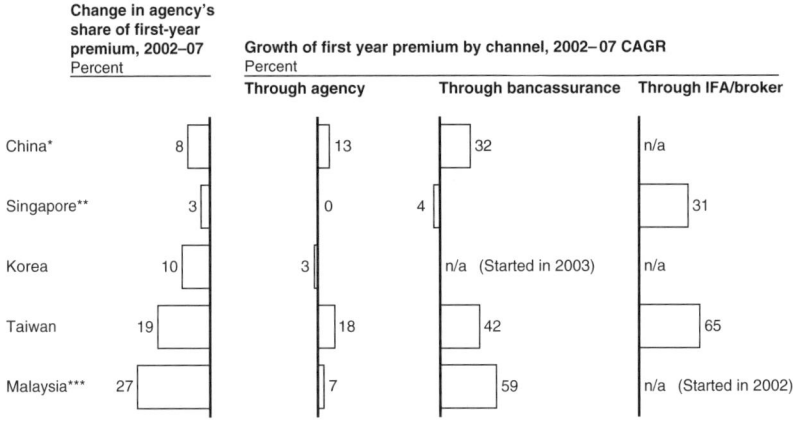

*By GWP due to data availability
**2002 figures for IFA and agency not available. 2002 IFA figure calculated assuming
   linear growth between 2001 and 2004 IFA sales
***Change calculated for 2002–05 as 2006 & 2007 distribution data yet to be released

Figure 2.7 The tied-agency channel is still growing in most markets

Source: Korea Life Insurance Agency; China Insurance Regulatory Commission; Monetary Authority of Singapore; Taiwan Insurance Institute

higher interest rates for life products. We believe that bancassurance in Asia will remain a key channel but growth rates will soon plateau. Some countries, such as India, will continue to see fast growth, especially where markets are not fully deregulated yet or banks have not all taken up this product, but in general we think that in many markets the banks have captured the low-hanging fruit with simple investment products and will find it much more difficult to sell more complex regular premium and protection products.

For the insurers, bancassurance is both an opportunity and a threat. On the one hand, insurers can extend their reach into previously untapped customers through partnering with banks by providing products and expertise. In particular, for those insurers without a large agency sales force, the banking channels can provide them with a quick way of ramping up volume. On the other hand, bancassurance does pose a threat. Overall, banks have recognized their superior bargaining position vis-à-vis the insurers. Consequently, they are demanding a much bigger share of income from bancassurance sales. In many markets, profitability of bancassurance products has deteriorated sharply—in some markets, for instance in China, the bancassurance channel barely breakevens for the insurers.

Recently, in some markets where regulation has allowed integration between banking and insurance, banks have actually started their own life insurers, thus shutting out traditional insurance companies from this channel altogether. The global experience of insurance/bank mergers has not been overly positive though, with many large, integrated, financial conglomerates spinning off the insurance entities after a few years (such as Citibank/Travelers, Credit Suisse/Winterthur, and Allianz/Dresdner). Most of these integrations have failed due to the difference in culture of the insurance and the banking entities, limitation of the cost and revenue synergies beyond the obvious distribution benefits, and different economic models, which are incredibly difficult to communicate to shareholders.

Changing the Product Mix Due to the New Needs of Asian Consumers

With the growing penetration of life insurance and the increasing wealth levels in Asia, it is natural that life products have been evolving. As one would expect, the product trends vary according to the maturity of the markets. While 10 years ago most insurers were selling basic protection and long-term savings products, the rapid wealth accumulation and increasing sophistication of consumers and booming equity markets have led to massive demand for investment-linked products in recent years (also known as unit-linked products). As such, insurers have been quite successful in penetrating the wealth-management market, which is probably the single largest market opportunity across Asia. For even more mature markets, such as Japan, with aging populations, retirement and health are likely to emerge as significant growth segments. Finally, niche areas such as Islamic insurance (*takaful*) are relevant for pockets of consumers whose needs are not met by the traditional insurance offerings.

The increasing diversity of products and consumer needs is forcing insurers to stay on top of these developments. To succeed in these new areas means proficiency in product development and marketing, as well as further training of those working in the distribution channels. These trends have also enabled latecomers in the market to gain share. For example, the overall growth of investment-linked products has provided an unprecedented opportunity for multinational insurers to grab market share from local incumbents across many countries. Most of them have grown disproportionately through training a younger and more sophisticated sales force targeted at selling these more sophisticated products.

Investment-Linked Products

The rapid growth of investment-linked products has blurred the divide between life insurance and investment products. While most of the investment-linked products have some form of protection element built into the product, the bulk of the policyholder premiums are invested in various local and international asset classes. In fact, many of the sales agents are marketing these policies as investments and asset allocation instruments, capturing the investment appetite of the Asian investor.

Why have investment-linked policies experienced such considerable growth in Asia? First, deregulation provided the environment for investment-linked policies to be created, giving insurers the opportunity to participate in the market. Second, investment-linked policies form part of the general rise in wealth-management products, as Asian customers turn from "savers" into "investors." This trend has been further accelerated by the boom in Asian equity markets during 2002–07. The demand for such products has pushed life insurers to adapt quickly and compete with asset management products such as mutual funds for a share of this market. Last, in some jurisdictions, there are also tax advantages for investors in investment-linked products that give them an unique selling point over traditional asset management products (see Box 2B).

Life insurers started selling investment-linked products in most Asian countries in the late 1990s and early 2000s. In 2001, investment-linked sales in Asia were only around US$12 billion, and were marginal relative to the sales of other products. However, by 2007, the figure surged to US$100 billion, accounting for around 65 percent of absolute gross-premium growth in the region. In Hong Kong, Taiwan, India, Malaysia, Singapore, Indonesia, and the Philippines, investment-linked sales accounted for 30 percent of gross premiums. This gave rise to two interesting phenomena: first, investment-linked has become the key growth component in overall sales and second, foreign players have tended to dominate this market.

2B—A primer on the development of investment-linked products

As recently as the early 1990s, when people discussed life insurance products in Asia, it was solely about protection (term life, whole life), annuity, endowments, and similarly traditional life insurance products. Participation products (that is, products giving policyholders a share of the earnings from the investments made on their behalf) were a rarity—investment-linked products were unheard of. Customers came to life insurers with protection in mind, and life insurers happily fulfilled this requirement. That changed in the late 1990s, when life insurers came to realize that the booming wealth-management market was ripe for capture.

Investment-linked products grew out of life insurers tapping into the wealth-management market. They are, in effect, a mutual fund combined with a life protection wrapper. This makes the life insurance company into a broker for the mutual fund and an underwriter of the assurance part

(continued)

2B (continued)

of the contract. Some life insurance companies might not agree with this description but it is a rough reflection of the investment-linked market.

After a customer has purchased an investment-linked policy and the premium has been deducted for commissions, provisions, and operational costs, the remaining investment portion is placed into a special account, or investment pool, and is managed like any other asset-management product. Life insurers can act either as a pure arranger, meaning they outsource the funds they have collected to third-party mutual funds, or they manage the assets themselves through their asset-management arm.

Investment-linked products offer both life insurers and policyholders an interesting alternative to traditional life insurance. For life insurers it means they are able to act as intermediaries in the asset-management business while not having to take on the investment risks involved or run a large asset-management business. The result is a fee-based business with stable margins and less deployment of risk capital.

Compared with mutual funds, investment-linked products have unique characteristics. The two products differ in terms of investment returns and fee structures.

First, due to the addition of a protection wrapper—the industry's description of death coverage for the insured—around its products, investment-linked insurance is never a pure investment product.

Second, the commission and cost structures differ, making investment-linked insurance more attractive for certain types of investors (typically those with a longer investment horizon).

For example, we calculated that for an investment in India with an annual contribution of US$2,500 for 15 years and a sum assured of about US$20,000, the cost of an investment-linked policy is more expensive than a mutual fund until the eighth year, after which, the investment-linked is a better bargain. By year 15, cumulative costs to the customer (load + annual management charge + mortality cover) would have amounted to about US$14,000 on the investment-linked, but US$16,000 for the mutual fund.

Investment-linked sales, plus bancassurance, are the biggest drivers behind life insurance premium growth across Asia. In Japan, for example, sales of variable annuities grew annually by 44 percent between 2002 and 2006. This is a staggering growth number considering that Japan is a mature market with shrinking total premiums. Similarly, in South Korea, the sale of variable products skyrocketed by 87 percent between 2002 and 2007, while sales of endowment policies shrunk to 60 percent of their 2002 figures.

The characteristic of investment-linked products presents a double-edged sword for the insurers in the region. On the one hand, insurers find the product attractive because it carries lower risk. Since the investment portions of the funds are passed through to mutual fund houses, insurers are not carrying the guaranteed liabilities on their balance sheets. In most of the Asian markets, where there is a lack of long-term assets to match long-term liabilities, the asset–liability mismatch often carries substantial risks. Therefore, investment-linked products lessen the already-substantial burden of these insurers to underwrite these investment risks. On the other hand, insurers find these products to be less profitable on an actuarial basis compared with traditional products. It is not uncommon to hear Asian actuaries complaining about the low profitability of investment-linked products. However, it is much less clear whether these actuaries are considering them from a risk-adjusted basis, given that it is almost impossible to hedge the long-term investment risks.

In general, foreign players are more active and aggressive in capitalizing on the demand for investment-linked products. This is probably because foreign multinationals know these products better than their local competitors, who have only recently been allowed to engage in this business as a result of deregulation. Therefore, from a product design and structuring perspective, the multinationals have a substantial advantage over the locals—in most of the markets the products from the multinationals tend to be more innovative.

Moreover, the advantage of foreign players in investment-linked products is not only limited to product design. Investment-linked policies are essentially investment products, and thus require a lot more explanation of the risks and benefits to customers. Many of the local insurers, who built their sales forces over the past decades, have agents who are often less-educated, older, and part-time. Compared to the locals, the foreign insurers' agents can be more easily trained to sell these policies to customers due to the higher quality of their recruits. They also come across as more credible and professional. Indeed some multinational insurers focus almost exclusively on investment-linked products, offering aggressive equity products with high risk/return profiles.

While investment-linked products have been a big growth story for Asian insurers, they have their downsides. The unique strengths of life insurance companies, with their strong balance sheets, cannot be brought to bear here. Life insurers are distinctive from other asset managers in their ability to provide long-term guarantees and smooth, stable returns; however, in the investment-linked market, this advantage is not utilized and they find themselves in direct competition with mutual fund companies and their distributors, which are primarily retail banks. Furthermore, life insurers are relying on a very high-cost channel, tied agents, to compete against banks in selling these investment products.

Investment-linked products will surely continue to grow in the long term as the investment needs for Asian consumers can only increase. In the short term there will be volatility, depending on the performance of the equity markets. At times of equity market downturns the sales of investment-linked products tend to suffer. In particular, Asian investors' investment horizons are much more short-term than those in more developed markets—this is partially due to the fact that the Asian equity markets are much more volatile than those in the West. Figure 2.8 shows that on average, Asians hold mutual funds for much shorter periods than the Western countries. At the low end, Chinese investors hold mutual funds for seven months, whereas at the other end of the spectrum, US investors hold mutual funds for an average of five years.

Across Asia, we believe that the sensitivity of investment-linked products to swings in the equity markets will differ according to the maturity of the sales force and the customer base. In the more mature Asian markets (such as Hong Kong and Singapore) where the long-term growth trend is positive and policyholders are more mature and equipped with a long-term mindset, investment-linked sales are more likely to flatten out rather than significantly slow down, even in times of equity market downturns. In other Asian markets where the long-term growth trend is steep but investors are less sophisticated and more speculation-minded, investment-linked sales are likely to fluctuate more with equity market booms and busts.

Over the past few years, investment-linked products have given life insurers a big boost in growing the overall size of the market. This has undeniably been aided by a benign economic environment and very high returns

Holding period of mutual funds
Number of years

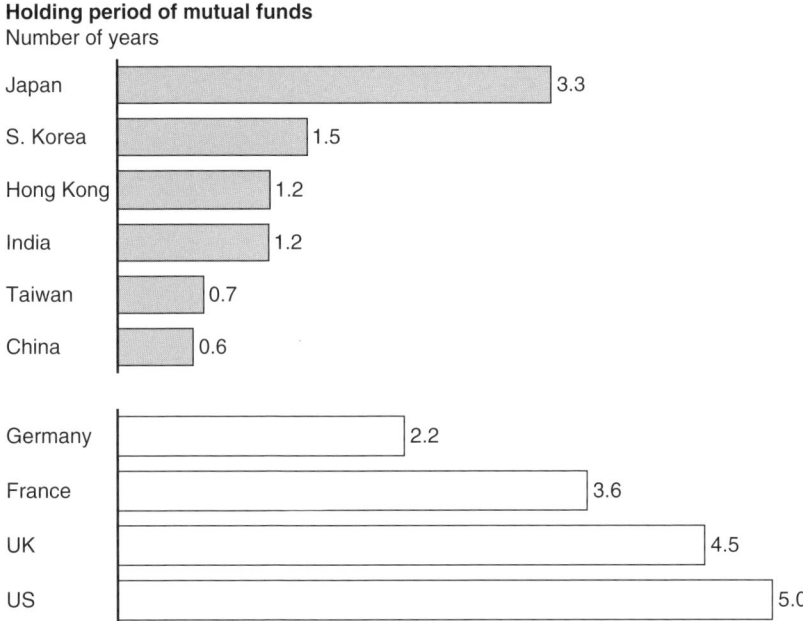

Note: 2006/07 data, depending on availability

Figure 2.8 Asians are short-term investors

Source: AMCIC; IRDA; AMFI; Nikkei; The Investment Trusts Association, Japan; EAMS; Lipper; ICI Mutual Fund Fact Book 2007; Strategic Insight, HKIA; press search; McKinsey

in the local equity markets. Starting in 2008, the economic environment has shifted into an extremely bearish mode with significant volatility in the equity markets. This volatility will again remind investors of the risks in the equity markets, and the benefits of long-term savings and stable returns. In these markets it would not be surprising to see some shift from investment-linked products back to more traditional products.

One last caveat on investment-linked products: History shows that over aggressive "mis-selling" by insurers can have substantial negative effects on the market as a whole. This first happened in Japan where a series of mis-selling incidents turned the Japanese consumer away from these products. In the late 1980s, insurance agents pushed investment-linked products to unsuspecting customers without fully disclosing the risk of such offerings. In addition, the agents made alliances with banks to allow customers to take out large loans for the purchase of these products, thus further increasing the customers' risk exposure. When the Japanese stock market crashed in the early 1990s many saw their savings disappear.

From 1994, customers filed lawsuits against insurance companies and banks alleging a lack of sufficient explanation of the risks entailed in variable insurance. The impact on reputation was lethal. Sales subsequently stagnated for over 10 years.

Annuities

Annuities have traditionally been a small segment of the insurance market in Asia, despite their unique product characteristics. Annuity policies are the only products that protect one against longevity risk—the risk of outliving one's expectations. Although there are various flavors of annuities, typically these products provide a stable stream of income that is guaranteed for as long as the policyholder is alive.

The one country in which annuities have a large share of the market is Japan where, in 2006, the annuities business accounted for about 40 percent of annualized premium for new individual policies. In fact, annuities, as a segment, have been growing since the 1980s. The Japanese enthusiasm for annuities policies can be explained by the maturity of the market, a large aging population and the presence of many wealthy pensioners.

Other than Japan, the annuities business elsewhere in Asia has been minimal. For example, in Singapore it accounted for only 2.2 percent of gross-premium income in 2007 and 5.3 percent in Taiwan in 2006. A likely reason for this low level of business is cultural attitude. In most Asian cultures, old people traditionally rely on bank savings, real-estate profits, and their children for post-retirement income, thus diminishing the need for a product to provide a stable source of retirement funding. In addition, Asians tend to be less interested in annuities policies because those with wealth are keen to pass it on to their children rather than use up their accumulated wealth in their twilight years. Moreover, in certain countries, such as China, wealth resides with a much younger age group, who are not yet at the age where they are considering retirement expenses.

There have been pockets of growth though. In South Korea, the annuities business grew from US$9 billion in premium income in 2002 to over US$14.5 billion in 2007, representing a 10 percent annual growth rate. This growth is attributable to the decline of pension benefits relative to rising living standards, less enduring family structures that make pensioners less reliant on their children for income, and a growing retirement population. For example, South Korea has been worried about its public pension system going bankrupt for years; various organizations' estimates put the year when the national pension fund would dry up as somewhere between 2020 and 2060.[11] We suspect that as parts of Asia age quickly over the next decade, the potential growth of annuities as a product segment will likely increase.

Accident and Health

With its huge population Asia should have a substantial market for accident and health products. However, this market is deceptively small. For eight of the markets—China, India, Hong Kong, South Korea, Singapore, Taiwan, Indonesia, and Malaysia—the aggregate accident and health market was worth a mere US$25 billion in 2007, or less than 10 percent of their total life gross written premium (GWP). The compound annual growth rate (CAGR) from 2002 to 2007 was 15 percent.

There are many reasons for this relatively small market size. First, strong government presence and the dominance of public payor systems limit the growth potential of these markets. Second, as maturing markets, the median income levels still render private health insurance a luxury for many. Third, underdeveloped healthcare infrastructure hinders insurers with such problems as nonstandardized treatment protocols, lack of case management, and fraud. Therefore, the market remains underpenetrated, although there are pockets of growth within specific segments. For example, the affluent segment, generally, is willing to pay for better healthcare than that which the State might offer. Especially in the more mature markets, such as Japan, health insurance will emerge as a key growth driver in the mid term.

Healthcare is a large topic both in Asia and the rest of the world. In this book, we touch on health insurance only as it relates to life insurers, but the intricacies of healthcare and medical reform merit a separate study.

Islamic Insurance

Islamic insurance, or *takaful*, is a nascent, underdeveloped market segment within the global life insurance market, but its market potential is substantial given the worldwide Muslim population of almost 1.5 billion. In Indonesia, India, China, and Malaysia alone, there are an estimated

350 million Muslims. Indonesia has the largest Muslim population in the world, with an estimated 200 million believers.

However, insurance penetration in these countries has traditionally been low—in part because some aspects of life insurance policies are in violation of Islamic Law or *Sharia*, which forbids the earning and charging of interest. *Takaful* was developed as a means of complying with Islamic requirements (see Box 2C).

Due to its large untapped potential, many life insurers are now seeking to open this market, including international names such as Allianz and Prudential (UK). The market is still very small—*takaful* life insurance premiums amounted to US$600 million in Malaysia in 2007 and US$31 million in Indonesia in 2006 (8 percent and 1.1 percent of the overall market respectively). However, the growth of the *takaful* market has outperformed the overall market and the product has yet to reach a large proportion of Asian Muslims. For example, *takaful* life premiums grew 34 percent annually in Indonesia from 2001 to 2006, while the overall market grew 24 percent. With opportunities still available in China and India, both homes to large Muslim communities, it seems reasonable to assume that the *takaful* market has plenty of scope for growth.

2C—*Takaful* insurance in Asia

Takaful insurance was developed to meet the needs of Muslim customers whose investments are expected to comply with the requirements of *Sharia* or Islamic Law. However, *Sharia* compliance alone is not enough to capture this opportunity. By combining Islamic values with conventional banking attributes, financial institutions can gain a powerful competitive advantage. McKinsey research shows that most Islamic finance customers are not motivated solely by the desire to invest in *Sharia*-compliant products. A market research study on key buying factors for deposit products in Indonesia found that accessibility scored the highest in terms of importance, then yield, fees, and only finally *Sharia* compliance. However, at the same time, consumers indicated an 8x multiple in utility for *Sharia* deposit products compared to conventional products.[12] Indeed, Malaysia has proven that *Sharia*-compliant products do not need to be exclusively for Muslims. Due to equal, if not higher, returns, ethnic Chinese in Malaysia are also buying *Sharia*-compliant

(continued)

2C (*continued*)

products. A study of the Jakarta and Kuala Lumpur stock exchanges, between 2002 and 2007, showed that KLSE Syariah Index[13] performed equally as well as the Kuala Lumpur Composite, while the Jakarta SE Islamic Index actually outperformed the Jakarta SE Composite by 100 percentage points.

In essence, *takaful* works on the following principles. As far as participants are concerned they jointly guarantee to protect each other against a defined loss, meaning that participants do not buy policies from an insurer but instead donate to a pool of funds which helps all investors in the pool (including themselves). Profits and responsibilities are shared among all participating investors. The *takaful* operator (the insurer) contracts to administer and operate the funds on behalf of the participants and do so on a commercial basis. The operator is required to provide full transparency for fees and charges and to separate the company's funds from those of the participants. Investments can only be made in *Sharia*-compliant assets that do not involve the charging or earning of interest.

Given its early nature, the *takaful* market is not significant at present but it is fast-growing. As matters stand in Southeast Asia, it is only really noticeable in Malaysia where gross premium—both life and property and casualty (P&C)—stood at some US$770 million in 2007. Even in Indonesia, the world's largest Muslim nation, *takaful* premiums were only US$51 million in 2006. Outside this region, the largest *takaful* market is in Saudi Arabia where gross premiums totalled US$756 million. Estimates of where the market will be by 2015 vary considerably with projections ranging from US$7.4 billion to US$14 billion for both life and P&C combined. This compares with a current market size of some US$2.3 billion, of which US$0.8 billion is derived from the Asia-Pacific market. We believe the growth from *takaful* will be high (just a matter of how high) because the penetration levels in Southeast Asia (even Malaysia) are still low compared to the states of the Gulf Cooperation Council (GCC).

The development of this market is largely determined by a confluence of three factors. First is government stewardship, which often means specific encouragement to promote the development of *takaful*. Success in Malaysia has in large part been due to government leadership providing clear guidelines/transparency to players interested in developing this market. Second, customer demand will drive this market and it is likely that this will have to be stimulated beyond just enticing customers to invest on religious reasons. Providing a more comprehensive/compelling value proposition to make *takaful* competitive with traditional alternatives will be key. Third, the market will only

(continued)

2C (*continued*)

develop in line with the growing sophistication of Islamic financial institutions. For example, the lack of sophisticated Islamic financial institutions in Indonesia can explain the low penetration of *takaful* in this massive Muslim nation.

Most of the players in the *takaful* market are specialist Islamic financial institutions but a number of major, non-Islamic financial institutions have emerged (mainly in Malaysia), including HSBC, Prudential (UK), and Allianz; in most cases they have teamed up with Islamic financial specialists and their operations are supervised by Islamic scholars who ensure compliance with *Sharia* requirements. Having a *takaful* offering is useful for insurers who are looking for a broader product mix to cross sell.

With the Islamic insurance market growing by 15–40 percent per year, albeit from a very small base, a good opportunity has been provided for new players alongside the better established institutions who, in this market, are also newcomers.

China and India: Yes, Size Does Matter

	China	India
Macroeconomic		
GDP (US$ billions)	3,416	1,193
GDP per capita (US$)	2,586	1,018
PPP GDP per capita (US$)	8,217	5,264
Inst. assets under management (US$ bns)	n/a	16
PFA (US$ billions)	1,508	285
Foreign reserve (US$ billions)	1,166	196
Socioeconomic		
Population (millions)	1,314	1,120
# of households (thousands)	379,760	209,886
Median household income (US$)	2,930	2,600
# of households earning >US$10k p.a.	12,100	9,606
% of households earning >US$10k p.a.	3%	5%
Urbanization (% of population)	41%	29%
% of population older than 65 in 2005	8%	5%
% of population older than 65 in 2025	15%	10%
Life insurance		
GWP (US$ billions)	68	52
Life insurance penetration	2%	4%
Life insurance density (US$ billions)	162	123
Investment-linked %	8%	66%
Bancassurance %	34%	9%
# of life insurers	53	17
# of foreign life insurers	24	18
Foreign share %	6%	18%
Year foreign entry allowed	1992	2000
Life insurance assets (US$ billions)	318	217

Note–all figures for 2007 unless otherwise stated

On March 26, 2008, Beijing hailed the opening of its third airport terminal. Designed by the British firm Foster + Partners, the sleek, modern terminal is 3 km (1.8 miles) long, and 17 percent larger than all of London Heathrow's terminals combined, including Terminal 5, which opened the same week.[1] Built at breakneck speed in four years by an army of 50,000 workers, Beijing's Terminal 3 is an architectural masterpiece to marvel at, with a lofty ceiling, full-height glass windows, and a roof formed in the shape of a dragon.

It was not so long ago that travellers to China resigned themselves to backward terminals, squat toilets, passenger lines from counter to curb, and lounges blanketed by curtains of cigarette smoke. Fifteen years ago, Beijing's airport was a subsized airport located in paddy fields northeast of the capital. Serving 100 flights a day, the terminal was dark, dingy, cramped, and smoky. Passengers took crowded buses from the terminal to airplanes on the tarmac. In some regional airports, computerized check-in systems were nonexistent, and passengers elbowed each other to board the plane—there was no assigned seating. James Kynge, who chronicled the rise of the Chinese economy in his book, *China Shakes the World*, recounted the days "when CAAC was known as China Airways Always Cancels. They never took off if there was a hint of bad weather."[2]

By 2007, Beijing Capital International Airport was the ninth busiest airport in the world.

The evolution of Beijing Airport chronicles the rising significance of China and the other emerging Asian giant, India. For strangers to these countries, the statistics of China and India are often mind-boggling. The size and speed of development of these nations have captivated headlines in recent years. In aviation, China's air traffic is expected to double every five years and India has seen an increase of 29 percent in the number of flights taking off from its airports between 2006 and 2007. The Airports Authority of India estimated that 100 million people travelled by plane in India in 2007, compared to just 43 million in 2003–04.[3] Only a hermit living on a remote mountaintop can have failed to get the message that China and India are the "new superpowers" of economic development with real gross domestic product (GDP) growth set to expand by 8–10 percent per annum between 2007 and 2012. These growth rates are even more remarkable given that India and China comprise 37 percent of the world's population. Anyone focusing on China's 1.3 billion population needs to appreciate that India is on course to exceed this total.

Ask any historian though, and they will tell you that the significance of China and India is not a recent phenomenon at all. Figure 3.1 traces the development of the global economy since the first century AD. It is striking to see that China and India have been the leading producers in the world economy for over 1,700 years! It was only in the last two to three centuries that the two countries' economic production shrunk, as a percentage of global production. So what is normal? One interesting perspective is that China and India are merely regaining their historic position on the world's economic map.

The implication of China and India's growth for life insurers is that these two countries will represent much of the growth in Asia in the next decade and beyond, with likely sustainable double-digit growth rates. Today, large parts of the populations of both India and China are still poor but as incomes rise, more people will have the ability to save, and life insurance is often the first financial product these people purchase. For life insurers, the potential market is analogous to looking at a reservoir

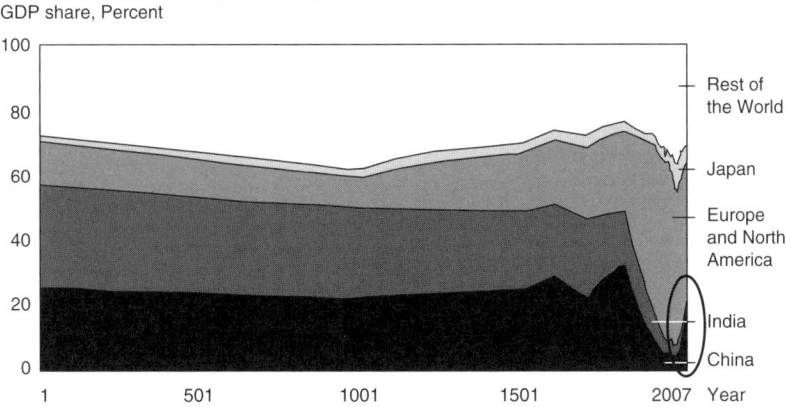

Share of total work GDP (1–2007 AD)
GDP share, Percent

Figure 3.1 What is "normal?"

Source: Angus Madison's "Historical Statistics for the World Economy: 1–2004 AD," Deutsche Bank Global Market Research

that goes on forever. This does not mean that there will not be hiccups along the way though. Volatility, a hallmark of Asia, definitely applies to both China and India, and it would be foolhardy to think that growth will develop in a straight line.

Although there is enormous potential for market growth, the environment is already extremely competitive. These countries are certainly not easier markets to penetrate than other parts of Asia—in particular, for foreign players who have to deal with significant regulatory constraints—but the potential rewards are much greater.

China opened the window to foreign insurers in 1992; India eased its window open only since the turn of the millennium. Both nations have thriving domestic life insurance companies and foreign joint ventures—how will these markets play out for them? This is certainly going to be one of the most interesting questions for these markets. Most of the major foreign life insurance players are playing in both markets, they are not choosing between India and China because they realize that they need a presence in both countries. And they know that if they want to make an impression in these markets they have to take a long-term view. Some Chinese local players are also beginning to become serious contenders on the world stage both in terms of clout and size. The Indian players are not far behind.

Despite the enormous growth potential, the current size of the China and India life insurance markets is still moderate. In 2007, China and India respectively ranked as third and fourth in Asia, with gross premiums of US$68 billion and US$52 billion respectively, significantly smaller than Japan's US$325 billion or South Korea's US$85 billion, and comparable to Taiwan's US$50 billion. In terms of growth expectations for the next five years, China and India are expected to continue to improve their position to second and third respectively in Asia and within the top 10 globally.

China's gross written premium (GWP) grew at 17 percent and India's grew at 30 percent annually from 2002 to 2007, and we expect them to grow at an average of 20 percent for the next five years. This tremendous market growth has also enabled the emergence of local players with global significance: The two largest insurers in China, China Life and Ping An, are now among the largest global insurers by market capitalization (on June 30, 2008, this was: China Life: US$99 billion; Ping An: US$53 billion). The Life Insurance Corporation (LIC) of India has 200 million policyholders and had 1.1 million agents in March 2007.

Market Trends Common to China and India

Many local and international players are attracted by China's and India's market prospects—we are seeing three main trends that describe the environment they will have to operate in:

- High growth potential in both markets
- Competition is intensifying rapidly
- Regulatory obstacles remain

High Growth Potential in Both Markets

Both China and India, despite their phenomenal growth over the last decade or so, retain significant growth potential. Penetration remains relatively low; the demographic trends are favorable; and these nations are in the middle of an incredible, sustained economic boom.

Insurance penetration, as a percentage of GDP, was 1.8 percent and 4.3 percent respectively in 2007, which is low compared with the more developed nations in the region. Hong Kong, for example, was at 10 percent, while Taiwan was at 13 percent—which might be an indication of what is still to come in China and India. Per capita premium is also low, at US$47 per person per year in China and US$46 in India, a mere 2 percent of equivalent expenditure in Japan.[4]

These statistics suggest enormous latent demand which is in the process of being converted to sales, especially among the growing, and increasingly wealthy, middle class. Nominal per capita GDP is expected to nearly double between 2007 and 2012 in China to around US$5,000 per year, and in India to US$2,000. It is estimated that in China another 70 million households, earning more than US$10,000 per year, will join the ranks of the burgeoning middle class in just another five years.[5] That figure will be nearly 30 million in India. Furthermore, this growth is expected to continue beyond the next decade. The McKinsey Global Institute's publication, *The Bird of Gold: The Rise of India's Consumer Market*, predicts growth of the average household disposable income in India to accelerate both in urban and rural areas (see Figure 3.2). For urban households, disposable income will increase by 5.8 percent annually in real terms from 2005 to 2025—accelerating from the 4.6 percent annual growth rate over the past two decades. Rural income would grow at a slower rate of 3.6 percent, but will nevertheless surpass today's average urban household income by 2025. In China, 65 percent of urban households will have an annual income over US$2,700 by 2025. In the same year, urban China will comprise of about 940 cities and towns with a total urban population of around 930 million people.[6]

As the two countries' per capita GDP grows, this will drive the penetration of financial services in general, and life insurance in particular. Household savings rates are high, at 14 percent and 27 percent, in 2007, for China and India respectively, compared with 4.4 percent and −1 percent in the US and UK.[7] This will accelerate insurance penetration

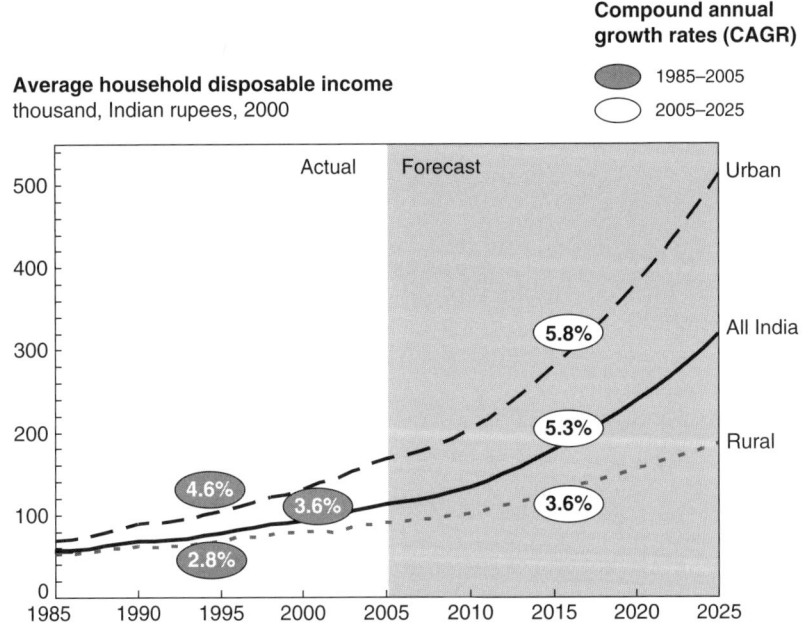

Figure 3.2 Household income growth will accelerate across India
Source: McKinsey Global Institute

and per capita coverage. In our Personal Financial Services surveys, conducted over the past decade in Asia, insurance comes out every time as one of the first financial products bought by the emerging, Asian-middle-class customers. As such, there is no doubt that the demand for savings, protection, and investment products will continue to grow rapidly over the next decades.

Competition is Intensifying Rapidly

China and India's life insurance markets share a common history of state-owned monopolies dominating the home markets.

The Chinese life insurance industry was nationalized after the establishment of the People's Republic of China in 1949, leading to the formation of a single entity—the People's Insurance Company of China (PICC). This company was later divided into two entities—PICC and what became China Life (see Box 3A).

3A—A brief history of China's life insurance market and the emergence of China Life

Today's insurance boom in China is in fact the country's second spring. The insurance industry has undergone many big changes over the last century, and the organization that is China Life today has been center stage for most of this time.

Prior to the formal establishment of the People's Republic of China (PRC) in 1949, China had some 240 insurance companies, approximately 180 of which were domestically owned.[8] With the establishment of the PRC, however, the government consolidated all insurance interests and established the People's Insurance Company of China (PICC). Many domestic companies abandoned their domestic assets and fled abroad to rebuild their businesses.

In the ensuing three decades, PICC operated a monopoly in a market where the state provided most necessities. There was negligible need for domestic insurance.

Deng Xiaoping's economic reforms, in the early 1980s, revived the stagnant insurance industry. In 1982, PICC offered life insurance again, and the

(continued)

3A (continued)

market was opened to private competitors in 1988. China Pacific came into being in that year, as well as Ping An. The two newer companies gained significant share in the early years through the development of branch offices and tied agencies, which PICC, as a state-owned enterprise, was initially barred from doing.

In 1996, PICC was reorganized into a holding company with three subsidiaries—PICC Life, PICC Property, and PICC Reinsurance. Two years later the three split and became independent entities: China Life, PICC, and China Re.

China Life was listed on the Hong Kong and New York stock exchanges in 2003. The listed company excluded the holding company, which was left with a highly unprofitable in-force business. China Life was the largest life insurer by gross premium in 2007 and its market capitalization exceeded US$100 billion as of December 2007. Ping An listed in Hong Kong in 2004 and later in Shanghai; China Pacific listed on the Shanghai Stock Exchange in 2007.

Similarly, India's LIC enjoyed a monopoly for nearly 50 years. The Indian life insurance industry was nationalized in 1956 when frequent insurance fraud attracted the attention of Indian legislators. LIC was formed with the intention to protect policyholders and was created by consolidating 245 private life insurers and other entities offering life insurance services.

In both markets, recent deregulation opened the doors to new, aggressive attackers. As of 2007, there were 53 life insurers in China, whereas in 2004, there were only 28. India started with only 4 private insurers when the market opened in 2000—by mid-2008, there were 20.

Life for new attackers is not easy. In both markets, it is becoming increasingly difficult to capture additional market share. With incumbents fighting back and private domestic and foreign joint ventures innovating and bringing world class practices into these markets, the cost of competing keeps rising. Indeed, the "landgrab" phase for these markets might end much earlier than expected and a stronger focus on value creation will prevail.

The challenge is enormous for new entrants, or those looking to enter these markets. Playing catch up with a "me-too" approach is an increasingly difficult option; new entrants are already considering the adoption of more focused approaches. In India, some new entrants are deliberating strategies that will pinpoint specific customer segments or product classes (for example, pensions and health insurance). Nonetheless, both China and India are still very much at the beginning of their growth curve. This should continue to offer very attractive long-term opportunities, even for late entrants—if they can overcome the operational challenges and adopt a long-term perspective.

Regulatory Obstacles Remain

China and India remain two of the more tightly regulated markets in Asia; deregulation came much later than in most other markets. In China, waves of liberalization have allowed new players to compete for market share following the end of China Life's monopoly. In the late 1980s and early 1990s, we saw the emergence of domestic insurers such as Ping An and China Pacific, and, in 1992, AIG was the first foreign insurer to re-enter the China Life insurance market. By 2007, China Life's market share in new life insurance premium decreased to 40 percent. In India, at least 20 private life players have entered the market since 2000, most of them foreign–domestic joint ventures. Over the last 7–8 years, these private players have grown rapidly, taking about 50 percent of new business on an annual premium equivalent (APE) basis for 2007–08.

Although regulations have eased, they are—in particular, for foreign competitors—still more restrictive than in many other Asian countries where foreign ownership of life insurers has been largely deregulated with a few exceptions. In China, foreigners are limited to a 50 percent equity stake for a joint venture but equity stakes in local companies are restricted to 24.9 percent. A single foreign investor is limited to a maximum of a 20 percent stake, but the China Insurance Regulatory Commission (CIRC) sometimes grants exceptions, such as the Fortis investment into Taiping Life, in which the Benelux firm took a 24.9 percent stake. In India, the limit on foreign ownership is even lower at 26 percent, although this has not prevented foreign players from having effective operating control in some instances. These regulatory constraints mean that foreign players have no choice but to find suitable joint venture partners. Today, foreign joint-venture insurers' shares of the Chinese and Indian markets are still relatively small compared with the rest of Asia—in China they had an 8 percent market share[9] in 2007 and in India, foreign joint ventures had 18 percent of market share in 2006.

The preceding few pages described some of the commonalities between China and India. Yet despite the inevitable comparisons, China and India are very different markets, with more differences than similarities. We will now highlight the rapid development of these two countries—arguably the most important two markets for global insurers in the next decade.

China: Emerging Giant

China is without doubt the most important growth story in the life insurance world—as it is in so many other industries. A mid-sized market today—smaller than the Italian market—it will likely become one of the largest insurance markets globally in the next several years. With annual growth rates projected at around 19 percent, the Chinese life insurance market will be larger than Germany's by 2010, and by 2015, it will have overtaken the United Kingdom as the third-largest market in the world, after the United States and Japan. Of course, this will not be straight-line growth, and there will be volatility along the way, but we are convinced that the growth of the life insurance market is broad-based and founded on solid fundamentals. The high national savings rate, and the enormous pace at which the economic development of China is producing households that for the first time have the means to invest in savings and protection products, will continue to fuel growth for a long time. First, China currently has about 12 million households with an income of more than US$10,000, mostly in urban centers, and this figure is expected to increase nearly sevenfold over the next five years. Second, the economic development is spreading from the urban centers where it started—the Pearl River (around Shenzhen), the Yangtze Delta (around Shanghai), and in the area of Beijing—westward to reach deep into the hinterland, where the majority of the population currently resides.

In absolute terms, most of the growth in Chinese life insurance will come from second- and third-tier cities and even rural areas.

On the distribution side, the big growth story of the last five years was the explosion of insurance sales through banks. Bancassurance accounted for 40 percent of 2005 first year premium (FYP) and 55 percent of 2006 FYP, a 42 percent increase. Over the same period, year-on-year growth of FYP was only 3.6 percent. It is not hard to see the reasons behind this. Chinese bank branches have long been underutilized distribution channels, mainly serving as collectors of deposits from retail and corporate customers, and lenders to local companies and government entities. In the last few years, with an increasing emphasis on fee-based income, banks have mobilized their branches to sell retail financial products, of which bancassurance became the big focus. However, sustaining profitability in this channel for life insurers looks increasingly challenging. As in many markets, the banks have realized they are in a strong negotiating position and are getting the lion's share of margins. For the insurers, the market-share numbers and growth often mask the less attractive profit numbers.

In terms of products, investment-linked policies grew at a combined annual rate of 27 percent while the market, overall, grew at 17 percent annually during the period 2002–07. Similar to other Asian markets, the investment appetite of Chinese customers remains strong. Meanwhile, some insurers are dabbling in the still nascent health insurance segment. While China has started to rebuild its state welfare system with some basic pension and healthcare provision, the Chinese are well aware that this is very basic cover at best. As the middle class emerges, they will likely seek greater protection (see Box 3B).

3B—China health insurance: From ugly duckling to swan?

With its 1.3 billion population, strong GDP growth, rapidly increasing wealth levels, and erosion of the traditional social security system—the so-called "iron rice bowl." China should be a highly attractive market for private health insurers. However, in 2007, the market size in total premiums was only US$4.9 billion. The reason lies in an underdeveloped provider sector and a rapidly growing public payor system. Similar to many European markets, private medical insurance (PMI) in China is largely supplementary to

(continued)

3B (continued)

government schemes, rather than a primary provider per the US system. As a result, health insurance premium accounts for only a small proportion of overall healthcare expenditure. In 2006, PMI accounted for about 4 percent of total healthcare spending.

The Chinese healthcare system is covered by five types of insurance—basic medical insurance (BMI), public insurance, urban citizens medical scheme (UCMS), rural cooperative medical scheme (RCMS), and PMI, but less than 50 percent of the Chinese population was covered as of 2006. Of the five schemes, the first four are government-sponsored plans for various segments of the population—urban residents, government employees, rural residents, etc.—and make up the bulk of coverage in China.

Looking forward, the government plans to focus on broader insurance penetration among the population, but less on depth of policy coverage. In 2006, 57 percent of urban employees were covered by BMI; by 2010, the government aspires to cover all urban employees and retirees. However, this insurance is positioned to meet "basic" medical needs only. Drugs or treatments regarded as nonessential, which are typically more expensive, are not covered.

This gives PMI players opportunities to provide add-on products to fill in the coverage gap. Between 2001 and 2006, health expenditure in China grew at a 14 percent compounded annual rate to US$135 billion, and is expected to reach US$204 billion by 2010. In particular, the Chinese PMI market has been growing by 32 percent annually from 2004 to 2006, and is expected to continue outpacing the overall expenditure. Swiss Re expects the market to be worth US$60 billion by 2020.

Growth momentum in the Chinese PMI market is strong. The major growth drivers are: substantial BMI coverage gaps, demand for better medical service, and demand for global coverage. Though about 57 percent of the urban population has been covered by BMI, there are still substantial coverage gaps, such as deductibles, co-payments, and non-BMI-accredited treatments. In Beijing, for example, a BMI policy comes with a US$275 deductible, and a 50 percent co-pay. Payout is capped at US$5,750. Consequently, affluent individuals are increasingly seeking "beyond basics" services. Significant patient dissatisfaction persists against the Chinese public provider system, mainly due to long waiting times. A McKinsey patient survey showed that 57 percent of urban patients are dissatisfied with the choice of providers, 62 percent with medical practice, and 64 percent with service

(continued)

3B (continued)

levels. In a Shanghai hospital, the average waiting time for a consultation was 78 minutes, as opposed to an international benchmark of 30 minutes. Finally, a premium customer segment is emerging in China. Foreigners working in China, senior executives, wealthy individuals, and outbound employees are seeking global coverage. Though such high-end products have emerged in the Chinese PMI market, their availability is still limited and awareness relatively low.

Meanwhile, the market is becoming increasingly competitive for insurers. As of 2006, 79 insurance companies, including life, property and casualty (P&C) and dedicated health insurers, have been active in the Chinese PMI market. In addition to insurance companies, there are another four parties relevant to Chinese PMI market dynamics: the All China Federation of Unions provides mutual insurance to its members; TPA companies provide product development and claims management; health management companies provide add-on services such as health check-ups and evaluation, and finally, insurance brokers are powerful intermediaries to the health insurance market. Nevertheless, life insurers still dominate the Chinese PMI market, with 95 percent market share in 2006. Among these, Ping An and China Life are the top two players, with a combined market share of 66 percent in 2006.

Private health insurers are also suffering from an underdeveloped provider sector. Difficulties in case management, low bargaining power, overprescription, and fraud plague PMI players under the current provider system. Due to the lack of a primary care system and standard treatment protocols, insurers find implementation of utilization management and case management difficult in China. Although there are some standard treatment protocols, many Class III hospitals[10] do not implement them due to doctors' reluctance to change and differing opinions on certain treatment practices. Insurance companies also have little bargaining power in negotiating fee schedules, since China's provider system is dominated by large, public hospitals. Concurrently, a reliance on drugs and device sales for funding leads public hospitals to overprescribe. In 2005, 42 percent of an average hospital's revenue was derived from device or drugs sales, which compensates for money-losing medical services. Only 9 percent of a hospital's revenue originates from government subsidies. As a result, doctors try to push for greater drug and device sales. In 2006, China's antibiotics sales accounted for 36 percent of the total pharmaceutical market, compared with a worldwide total of 5 percent.

(continued)

3B *(continued)*

But leading market-minded hospitals are starting to show interest in collaborating with insurance companies, especially for VIP patients brought in by PMI players. For example, the leading hospital in Shenzhen offers preferential services to PICC and Ping An customers, including priority check-in and a dedicated guide. Similarly, the university-affiliated Fudan Hospital Group in Shanghai signed an alliance agreement with PICC Health in 2006. There has been a steady growth in VIP wards in public hospitals, driven by demand for higher service levels by affluent patients and by the hospitals' need to create additional revenues. VIP beds in first-tier cities jumped from around 14,000 in 2001 to nearly 18,000 in 2005.

In addition, the government is also piloting healthcare system reforms to privatize hospitals and separate pharmacies from hospitals. To make medical services more affordable for patients, the government has been conducting pilot schemes that separate pharmacy services from the public hospitals in a few cities since 2000. Nanjing is regarded as a successful example of hospital pharmacy reform. It has managed to spin off the pharmacies from most Class I hospitals and 50 percent of Class II hospitals.

Some product segments are more attractive than others for insurers. Currently there are four types of health insurance cover available in the Chinese PMI market—dread diseases, medical expenses, disability income, and care. Disability income and care products are just new to the Chinese market. Dread disease products and medical insurance products are still the best sellers. According to a Swiss Re survey, about 81 percent of premium is contributed by dread disease products in the individual segment, whereas 93 percent of premium is from medical insurance products in the group employer segment. High-end products targeting expatriates senior executives, and high-net-worth individuals, have emerged in the Chinese PMI market, providing global coverage and having similar product features to overseas products—however, this segment is still very small. The group employer segment, especially the MNC employer subsegment, is highly competitive. Most insurance companies have entered this market, as the quickest way to grab market share, but their product offering is highly undifferentiated, leading to a "price war" effect. Profitability of group business varies by subsegment. Usually, the high-end subsegment is very profitable (with a loss ratio of 30–40 percent), but the general staff subsegment is mostly money-losing (with a loss ratio of up to 100 percent). However, health insurance products are usually bundled with other life or

(continued)

3B (*continued*)

P&C products as a full insurance package to employers; health insurance products are often seen as a loss leader to get the profitable life or P&C business. Therefore, most insurers only calculate the holistic loss ratio of the insurance package, and do not separate the loss ratio of the health insurance product. The retail segment, especially in the mass market, is still relatively underdeveloped. Most product offerings only provide hospitalization coverage. There is still a product gap for the highly demanded outpatient coverage. Due to limited coverage and low utilization, the individual business is reported to be profitable.

China's health insurance market will be a very significant opportunity. Despite the immediate challenges, the future payoff is real and very substantial. As with most opportunities in Asia, this one will only go to those who have the patience and foresight to be well-positioned when the duckling turns into a swan.

We are not alone with this assessment of China's growth potential. Every major multinational insurance company has made the Chinese market a priority for expansion. As of June 2008, eight of the world's top 10 insurance companies by revenues[11] have already entered in China. However, strict regulation, limiting foreign companies' development of the Chinese market, has benefited the local players. When China joined the World Trade Organization (WTO), it agreed to open its insurance market, in stages, to foreign companies, but restrictions, mostly on geographic expansion and ownership, remain in place that prevent foreign players from competing on a level playing field with local companies. Initially, only five cities were open to foreign insurers: Shanghai, Guangzhou, Dalian, Shenzhen, and Foshan. This was followed by the opening of another 10 cities: Beijing, Chengdu, Chongqing, Fuzhou, Suzhou, Xiamen, Ningbo, Shenyang, Wuhan, and Tianjin. In 2004, all geographic constraints were lifted, but foreign insurers applying to enter new geographies still need to secure regulatory approval from all tiers of CIRC, the insurance regulator, at central, provincial, and city level. The entire application process can take years and the number of new provinces and cities that a foreign player can enter in a given year has in effect been limited to three to six cities per year. In a market where the bulk of growth is expected to come from hundreds of second- and third-tier cities, this restriction severely confines the capability of foreign players to capture top-line growth at a national level quickly. As a result, the combined market share of all 24 foreign companies was only 8 percent in 2007, with AIA accounting for 1.8 percent and every other player remaining below the 1 percent mark.

Consequently, the China insurance market remains dominated by the domestic "Big 3" players, with a combined market share of 70 percent in 2007. While, to some people, names such as China Life, Ping An, and China Pacific are still not familiar, these dominant Chinese players have grown to enormous size and have begun to wield their newfound clout, leveraging their domestic strength and high valuations to make investments globally.

However, the competition has been catching up. In 1988, the Chinese government opened the life insurance market to domestic competition but at first only allowed another two competitors—Ping An and China Pacific. These two first movers, along with the state-owned incumbent, China Life, dominated the market in the early 1990s. Gradually, regulators allowed more companies to enter the market and, in 2001, foreign entries increased as a result of China's WTO accession. This has led to a systematic loss of market share for the Big 3 within the past several years. In 2007, China Life controlled only 44 percent of the market, down from 57 percent in 2001. If we add Ping An and China Pacific, the combined market share of all three declined from 95 percent in 2001 to 70 percent in 2007. This loss in market share was particularly acute in the large cities where droves of foreign insurers entered (for example, Shanghai), and was aggravated by the fact that the Big 3—after their rapid expansion based on the growth of enormous, nationwide sales forces—faced significant organizational strain in managing their huge and rapidly grown organizations. The numbers testify to the enormity of this challenge: China's new-agent turnover rate was 80 percent, compared with 20 percent in Europe's more mature markets—and agents are counted in the hundred thousands.

In their own ways, the Big 3 have been forced to retrench and fortify their positions. Ping An, for example, consolidated and downsized its agent sales force from over 267,000 in 2001 to less than 200,000 in 2004 in order to improve agent productivity. China Life has also slowed the growth of its agency force, although not to the extent of Ping An.

And their public listing has further accelerated their transition from a pure, growth-focused, "landgrab" mindset to a focus on value creation. Consequently, they stayed away from some of the fastest-growing but less profitable segments in the market, such as bancassurance and group business. This has created opportunities for local and foreign competitors to build share in the market.

As the growth of the Big 3 slowed, domestic attackers captured a greater share of the growing pie. In 2007, their combined market share was 22 percent, up from 8 percent just five years before. More significantly, the number of local players also multiplied. Whereas in 2002 there were only six local life insurers, including the Big 3, by 2007, there were 28 active players. Among the new players are New China Life, Taikang Life, and Taiping Life, who have built national presences and a market share of around 3–7 percent each. They have managed to succeed by heavy reliance on bancassurance and aggressive investment-linked sales. As much as 80 percent of the business of newer players is derived from participating or investment-linked policies, while China Life and China Pacific have only just begun to offer investment-linked products. In addition, these attackers relied heavily on poaching executives from the Big 3 to fill their talent ranks—the entry of these domestic attackers has greatly exacerbated the talent problem in the Chinese life insurance market.

However, this batch of small but rapidly growing domestic players, are also beginning to face some of the problems confronted by the Big 3. They too find the rapid growth of their organizations and agent networks unwieldy and difficult to control. Having jumped from being small, nimble enterprises into larger, more bureaucratic organizations, they now need to relook at their management style and standardize their operating model. Without this exercise, many of these players will find it hard to sustain the high levels of growth they have enjoyed in recent years.

Not all attackers are successful. While companies like New China Life, Taikang Life, and Taiping Life have pulled away from the pack, many local attackers' market share is still below the 2 percent mark. With distribution forces numbering in the hundred thousands, the market leaders still dwarf the smaller players, giving them a big advantage in reaching into China's fast-growing, third-tier cities and even its rural areas. For example, Taiping Life has 44,000 agents spread across the country, compared with China Life's 680,000 agents (see Figure 3.3).

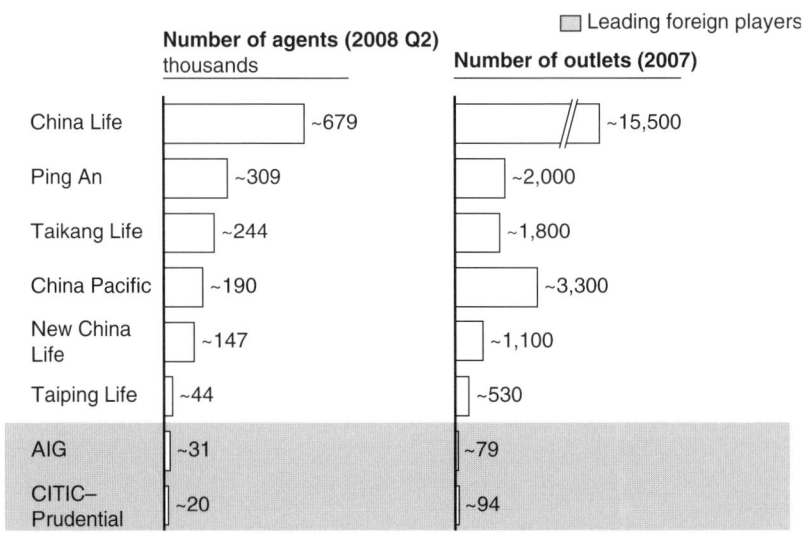

Figure 3.3 Massive sales forces in China

Source: Almanac of China Insurance; literature research; telephone interview; McKinsey analysis

Returning to the category of foreign players, all is not lost. If we look at the cities where foreign companies had more access and a longer history, their market share is significantly higher, implying that the regulations mask the true level of success for these players. Between 2001 and 2006, foreign insurers collectively entered approximately 30 cities in China. As in many other markets, once the markets were accessed, foreign players would capture market share through better execution than the locals. During this period, foreign players grew 4 percent in market share, or 53 percent compound annual growth. In terms of new business, the foreign share will of course be even higher, although this data is not published in China. For example, in cities where foreign companies have had time to establish a presence they have performed extremely well, generating 30 percent of gross premium in Shanghai by 2007 and 23 percent in Beijing (see Figure 3.4).

Generally foreign players are more focused on sales of investment-linked products than their local competitors, which led to strong growth on the back of high-performing stock markets during 2004–07. In 2006, 31 percent of their combined premium portfolio was derived from

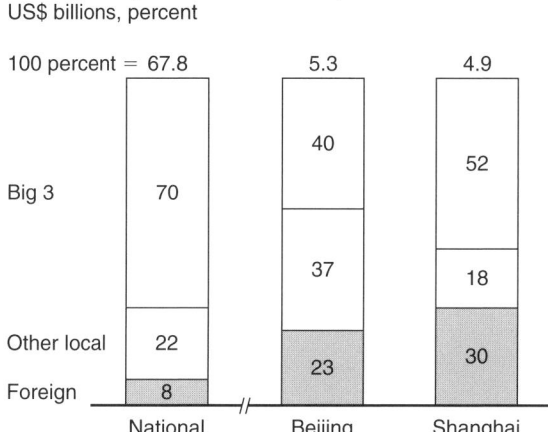

China gross premium breakdown, 2007
US$ billions, percent

Figure 3.4 Foreign insurers are already strong in the cities
Note: Big 3 = Chinese Life, Ping An, and China Pacific
Source: Chinese insurance Regulatory Commission (CIRC)

investment-linked policies, as opposed to 10 percent for domestic companies. Consequently, they have managed to secure 16 percent of the 2006
market in these products. It is important to note that in a downturn scenario in equity markets—as we are experiencing at the time of writing—
these portfolios are usually the hardest hit. How sustainable this strategy is
in a bear market depends on the quality of the sales force.

The foreign players' journey in the China market is not without its
challenges. The key challenges all involve people and regulations. On the
people side, recruiting the right executives to manage the sales force and
develop the newly licensed cities is proving to be a major challenge. When
we study the performance of various foreign players in China, it is striking
how much the quality of the specific management team in each city deter-
mines the success of that multinational in that specific geography. It is not
uncommon to find a foreign player perform very well in one city and very
poorly in another—and the key difference centers on a few top local executives. In addition, recruiting sales agents at a rapid pace is also increasingly
difficult. A few foreign players have tried to develop a higher quality agency
force based on better agent qualification and training, with hopefully less
turnover. But so far no one has succeeded in enlarging this kind of model to

a relevant scale. On the regulatory side, with restrictions on rolling out to tier two, three, and four cities, foreign insurers are still struggling to establish critical mass across China in their geographical footprint. Most foreign insurers have underestimated the challenges in dealing with the regulator.

With these obstacles, foreign insurers are likely to remain marginal players in terms of national market share in the medium term, but their growth rates will likely remain above the national average in cities where they have a presence.

For foreign companies still not in the market this may be the last boarding call. There are now 24 foreign companies in the Chinese market and as they become better established, the winners will pull away from the also-rans. The coastal markets are already nearing saturation; competition is both intensifying and moving further inland. The new wave of foreign joint ventures are increasingly looking further afield, either northward to the northeastern provinces (for example, Jilin, Heilongjiang, and Liaoning), or westward, most notably to Sichuan.

India: Rediscovering Private Insurance

The year 2000 was a watershed for India. After 50 years of state monopoly, the market was reopened to private insurers. With that reopening, the Indian life insurance market ballooned from US$9 billion in gross premiums in 2000 to US$52 billion in 2007. It is rapidly catching up with the rest of the large Asian markets, and we would expect it to become Asia's third-largest insurance market by 2012, and feature in the top 10 globally. Market penetration remains modest by international standards at 4 percent of GDP but it is already higher than levels that prevail in China, while GWP per capita of US$46 is at par with China and significantly greater than Vietnam, the Philippines, or Indonesia. With a forecasted real GDP growth of around 8 percent, India is offering similar long-term growth potential to China. Equally, economic development is spreading from the large urban centers to smaller towns and even rural areas, and households are entering the ranks of the middle class at breakneck speed. For example, households earning more than US$10,000 per annum are expected to grow from 9.6 million in 2007 to 32.8 million in 2012—creating a whole group of customers who can afford life insurance.

The tied sales force remains the dominant sales channel, accounting for nearly 90 percent of new individual business sales[12] in 2007. Major players have aggressively scaled up their sales forces over the past seven years. LIC still has the largest sales force in absolute numbers, with roughly 1.2 million agents; those of most other players have been growing by mid-double digits. Meanwhile, bancassurance grew from 6.2 percent of new business premium in 2004 to 9 percent in 2007. This is still low compared to other Asian markets, and in India many state-owned and rural banks have not yet started to sell insurance products at all. But as more and more banks take up bancassurance, this is expected to be among the biggest growth drivers in the future.

In terms of products, the aggressive push to sell investment-linked policies has contributed to the fast growth of the Indian market. Investment-linked sales grew from 9 percent of new business premium in 2004 to 75 percent in 2008. Investment-linked sales alone contributed to around 92 percent of absolute new business premium growth during that period. The perception of life insurance being an investment tool, as opposed to a means of regular saving has also been a major driver of this trend. Indian customers appear to be more speculative and short-term driven, based on a survey of insurance agents in seven countries.[13] These products have done very well because of the strong performance of the local stock market. It remains to be seen what will happen to investment-linked, single-premium products as the stock market weakens. In particular, the trend of some private insurers to sell investment-linked policies on a negative embedded value (EV) basis is worrisome. Investment-linked products account for more than 85 percent of premium from private players; for players wanting to build market share, these are the easiest products to push into the market.

Since the deregulation of the Indian market in 2000 there has been a major shift in the competitive landscape. LIC's market share of new business premium dropped from 100 percent to 64 percent in 2007, as at least 20 private players entered the market including international insurance companies such as Prudential (UK), Allianz, and Standard Life. Nonetheless, LIC, which is still state-owned, is holding onto its leadership position and is trying to fight back. Despite an initially steep decline in new business share to 71 percent from 2000 to 2005, LIC still generated 74 percent of new business premium in India for 2006. LIC fights to maintain market share by drawing on what worked for the new entrants (that is, product innovation and aggressive hiring of more agents) and leveraging its formidable brand (India's most recognized financial services brand) and massive distribution. LIC has 2,048 branches, 100 divisional offices, eight zonal offices and, as we have discussed, retains over one million agents. In the fiscal year 2006–07, LIC's number of policyholders is said to have exceeded a whopping 200 million (collectively, the policyholders could become the world's fourth most populous nation). McKinsey's consumer research confirms that over 97 percent of consumers are aware of LIC without any kind of prompting and over 90 percent of Indian consumers are inclined to approach LIC when in need of insurance (see Figure 3.5). There has also been a conscious push to improve agent productivity. Based on our research we estimate that the value of new personal business per active agent rose by an impressive 70 percent from 2005–06 to 2006–07.

Nevertheless, LIC's market share may still be on a long-term declining trend. To hold market share, LIC actively pushed single-premium policies. When regular-premium products regained popularity, LIC experienced a steep dive in market share, dropping to 45 percent in April and May 2008. At the time of writing, LIC was still struggling with the fall in market share. The final outcome is yet to be decided.

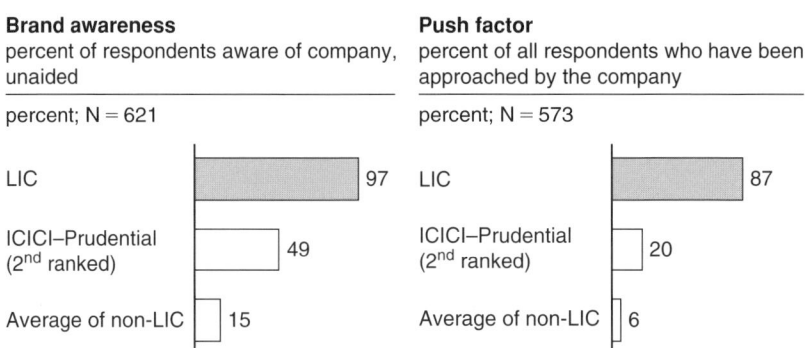

Brand awareness
percent of respondents aware of company, unaided

percent; N = 621

LIC — 97
ICICI–Prudential (2nd ranked) — 49
Average of non-LIC — 15

Push factor
percent of all respondents who have been approached by the company

percent; N = 573

LIC — 87
ICICI–Prudential (2nd ranked) — 20
Average of non-LIC — 6

Note: Unaided awareness refer to top-of-mind or spontaneous awareness, without showing any list to respondent. Aided awareness refers to recognition after showing the list of options to respondent.

Figure 3.5 LIC is synonymous with life insurance to Indian customers
Source: Proprietary McKinsey market research, 2007

At the same time, some private-sector players have reached a meaningful scale. The largest among them have written almost two million policies in over 500 locations across the country.[14] The two largest private life insurers—ICICI–Prudential and BAJAJ–Allianz—accounted for nearly 50 percent of non-LIC market share in 2006. Significantly, these players are entering second- and third-tier towns, and even rural areas. For instance, ICICI–Prudential, through a bancassurance tie-up with 10 regional rural banks, has access to about 10,000 rural and semi-rural bank branches in five Indian states. Most of the private-sector players are growing either through bancassurance or increasing their sales forces. The massive size of these sales forces mirrors the challenges in China. In fact, we were struck by the similarities of the nature of these sales forces in both markets. Saddled with low productivity, high turnover, part-time agents, and nonstandardized practices, the Indian insurers face exactly the same challenges as Chinese insurers do. They will need to standardize operating practices across the country, reduce turnover by focusing on better recruiting processes, and focus on upgrading professionalism over time. Investment in management talent and supporting infrastructure will also be required. More will be discussed below.

New entrants continue to be interested in the market, with most domestic entities choosing to partner with a foreign insurer. Despite a 26 percent foreign ownership cap for life insurance, only two out of 20 private Indian insurers in 2007 were 100 percent domestically owned. There is talk of the government moving to increase the maximum foreign share in joint ventures from 26 percent to 49 percent. If this is so, it is likely to attract even more foreign insurers who are currently hesitant due to the 26 percent ownership cap. Market insiders believe that foreign insurers are not, and really should not, be deterred by the ownership cap. The current regulatory situation has not prevented some foreign insurers from effectively controlling the management of their joint venture partnerships, such as the BAJAJ–Allianz venture, which is in essence run by Allianz. But it is important to note that more often than not, it is the domestic Indian partner who has management control.

Once in the market, a single license allows access to all Indian cities and towns with no geographical restrictions (a situation very unlike that of China).

Similarly, there are no restrictions in terms of the number of branches an insurance player can open and the product lines that the branches can sell.

There are, however, regulatory challenges that players in India must contend with. One key challenge is the current bancassurance regulation, which restricts any bank to distributing the insurance products of only one life insurer. This creates tremendous competition for distribution deals with the better banks in the country (deals are typically renegotiated every three years). An open architecture regulation that will allow banks to market multiple manufacturers' products has been discussed but its timing is uncertain.

Players in India are also coming under increasingly vigilant regulations in terms of selling investment-linked products. In order to prevent mis-selling, the regulator is beginning to introduce more stringent customer disclosure practices as well as modifications to product features that discourage investment-linked products from merely acting as a substitute for mutual funds.

Looking forward, the Indian life insurance industry is at a unique point in its evolution. Momentum from accelerating economic growth and India's favorable demographics will drive insurance premium growth, making it one of the most attractive financial services markets in the world. We forecast that the Indian insurance market will grow at close to 19 percent per annum from 2007 to 2012. In addition, in the midst of this massive growth phase, the market is witnessing significant shifts in competitive dynamics: customer needs are evolving, untapped segments of the market are emerging, and competition has become more sophisticated. To win in the next decade in India, players must be able to outperform the rest of the competition.

Key Challenges to Growth for Life Insurers in China and India

The sustained growth of China and India's life insurance market presents exciting opportunities in size and scope. But newly emerging market segments and intensifying competition make traditional approaches insufficient to capture their full potential. Players who can innovate and identify differentiated models for different customer segments are most likely to succeed. We see the following key challenges that life insurers in China and India will have to deal with in the next decade:

- Regulatory restrictions for entrants
- Operational challenges
- Increasing complexity in managing the product portfolio
- The need for distribution excellence

Regulatory Restrictions for Entrants

We have already laid out above that, foreign players in particular, have to deal with significant regulatory constraints in both China and India. The stringent ownership requirements for foreign insurers make the choice of an entry model a most critical decision. For foreign players, entry into India generally means one of two choices: a 26 percent "active" stake or a 26 percent "investor" (more passive) stake. China entry is more varied: players can choose between a 50 percent joint venture or a minority stake in a local insurer, as Zurich has with New China Life.

But this is not merely a choice for the foreign partner. Joint-venture partnership is also a key decision for Indian and Chinese enterprises choosing to enter the insurance market for the first time. In India, there are few local insurers with the right know-how. As a result, firms choose to acquire that technical expertise through partnerships with foreign insurers. In China, despite already intensive competition, nonfinancial Chinese enterprises, state-owned or private, continue to be interested in diversifying into the insurance sector. While some of these, such as State Grid Corporation of China, developed their own wholly-owned insurance subsidiary (Yingda Taihe), many more chose to partner right from the beginning, such as the PetroChina–Generali joint venture. Consequently, foreign joint-venture partnerships with nonfinancial firms have increased over the years—between 2000 and 2006, the proportion of life insurance joint ventures with nonfinancial local partners increased from 33 percent to 71 percent.

So what is the right choice for a new entrant? What type of a partner would be the best fit? For China entry, should one look at a joint-venture partnership or merely buy into a minority stake? Not surprisingly, there is no single answer. First, an entrant, domestic or foreign, needs to establish how investment in the China or India market fits into its corporate portfolio or strategy. That would dictate the degree of control required and the type of partner as well. For example, foreign insurers seeking a large degree of control will find local nonfinancial companies attractive partners due to lower managerial conflict, potential synergies in cross-selling to the partner's customers, and lower premiums for any transaction. Our analysis shows that investors paid a premium as much as four times the normal rate for established life insurance firms.

Some foreign insurers seeking to break into the China and India market lament the amount of upside, technical know-how, and control that must be yielded in a joint venture for a relative small stake. However, it is important to bear in mind that no joint venture is permanent. Rather, it is a temporary construct where both sides seek some benefits within a certain period of time. For domestic partners, that benefit is often the industry knowledge from more developed markets. For the foreigner, it is the opportunity to capture local market knowledge, while waiting for further deregulation. Japan's SONY–Prudential is a classic example where both sides of the joint venture gained from the partnership and went on to prosper individually. Our observations show that success in a joint venture requires good implementation of the following elements:

- *Developing early spikes in channels or products.* For example, Manu-life–Sinochem focused on the Chinese family/retirement-planning market, while CMG–Cigna chose a strong focus on telemarketing, avoiding direct competition for scarce, quality tied agents.
- *Finding partners who are committed to the long-run.* China International Trust and Investment Company (CITIC) believes life insurance is a strategic focus for its financial arm and explicitly wants its CITIC Prudential joint venture to be a long-term venture (it has been in operation since 2000) and capital invested has been over US$246 million (among the largest of all joint ventures).
- *Taking care when transplanting a foreign model.* China's insurance joint ventures are full of examples where foreign insurers were too eager to transplant their home models. For example, at least two foreign insurers have tried to transplant their sales incentives system to China, but underestimated the difficulties in localizing the system.
- *Demarcation of powers between partners.* Clear demarcation of power at the onset of a partnership can avoid misunderstandings and conflicts. While horror stories about Chinese joint-venture partners

have been well-documented in the Western media, we have found that fault often lies with both sides right from the beginning of the partnership when misunderstandings are left unattended.

Finding the right joint-venture partner is not always easy. A partnership search is akin to courtship, where both sides need to find a suitable match. Holding out for the right partner might delay critical time-to-market, but more often than not, entering an inappropriate marriage is even worse.

Operational Challenges

In the nascent markets of China and India, massive operational challenges exist in terms of geography and talent shortage. Despite the skyrocketing market growth, intensifying competition means operational efficiencies will increasingly matter. To grow further, players will need to overcome the challenges inherent in the China and India markets.

Large Geographic Expanses

The sheer size of both China and India is daunting. Each have hundreds of cities surrounded by vast rural areas, which are very hard to access. In its infant stage, life insurance market growth was driven out of the major urban centers, such as Beijing, New Delhi, Bangalore, Mumbai, and Shanghai. Today growth is increasingly coming from second- and third-tier cities and even rural areas. Furthermore, customers have increasingly heterogeneous needs and are gradually, but increasingly, becoming more demanding. All this has increased the potential opportunity but also made it much more difficult to capture.

To grasp the immense size and diversity of these markets, consider this: China comprises 31 provinces in a country that spans 5,200 km east to west. India has 29 states in a nation that spans 3,050 km from north to south. As of 2006, China has 119 cities with population over 1 million and India has 69.[15] The US has only 9 cities of that size and Europe has 36.[16]

Beyond the four best-known first-tier Chinese cities of Beijing, Guangzhou, Shanghai, and Shenzhen, there were another 854 urban centers in China[17] as of 2005—14 large cities with a population of over five million, 69 mid-sized cities of 1.5–5 million, and 775 small cities

and towns with a population of 0.5–1.5 million. According to the 2006
Census of India, there were five cities with a population of over four million, 22 cities of population range 1–4 million, and 43 third-tier towns
with a population of more than 500,000.

And wealth is by no means limited to the tier one cities. By 2025,
46 percent of China's "upper aspirant" segment[18] is expected to come from
mid-sized cities and another 9.2 percent from small cities and towns. Sixty
percent of the population in mid-sized and small cities will be considered
middle class; in the larger cities, as the affluent segment grows, about 50
percent of households would be middle class (see Figure 3.6). Similarly
in India, the McKinsey Global Institute estimates that 25 percent of the
middle class will come from the second- and third-tier cities by 2025.

In short, the growth story in China and India is expanding from first-
tier cities to include second- and third-tier cities and then the rural areas.
This presents an enormous growth reserve as this potential market is massive (for example, in China, approximately 770 million people are still
living on the countryside). But this also raises substantial logistical challenges for insurers who will have to deploy hundreds of thousands of
agents, scattered over a vast geographical expanse. Even today, the agency

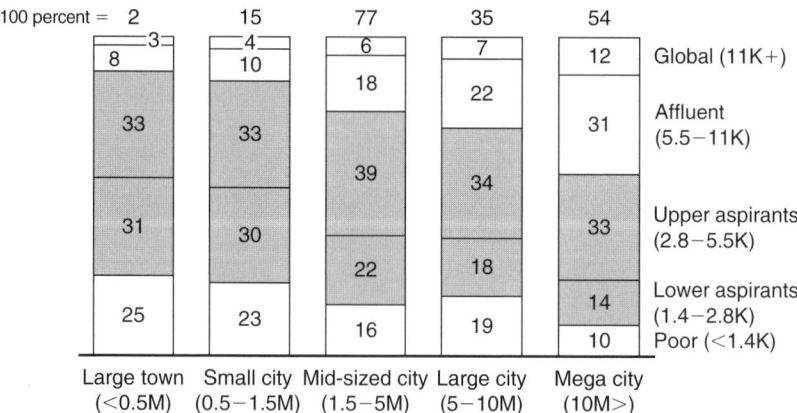

Figure 3.6 Middle-class households are growing beyond the megacities

Source: McKinsey Global Institute analysis, China-All-City model output—138 cities

networks of the leading players are already quite difficult to manage due to their geographic dispersion. In our experience, the majority of the insurers in these markets do not know (within a margin of 10 thousand agents) how many agents they currently have. In China, for example, one company accidentally discovered that one of its agents defrauded the company, claiming to have established an office from which subagents were deployed. However the office turned out to be his bedroom—and the agent pocketed the office rental payment. This small example provides a flavor of the even bigger problems of management that will come as the battlefield moves to the rural areas.

Rather than allowing themselves to be intimidated by the scale of the challenge, players are innovating to capture this growth opportunity. In India, micro-insurance and rural insurance initiatives in partnership with NGOs, rural distribution depots, and even the postal system are emerging to carry insurance into the hinterland. Further, players are beginning to innovate with "franchise" models—through which they appoint local entrepreneurs as "contract unit managers" and leverage their current employee base as agents (after training and certification), creating a win-win proposition for the entrepreneur and the insurer alike.

Talent Shortages

Both local and foreign companies often have difficulty finding sufficient talent to fuel their growth ambitions in China and India. This challenge of finding suitable recruits is even more acute in the life insurance industry, which is relatively new and lacks an established talent base. This has given rise to considerable poaching of talent and turnover rates are significantly higher than in other parts of the world. The problem is not likely to disappear in the near future.

Although China and India are obviously populous nations with large pools of talent in absolute terms, the demand for these candidates far exceeds the supply. This is even more acute for foreign players, who generally require higher standards for employment. According to a McKinsey survey, less than 10 percent of Chinese job candidates, on average, would qualify for employment with a foreign company. Effective managers are in short supply as well. We estimate that given the global aspirations of many Chinese companies, 75,000 leaders will be needed over the next

10–15 years who can work effectively in global environments; in 2005 there were only 3,000 to 5,000.[19] Multinationals operating in China, therefore, have had to import managers, often from Hong Kong, Taiwan, and Singapore due to their language capabilities.

Talent shortage is not only a problem at the management level. Agent recruitment has become vastly competitive and poaching is a common phenomenon. As a result, most companies have adopted a "whoever walks through the doors" approach to recruiting. In India, of 100 candidates recruited to become agents, almost 20 either fail the initial certification or leave immediately after initial training to pursue other options. Of the remaining 80 only 40 can be considered "active" with the remaining 40 largely dormant, though they remain registered agents of the company. Finally, of the 40 active agents, roughly 10 remain active beyond one year, selling at least one policy a month. Suffice to say that this practice is not sustainable in the long term; most insurers will need to find ways to improve their recruiting and retention practices.

Increasing Complexity in Managing the Product Portfolio

Most Chinese and Indian insurers are constantly challenged by the need to balance market-share growth with bottom-line profitability. There is a tendency to maintain growth and market-share gains at all costs. As a result, many players rely on low-margin and short-term products to maintain their share. Currently, high valuations seem to reward this focus on growth, but selling unprofitable products will come back to haunt life insurers in the long run. Therefore, insurers would serve themselves well by constantly reviewing and rationalizing the economics of the product portfolio.

Furthermore, life insurers with a one-size-fits-all product portfolio are increasingly faced with the diverging needs of very different customer segments in China and India. In India, for example, players are faced with the very different needs of at least three core segments of the market—high-net-worth customers, low-income urban groups, and the rural population. The high-net-worth segment will eventually want to move from a narrow range of proprietary insurance products to a broad, potentially open architecture product range that spans a broader set of investment products. To a certain degree, this is happening in distribution already, so insurers are faced with the option of entering into alliances for the full suite of personal financial services products, such as mutual funds, brokerage, real estate, consumer finance, and banking—or producing some, or all, of these products in-house. The low-income urban group requires very different products and operating processes. Products need to be simple, with documentation that is easy to understand and complete, subject of course, to meeting regulatory requirements. Payment terms need to be flexible with low upfront payments and openness to topping up thereafter, based on the consumer's more volatile income streams. Finally, the rural population will require life insurance players to offer a more appealing product suite by bundling products from a range of partners to satisfy the local needs. For example, life insurers could partner with general insurance players to create a bundled product that addresses mortality risk as well as health, crop, and property-related risk. Similarly, they could partner with banks or consumer-credit companies to provide a bundled home-loan product with life insurance cover.

Other product niches to explore include health insurance and pension offerings. In the absence of government-funded health insurance and state-sponsored pensions (excepting those for government employees), we believe there is a very substantial opportunity for these products.

The Need for Distribution Excellence

Success for Chinese and Indian insurance players will hinge on achieving excellence in distribution, in particular by raising agency productivity while simultaneously exploring new models in nonagency distribution.

In both China and India, tied agents, who operate at a very basic level of sophistication, make most sales. New competitors and incumbents, in principle, tread the same path here, although there are some degrees of difference in quality and training. In general, the agent turnover rate is extremely high, and productivity is skewed (the bottom third of these agency forces often produce less than 1 percent of sales). Productivity is low and the sales process is often a simple "product push." On the other hand, this also reflects the limited experience most customers in China and India have with financial products in general and life insurance in particular—especially in the mass market segment which is the key domain for life agents.

In India, the life insurance agency force has grown at a rapid pace, from approximately one million agents in 2000 to close to two million in 2007.

Similar to China, overall inactivity and attrition rates of 50–70 percent are causing big headaches for life insurers. With recruitment aimed at growing the base at any cost, productivity has suffered.

The good news is that there is significant room for improvement. With such scale, the difference between good and poor execution will make all the difference. Through the right set of interventions, players have proven that productivity can be increased, with large differentials between the top and lowest performing players. In 2006, the top-ranking company in terms of agent productivity,[20] among five domestic Chinese insurers analyzed by McKinsey, yielded an agent productivity of 2.8 times greater than that of the least productive company. Moreover, this productivity was not achieved by giving up growth.

As in all life markets, distribution is the key to success in China and India. However a blind rush to build scale will almost certainly be counterproductive in the longer run. The significant disparities in the productivity of the Chinese sales force and the diminishing efficiency of the Indian sales force illustrate that quality and quantity are both required to create sustainable value.

Another challenge in distribution is the need to tap into the growth opportunities in second- and third-tier cities and in rural areas. One way to capture this market potential is to design new innovative agency structures and approaches to recruiting and managing agents. Some Indian players such as BAJAJ–Allianz, ICICI–Prudential, and Reliance have employed a franchisee model to quickly expand their agent base. Targeting mainly rural areas and cities without current coverage, these models typically involve recruiting current insurance agents or entrepreneurs with an existing customer base (for example, car dealers) and providing the franchisee with training and some infrastructure (for example, an IT system). This franchise business is generally separate from that of the tied-agency channel. By 2007, ICICI–Prudential had around 35,000 agents in this system and Reliance had 40,000. However, it remains to be seen whether this model can stand the test of time, as quality and mis-selling issues from this model can pose significant risks to the franchise.

Further, there is a more complex game to be played in accessing consumers from different sociogeographic layers. Growth is not only generated by the expansion of economic development into third-tier cities and rural areas, but also by the rapidly growing and more affluent middle class. China and India will add another 100 million middle-class households in just five years.[21] Their needs are diverse and their full potential will only be captured by companies who recognize these differences and evolve their distribution structure to address them.

This means that players in these markets should look to professionalizing their agency, innovating to maximize reach, and tailoring their value proposition to cater to specific, high-potential market segments.

But beyond the professionalization and innovation of the agency force, differentiated product offerings coupled with innovative sales channels will create new distribution opportunities. Benefiting from an existing branch network, bancassurance will certainly play a role in opening second- and third-tier markets as well as catering to more affluent segments who rely more heavily on their relationship managers and the banks' wealth-management offerings.

In China, bancassurance has provided a means for new players to capture market share from the Big 3. In 2007, the three biggest attackers—New China Life, Taikang Life, and Taiping Life—sold 50 percent or more of their business through bancassurance, compared to 29 percent for the Big 3 and the 34 percent share of bancassurance in the overall market (see Figure 3.7). However, volume expansion into bancassurance has come at the expense of profitability, as retail banking distribution is still dominated by the four large banks (Agricultural Bank of China, Industrial and Commercial Bank of China, Bank of China, and China Construction Bank) who have enormous bargaining power over the life insurers in sharing economics from new sales.

In India as well, LIC sells only 1.2 percent of its premiums through bancassurance—while private players see 22 percent of their premiums coming through this channel.

We believe bancassurance, as a percentage of new sales, will probably stay at its current level in China. The reason is that most major banks are already selling life insurance and have collected the low-hanging fruit. While they are good at selling simple investment products, it is hard for them to move up the value chain and sell more sophisticated policies because their staff lack the expertise required to engage in sales of this kind. In India, however, bancassurance is at an earlier development stage and we expect it to continue to grow from the current share of just over 9 percent of new business to over 20 percent by 2012 as more banks take up

Channel breakdown by gross written premium (GWP), 2007
percent

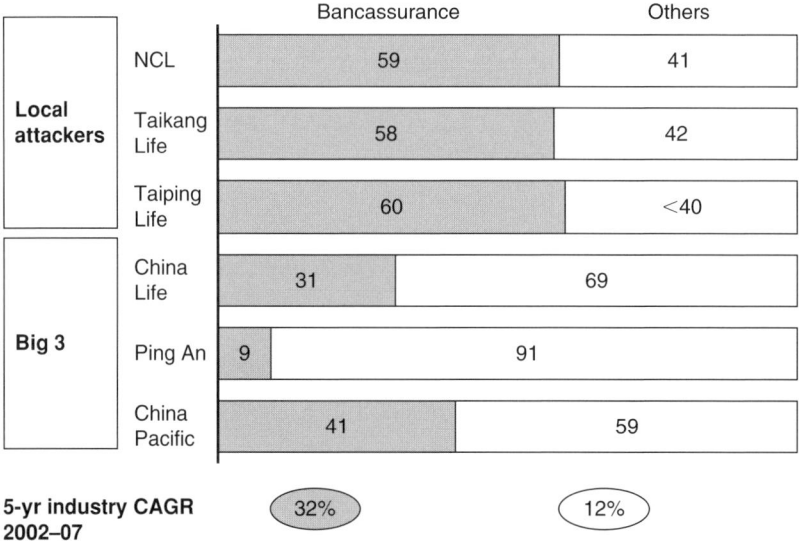

Figure 3.7 In China, local attackers grew through bancassurance
Source: Annual report; China Insurance Yearbook; CIRC; NIICC, McKinsey analysis

bancassurance and improve their ability to sell insurance products to their consumers.

Beyond agency and bancassurance, we have also begun to see players experiment with new distribution and service models that are more aligned with specialized customer segments. For example, India's Future–Generali India Life Insurance and Future–Generali India Insurance (non-life venture) are targeting 30 percent of their business to come from malls operated by the Indian partner, Future Group. These malls had a combined footfall of 140 million in 2006. The policies will start at a low unit cost catering to this segment of customers. "Future–Generali has designed simple insurance covers that can be easily understood by the customer and can be sold over the counter," said G.N. Bajpai, chairman of Future–Generali.[22] Similarly, Bharti–AXA is exploring a "shopassurance" model with its retail joint ventures. This model has been successful in the UK with retailers like Tesco. These experiments are in their early stages, and time will tell whether they are going to succeed in these markets.

China and India are markets with enormous long-term growth potential and are critical for the world's leading life insurance players. These are also markets where leading local players will gain enough size and clout to start competing outside their own markets. Simply put, these are markets where the competitive outcome will not only have repercussions within the domestic market, but have the potential to reshape the global life insurance landscape.

Japan: New Tricks in an Old Market

4

Macroeconomic	Japan

GDP (US$ billions)	4,603
GDP per capita (US$)	36,031
PPP GDP per capita (US$)	33,325
Inst. assets under management (US$ bns)	3,765
PFA (US$ billions)	12,482
Foreign reserve (US$ billions)	914

Socioeconomic	
Population (millions)	128
# of households (thousands)	49,390
Median household income (US$)	45,770
# of households earning >US$10k p.a.	49,390
% of households earning >US$10k p.a.	100%
Urbanization (% of population)	66%
% of population older than 65 in 2005	20%
% of population older than 65 in 2025	28%

Life insurance	
GWP (US$ billions)	325
Life insurance penetration	7%
Life insurance density (US$ billions)	325
Investment-linked %	n/a
Bancassurance %	n/a
# of life insurers	41
# of foreign life insurers	17
Foreign share %	18%
Year foreign entry allowed	1954
Life insurance assets (US$ billions)	2,137

Note–all figures for 2007 unless otherwise stated

Some call him the "Bad Boy of Sumo" for his youth and unreserved fighting, but none can deny that Asashoryu Akinori is the 68th Grand Champion of sumo. Born in 1980, he started wrestling at the age of 15. In 1999, he entered Meitoku Gijuku High School to study sumo wrestling and became a disciple of Takasago-beya (then-Wakamatsu-beya). In January 2001, the youth entered the top division of sumo for the first time and in 2002, he became the fastest wrestler to reach the rank of *ozeki* (the second highest rank in sumo) since the current system was introduced in 1958.

Asashoryu Akinori is one of the greatest contemporary grand champions of the quintessentially Japanese sport of sumo wrestling. Known simply as Asashoryu, he is joined by another formidable master of this sport known as Hakuho. Indeed, the two of them are credited with bringing about a revival of this ancient sport. The surprising fact is that neither of these men is Japanese; both men are Mongolians. The irony is that while foreign sumo wrestlers seem keen to accept the discipline and lifestyle of this demanding sport, young Japanese are hesitant to enter the ring and the older Japanese wrestlers are finding it increasingly difficult to compete with the younger, stronger Mongolians. Thus what appears to be a uniquely Japanese endeavor is now dominated by two foreigners.

Sumo's Mongolian champions are not alone in providing a somewhat counter-intuitive perspective of events in Japan. Deceptive appearances also muddle much of the thinking about the Japanese life insurance industry, which appears stagnant and lacking in space for growth. In reality, there are significant forces driving the Japanese market.

It cannot be denied that the Japanese life industry was hit badly by the economic downturn that gathered force in the 1990s. Indeed, many companies have come close to collapse following the sharp interest rate rises; overall market growth has stagnated ever since.

This leaves a present-day picture of a Japanese life insurance market that, at first sight, looks like a huge, unchanging monolith, very much dominated by incumbent players and leaving little room for anyone else. But, as is often the case with perceptions of Japan, this picture is incomplete because the Japanese insurance market does have zones of growth and even foreign companies are managing to capitalize on them. A glimpse of these opportunities for smaller players can be seen in the fact that from 2000 to 2006, smaller players gained 36 percent market share[1] at the expense of the four large, local incumbents and the postal system. These include foreign insurers such as The Hartford and ING who focused on variable (investment-linked) annuities.

Japan is the largest market in Asia by far. Its 2007 gross premium was around US$325 billion,[2] which was equivalent to four times that of South Korea, the second-largest market, and five times that of China, the third-largest market. However, the Japanese market as a whole has been stagnant for years; during 2002–07 there was a compound decline of 2 percent, while other markets in Asia grew by an annual aggregate rate of 15.7 percent.

To understand Japanese insurance, one must first have an understanding of the different parties that make up the Japanese industries. The traditional players still dominate, including the postal system, mutual cooperatives, and large private incumbents. In particular, Japan Post Insurance Co. (*Kampo Seimei Hoken*), which raked in US$80 billion in premium or 23 percent aggregate market share[3] in 2007, plays a large role in the industry. It used to be that Japanese consumers bought mostly savings-type insurance, such as endowments, through postal outlets. Japan Post Insurance's average per policy face value is smaller than its private peers but with the sheer number of policies, the postal system used to dominate the market. However, with shifting consumer behavior in Japan, Japan Post Insurance's premium income has steadily declined. In 1999, sales through Japan Post Insurance accounted for 33 percent of all life premiums.

A second category of life insurers in Japan are insurance cooperatives named *kyosai kumiai* (mutual societies). The *Cooperative Insurance in Japan 2007 Factbook* describes a *kyosai* as:

> A cooperative is a nonprofit-making organization established by a group of people with the desire to improve their living… In Japan, agricultural cooperatives (JA), fishery cooperatives (JF), consumer cooperatives, and cooperatives of small- and medium-sized enterprises, and so forth, are monitored by the relevant authorities… As such, the types of cooperative insurance, upper limit of the amount insured, utilization by nonmembers, accounting (various reserves, surplus regulations, asset operation procedures, etc.), and inspections by competent authorities are regulated in law.[4]

Due to their private nature, there is no comprehensive data on how much life insurance they sold, but a survey of 59 *kyosai* cooperatives suggested that together they collected over US$38 billion in life insurance premium in 2006.

Finally, private insurers make up the third and largest category of players in Japan, with premiums clocking in at almost US$250 billion in 2007. Large traditional players dominate this group; Japan's biggest insurer, Nippon Life, made US$45 billion in premium in 2006 alone—more than the entire Taiwan market combined! The top five players—Nippon Life, Dai-ichi Mutual, Sumitomo, Meiji Yasuda, and Mitsui Life—are all well-known names in Japan, with company histories going back over 100 years. In 2006, the forerunner, Nippon Life, earned 3.5 times more premium than the largest foreign insurer, ALICO Japan.

The industry still focuses on traditional insurance products such as term and whole life, but this is slowly declining. In 2000, traditional products[5] accounted for 70 percent of new private insurance policies by sum assured; by 2005, the figure was down to 60 percent.

The stagnation of Japan's life insurance market is likely to persist for some time due to the following factors: i) a shrinking population; ii) economic stagnation; iii) the erosion of sales power because the housewife-based sales force is not equipped to cater to customer's changing and more sophisticated needs; and iv) an already high insurance penetration and density, amounting to approximately 7.5 percent of gross domestic product (GDP) and US$2,500 per capita in 2007.

But the overall stagnation of the market is masking some of the forces driving growth in the market. Liberalization of market-restrictive laws continues to shape the market. For example, reforms in the medical system are giving rise to new product offerings. There are also signs that regulators are seeking more vigorous customer protection, which will lead to changes in sales practices. In the past, mis-selling or poor selling (lack of product information) were not uncommon in this market. The Financial Instruments and Exchange Law (FIEL) was implemented in September 2007, bringing greater protection to buyers of financial products. The law stipulates that banks and brokerages must explain and disclose, in marketing materials, the risks inherent in certain investment products. Meanwhile, other regulatory changes may lead to more competition from other financial institutions.

As a result, there are a number of niche opportunities, which are small compared to the size of the total market, but are equivalent to the size of an entire market elsewhere in Asia. Take the market for individual annuities as an example—in 2006, premium income was US$66 billion, up from

US$19 billion just five years earlier, and it is now larger than the size of Taiwan's entire market.

New opportunities are mainly to be found in the following areas:

- *The retirement market*: Japan is the most rapidly aging society in Asia with needs that mirror those of Western markets. We are already seeing a reflection of this in the rapid growth of the annuity market and, if the Western experience is anything to go by, other retirement offerings will follow.
- *Health insurance*: Japan did not have medical insurance prior to the 1970s as the government offered a universal healthcare system. However, as medical needs grew, the demand for insurance complementary to the public healthcare system also grew, and insurance firms started selling private medical insurance. With an aging population, the need for health insurance is expected to continue its growth trajectory in Japan.
- *Investment-related products*: As in other Asian markets, an attitudinal change to personal finance management is underway in Japan, leading to a demand for investment products. Between 2002 and 2006, the Japanese moved 7 percent of their personal financial assets, or US$50 billion, away from cash or deposits. Looking at it in a different way, personal assets in higher yield (nondeposit) financial vehicles grew by US$1.5 trillion over that period, including both new injections of funds and capital appreciation. Japanese insurers had suffered a reputational hit in the 1990s on investment-linked insurance, but the product has returned in recent years, repackaged as variable annuities.
- *Bancassurance*: In the wake of deregulation, distribution through banks swelled, having been well received by customers. It seems likely that Japan will share the experience of other Asian markets and see an even greater growth of this business, which is still relatively new in Japan. Indeed, full deregulation only occurred at the end of 2007, following a first wave in 2002 when banks were allowed to sell annuities.
- *Channel innovation*: There are some interesting examples here, albeit not widespread. For instance, there are insurance outlets in retail stores (known as shopassurance), kiosks in high-traffic areas like train stations, mail order and TV shopping, and online sales.

Based on these trends, we see a distinctly mixed picture emerging in Japan characterized by the following themes: continued decline in the overall market, slow decline of incumbents, emerging sizeable opportunities in certain product submarkets, increasing scope for innovative sales models, and rewards for innovative players with perseverance.

Continued Decline in the Overall Market

In October 2006, the in-force value of private individual life insurance policies[6] in Japan hit an 18-year low, falling below US$10 trillion for the first time since March, 1990. This was primarily the result of a severe downturn in the traditional life insurance market, including whole life, term life, and endowments. Because this segment had accounted for over 50 percent of gross premium from non-Japan Post[7] insurance, its decline created a significant drop in the total market size. Factors driving this downward spiral include a shrinking addressable population, market saturation, and shifting customer demand towards such alternative products as mutual funds.

Shrinking Addressable Market

Japan's 2012 population is projected to be 127.2 million, approximately 0.6 million less than in 2007. While this does not sound like a big difference, the population comprising life insurers' primary addressable market, that is those between ages of 15 and 64, is projected to be only 80.3 million in 2012, a drop of 3.5 million or 4.3 percent from 2007. At the same time, the population of all those over the age of 65 is expected to increase by four million people. With a shrinking population and a demographic trend that is not in favor of life insurance, the traditional life insurers' addressable market is steadily declining.

Market Saturation

Customer surveys show that penetration of life insurance for death coverage has peaked. Around 70–80 percent of the population aged between 20 and 60 has some form of death coverage. The coverage ratio of males between 30 and 60 has already surpassed 90 percent.

Not only is the coverage ratio high, but in addition a lot of middle-aged Japanese have actually come to realize that they have more death coverage than they need. In other words, they feel over-insured, particularly by whole-life products. Average benefits per whole-life policy have been continuously decreasing. Since whole-life products account for nearly three-quarters of sum assured from traditional individual policies,[8] the decrease in average benefits has a severe impact on total premium intake from the traditional category. However, it is also interesting to note that term life has been on a slight incline, both in the number of policies and benefit per policy. Term-life growth is mainly driven by increasing penetration in the profitable small- and medium-size enterprise owner segment where policyholders can obtain tax benefits. However, a reduction in tax benefit from new regulations in February, 2008 is expected to cause some impact to this segment.

Shifting Customer Demand

The decreasing fertility ratio is also a problem for insurers. As younger generations of Japanese choose to marry later and have fewer children, the fertility ratio dropped from around 1.5 in the early 1990s to less than 1.3 today. A declining fertility ratio shrinks demand for death protection as fewer potential customers have children for whom they are responsible.

Lack of Economic Growth

Unlike other nations described in this book, Japan is expected to experience 1.6 percent real GDP growth per year between 2007 and 2012; in contrast, the other 12 countries will grow at an average annual rate of 6.8 percent, a key driver to fundamental demand for insurance.

As a result of the above factors, gross premium in Japan is expected to remain at the same level over the next five years, as the aging population causes a depletion of insurance assets. This will cause some reshuffling of the industry while competition intensifies. Whole life and other traditional products are likely to be hardest hit, as has been the case in other more developed markets.

Large incumbents such as Nippon Life, Sumitomo, and Meiji Yasuda, whose portfolios are dominated by these products, will be increasingly pushed to reinvent their business models. Once a whole generation of loyal insurance customers reaches retirement age they will find it hard to create new business to make up for this depleting in-force book.

The Slow Decline of the Incumbents

Nippon Life, Sumitomo, Meiji Yasuda, Dai-ichi Mutual, Mitsui Life—these are the names of what were, 15 years ago, the largest insurance companies in the world. The business of each of these companies exceeds that of the size of whole markets in most other Asian countries. However, due to the lack of growth and difficult economics, the future prospects for these companies are very challenging, as indicated by their market value. For example, Dai-ichi Mutual and Sumitomo ranked 16th and 23rd among all insurers by 2006 revenue,[9] but only 33rd and 56th respectively by value.[10] Their estimated values were US$21.6 billion and US$13.0 billion.

It is undeniable that these companies are in a state of decline, despite their impressive size and prestige. Some have even gone through a phase of facing bankruptcy because of the need to meet high-guarantee policies. Their fate may have been worse if not for intervention from the Japanese government, which was loath to lose some of the nation's leading financial institutions during the long period of economic recession in the 1990s. By any standard these companies have weathered an economic environment that would test even the hardiest of contenders. It is, therefore, easy to understand why these companies have focused on survival and sustainability rather than expansion (see Box 4A).

The weakness of Japanese insurance companies gave rise to a number of acquisitions of illiquid and bankrupt mid-size insurers in the late 1990s and early 2000s. GE led the way with the acquisition of Toho and was followed by AIG buying Chiyoda Life, AXA acquiring Nichidan, Prudential (US) buying Kyoei Life, and Manulife's successful acquisition of Daihyaku. This is a major change to the market; with foreign players cleaning up the companies in the last 3–4 years, these insurers are likely to become strong competitors to the large incumbents in the near future.

4A—The life insurance industry in Japan in the 1990s

The Japanese life insurance industry has undergone a lot of pain in the past two decades, and credit must be given to those who survived the crisis.

Japanese life insurance companies became important leaders in international finance in the late 1980s. More than 90 percent of the Japanese population owned life insurance and the amount held per person was at least 50 percent greater than in the United States. Many Japanese used insurance companies as savings vehicles. Insurance companies' assets grew annually at a rate of more than 20 percent per year in the late 1980s. By the end of the 1988 financial year, the invested assets of private insurance companies (excluding Japan Post Insurance and *kyosai*) had reached US$850 billion at today's exchange rate. The life insurance companies moved heavily into foreign investments as deregulation allowed them to do so and as their resources increased through the spread of fully funded pension funds. These assets permitted the companies to become major players in international money markets. Nippon Life Insurance Company, the world's largest insurance firm, was reportedly the biggest single holder of United States Treasury securities in 1989.

But the rosy picture did not hold up for long. Many insurance players' policies in force—contracted during the 1980s—guaranteed high yields. As the bubble economy collapsed in the late 1980s and interest rates tumbled, these contracts started to incur massive losses (see Figure 4.1). As the Japanese government maintained the low-interest-rate environment, many insurance companies were unable to sustain the massive losses due to the negative spread. Seven large insurers eventually declared bankruptcy in the early 2000s, including Kyoei Life, which was the largest bankruptcy in the world at the time. Of the 31 members of the Life Insurance Association of Japan in 1996, only 15 remained in 2005. The rest had either been acquired, merged, or declared bankrupt.[11]

In the aftermath of these large collapses, the government stepped in and restructured many of these policies, reducing policyholder benefits by as much as 70 percent and surrender values by as much as 20 percent.[12] In 2003, the Insurance Business Law was revised, allowing insurers to lower expected rates of interest prior to declaring bankruptcy. This controversial

(continued)

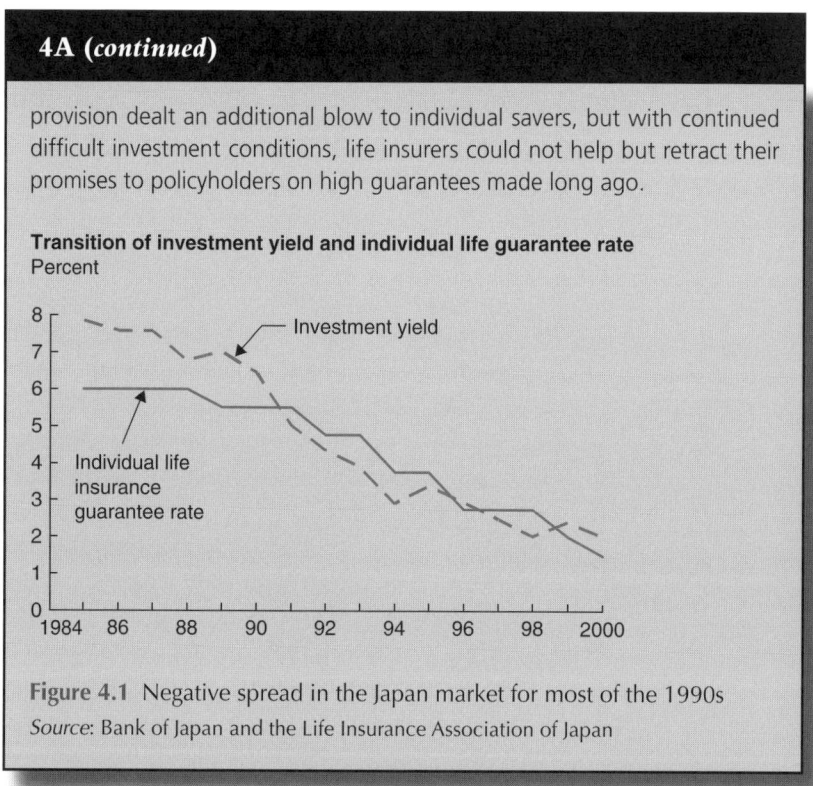

4A (*continued*)

provision dealt an additional blow to individual savers, but with continued difficult investment conditions, life insurers could not help but retract their promises to policyholders on high guarantees made long ago.

Transition of investment yield and individual life guarantee rate
Percent

Figure 4.1 Negative spread in the Japan market for most of the 1990s
Source: Bank of Japan and the Life Insurance Association of Japan

So why have local incumbents not taken action to revitalize their standing? First, local incumbents do not have a history of venturing into new product areas. They were not the first to enter the stand-alone medical market, nor were they eager to develop variable annuities. With a conservative investment outlook, the majority of these players' portfolios have remained in traditional life policies. Nippon Life, Sumitomo, and Meiji Yasuda together account for some 70 percent of the whole-life market, a sector that declined at an annualized rate of 7 percent from 2001 to 2006.

Second, these players' large sales forces are entrenched in their current form, making it very difficult for the sales forces to change their habits, including selling new products such as investment-linked policies. Japanese insurance companies own enormous housewife-based (*seiho lady*) sales forces, which were nurtured in the period after World War II, when societal pressures obliged large corporations to give women work. In 2006,

Nippon Life had almost 51,000 agents, while Meiji Yasuda, the fourth-largest insurer, had nearly 32,000 agents.[13] Having invented this model for selling life insurance and seen it produce decades of success, they are now encumbered with a legacy that has come to haunt them.

Third, a conservative corporate culture with long, decision-making processes prohibits these companies from taking swift action when markets turn. Most of the major Japanese incumbents are "mutuals," owned by their policyholders. Consequently, they are not subject to shareholder pressure, leaving the management to its own devices with a weak governance culture. There has been much talk about demutualization and in 2002 Daido became the first company to demutualize, but so far, the larger players remain mutuals. In particular, given their stronghold in the still-large traditional sector, management may eschew opportunities in the variable annuity or medical insurance markets on the grounds that they are too small. To put this in perspective, Nippon Life earned US$46 billion in premium in 2006, when the entire medical insurance market was estimated to be worth no more than US$19 billion.

4B—Incumbents are losing out in the corporate pension market

Developments in the corporate pension market illustrate how changing market conditions have challenged incumbents in Japan. Over the last decade, insurers faced head-on competition in the corporate pension market from asset managers and trust banks. Insurers had a 35.3 percent share of the corporate pension market in 1998, but by 2002, this figure was down to 23.6 percent. By 2006, insurance companies only had 18.9 percent of that market.[14] Gross premium from group annuity was US$35 billion in 2006, as opposed to nearly US$75 billion in 1997. The decline accelerated from 2001 to 2006, as the total market fell by an average rate of 10 percent per year. A combination of factors caused this decline, namely a proliferation of substitute products and the decreasing competitiveness of insurance company products.

Daiko Henjo, a change in pension law in 2001 that allowed corporations to fold their pension funds back into the government pension scheme,

(continued)

4B (*continued*)

shrunk the size of the overall market of pension funds under management. The change was the result of poor corporate pension performance in the 1990s. The government has thus far managed the majority of the funds in-house, but is increasingly seeking to outsource to third-party asset managers to seek better performance.

As the domestic investment environment continued its lackluster performance, insurers' products became comparatively less attractive. Low interest rates and losses from falling stock prices forced insurance companies to cut guaranteed yields. In 2002, life insurers cut guaranteed annuity yields to record lows, from the previous 1.5 percent per annum to 0.75 percent.[15] Also, in fiscal years 2001 and 2002, seven major life insurers skipped dividend payouts on corporate group policies for two consecutive years, as low interest rates and the stock market slump made their annuity yields negative. Consequently, life insurers' credit ratings were downgraded due to concerns that customers would pull out of funds fearing that life insurers would be unable to pay their obligations. There are signs that these insurers are improving their performance: Four of the insurers resumed dividend payouts from FY2004; more players resumed or increased payouts in FY2005–06. In addition, since 2004, many of the major players' credit ratings have been upgraded. Nippon Life was the first to raise the guaranteed yield by 25 basis points in 2006. However, despite these efforts, they have not been able to reverse the declining trend in the corporate pension market.

Emerging Sizeable Opportunities in Certain Product Submarkets

The Japanese life insurance market is not known for rapid change—but there are some new opportunities, albeit emerging at a distinctive (that is to say, slow) Japanese pace. Given the size of the Japan market, these niche opportunities are quite significant—after all, the Japanese life market is expected to still be double China's market by 2012.

The Retirement Opportunity

Japan has the single largest retirement market in Asia by far. In Japan, 21 percent of the population is over 65, as opposed to the rest of Asia where,

on average, only 7 percent of the population is of retirement age. The proportion of people aged 65 or older is expected to further increase to 28.4
percent of the overall Japanese population by 2020.[16]

A McKinsey retirement study showed that the next generation of Japanese retirees, those now between 40 and 55, does not have the same level
of savings as the previous generation. Therefore, it is likely that a significant retirement gap will emerge. Post-retirement expense is estimated to
be about US$800,000 in current dollars, but Japanese currently in their
mid-40s will face a shortfall of US$200,000 at the time of retirement. This
sum represents the gap between estimated financial resources and the cost
of retirement (see Figure 4.2).

Furthermore, the Japanese are well aware of the shortcomings of their
public pension scheme. Poor investment returns have hobbled Japan's public pension funds. Although the Japanese Diet has enacted successive layers
of pension reforms in recent years, there is a widespread lack of confidence
in Japan's pension system. Between April 2007 and January 2008, 37 percent of eligible Japanese did not contribute to designated public pension
schemes for the self-employed, farmers, fishermen, and students. There is

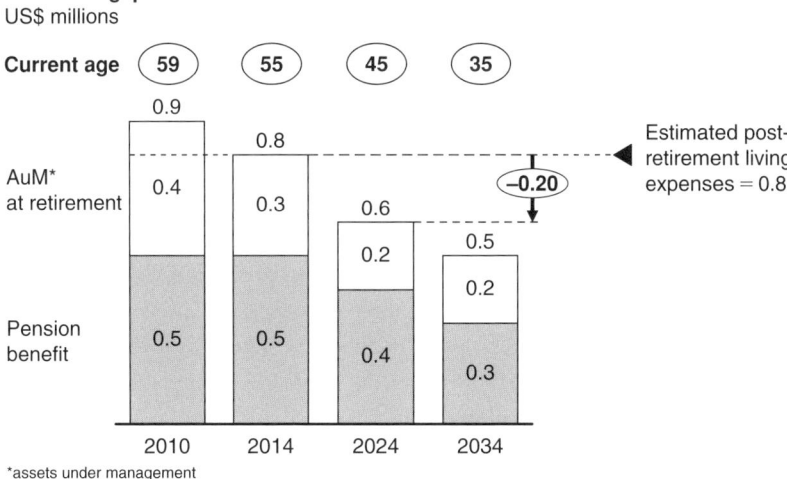

Figure 4.2 A huge retirement gap—but only for younger Japanese

Source: Public opinion poll regarding financial assets and expenses; National Survey of
Family Income and Expenditure

a general skepticism among young adults on whether a public pension will still be in place at the time of their retirement.[17]

Consequently, there is considerable awareness of this problem among the pre-retirement generation, leading to a widespread recognition of the need for post-retirement financial advice. As matters stand, none of the life companies has come forward with a holistic approach to meet this need, although annuities have exploited this opportunity on a stand-alone product basis. A survey by McKinsey in 2005 showed that 90 percent of Japanese do not have a financial advisor.

In markets with similar demographic characteristics, such as the United States, we have seen companies positioning themselves as retirement specialists. This has not yet happened in Japan, partially because large incumbent players have difficulty creating the advisory model required to succeed in this market. This gives rise to a significant opportunity for insurers and other financial institutions to brand themselves around the retirement theme, and develop a holistic retirement approach. This will include portfolio planning for different pre-retirement segments, consistent and periodic tracking of customers' evolving needs, products tailored to retirement needs, and a trained sales force that is able to provide the advisory services.

Individual Annuities

Sales of annuities are particularly befitting Japan's aging population. Japan's first baby-boomer generation, known as *dankai* seniors, are in their late fifties. Consequently, a large cohort is about to approach retirement and will be seeking financial products that can provide them with a safe, steady income stream. Annuity, with its unique decumulation characteristics, is set to be one of the biggest beneficiaries in the coming years.

Premium from individual annuity policies grew US$47 billion, from US$19 billion in 2001 to US$66 billion in 2006; to put this in context, that growth was approximately equal to China's total market size in 2004. Such growth is likely to continue—we estimate the individual annuities market in Japan could be worth up to US$80 billion by 2010.

While all other product categories saw negative premium growth between 2001 and 2006, individual annuity clocked an annualized rate of increase of 28 percent. This phenomenon can be attributed to product deregulation that allowed the sale of variable annuities in 1999 as well as the opening of the bancassurance channel to annuity sales in 2002. The role of bank distribution has been very significant—61 percent of individual annuities in 2006 were sold through banks. Meanwhile, in-force policies for fixed individual annuities grew by only 2 percent per year. In terms of sum insured from new policies, variable annuities grew 44 percent annually from 2002 to 2006, whereas fixed annuities grew 16 percent.

As interest in investment-type products grows among Japanese consumers, variable individual annuity is expected to be the stronger growth segment of the annuity market, even though it is dependent on the performance of equity markets and will have more volatile growth, especially during difficult market conditions.

Medical Insurance

Medical insurance is often overlooked as a niche sector within Japanese life insurance due to its small share; however, this niche market is vastly greater than its equivalents anywhere else in Asia. Furthermore, there is potential for even more growth as public medical system policy changes give rise to the need for more private medical care.

Japan did not have a medical insurance industry prior to the 1970s as the government offered a universal healthcare system. A government committee set the fee schedule for medical services, and patients chose their physicians and facilities, based on preference. Japanese nationals chose to participate in either an employer's health insurance program or a national health insurance program administered by local governments. However, as medical needs grew, the demand for supplementary insurance to the public healthcare system also increased, and insurance companies started offering private medical insurance schemes. It should be noted that medical insurance in Japan does not provide indemnity cover; instead it makes fixed, per diem payments to the hospitalized insured and helps offset surcharges and other expenses.

Our estimates show that healthcare products such as medical insurance, cancer insurance, and nursing-care insurance could be worth an estimated gross premium of around US$20 billion by 2010, which would be almost 20 percent of the premiums from private insurers' traditional policies.

The health insurance market in Japan consists of three different seg-ments: Cancer insurance only covers cancer, while medical insurance cov-ers illness and injury in general. Medical insurance has a limit on the number of hospitalized days covered, while cancer insurance does not have such a limit. The third segment, nursing insurance, covers the costs for medical and other services to patients who need constant care at home or in a nursing home. Medical insurance is the fastest expanding seg-ment of the healthcare insurance market; its number of in-force policies grew at an annualized rate of 5 percent from 2001 to 2006. Penetration is very low today—starting from a base of 2.7 million new policies each year or 2.1 percent of the population, this product line is well-positioned to continue its growth trajectory. Within medical insurance, stand-alone life medical insurance, which covers medical expenses for life without death coverage, is one of the faster growing products. In 1974, AFLAC started a unique medical insurance that covered medical expenses for cancer. This became the first stand-alone medical insurance approved by the ministry. In 1984, other foreign and local small- and medium-sized life insurers were allowed to underwrite cancer insurance, but the large domestic incumbents could not. From the beginning of the 1990s, the Japanese government considered deregulating third sector insurance (covering medical, nursing, etc.) as a trial run to full-scale deregulation of life and non-life insurance. However foreign players who had a pres-ence in the third sector (especially medical) opposed the plan and lobbied the Japanese government. The government eventually compromised and proceeded with the deregulation of life and P&C by allowing insurers to establish subsidiaries in other sectors. Domestic insurers were not allowed to underwrite stand-alone medical policies until 2001 when a US–Japan agreement was made. Stand-alone insurance has grown rapidly since then with increased competition from the local players such as Sumitomo, Dai-ichi Mutual, Meiji Yasuda, and Nippon Life. However, foreign play-ers remain the leaders in this area, with AFLAC, ALICO, and AXA tak-ing almost 50 percent of market share.

Other healthcare subsectors, such as cancer insurance and nursing-care insurance, are less promising and have registered negative growth, along with the rest of the insurance market. Without further product innovation, it is unlikely that there will be much growth in these subsegments.

As in most medical insurance markets, public policy will drive the growth of medical insurance in the coming years. At today's status quo, medical insurance will, at minimum, rise at the same rate as medical costs. Japan's Ministry of Health, Labor, and Welfare (MHLW) estimates that the total national cost of medical care will rise to somewhere between US$425–530 billion by 2025, representing a moderate growth rate of 2 percent per year.

However, it is likely that some healthcare reform is on the horizon. Given the aging population and funding strains, similar to those found in many Western markets, it is unlikely that the public healthcare system can continue to maintain today's coverage. Figure 4.3 shows that medical costs are expected to continue rising, while the compulsory insurance system will be increasingly unable to cover these additional expenses. Patients' co-payments and public funds have already taken up some of that slack. This is where private health insurance may be able to exploit an opportunity as Japanese patients find themselves increasingly required to pay for medical services. Government reform will create instant opportunities: for example, the recent policy change in 2003, which increased the ratio

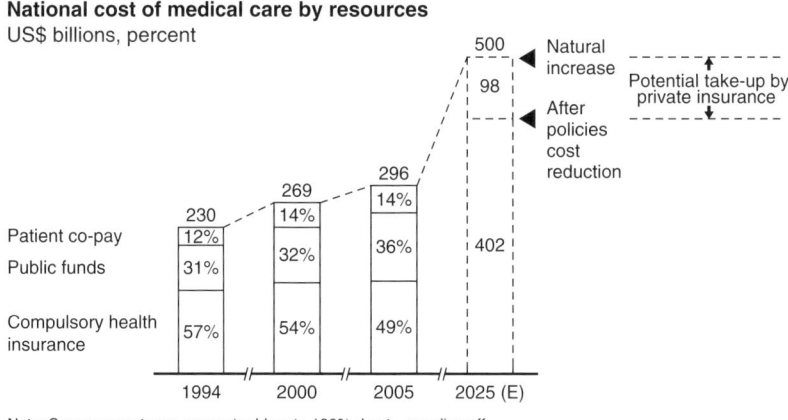

National cost of medical care by resources
US$ billions, percent

Note: Some percentages may not add up to 100% due to rounding off

Figure 4.3 Potential for private health insurers

Source: MHLW; literature search

of out-of-pocket medical expenses for company employees (salarymen) from 20 percent to 30 percent caused a spike in gross premium the year the policy was implemented, but then the growth rate flattened out in subsequent years.

Increasing Scope for Innovative Sales Models

Bancassurance has proved to be the most successful of the new channels for sales of life insurance. Partial deregulation in 2002, allowing banks to sell annuities, a few asset-formation products, and some P&C insurance, proved that large banks have incredible selling power through their branch channels. In 2006, banks accounted for 44 percent of annuity premium income sold by private insurers. As in most other Asian countries, the trustworthy reputations of banks and their established branch coverages have made them successful in cross-selling insurance products to their customer base. With complete bancassurance deregulation in December 2007, this channel has become even more important for life insurers, and its evolution is likely to reshape the power structure of Japan's life insurance industry. The power of the banking channel can be seen through the development of mutual-fund sales. From 1998, when mutual-fund sales through banks were deregulated, to 2005, approximately 43 percent of publicly offered, mutual-fund sales came through banks.

Besides bank branches, other sales channels are also gaining ground in insurance distribution (albeit on a smaller scale), including brokerages, retail storefronts, and direct sales—or a combination of the three. Retail storefronts are designed to serve as face-to-face channels for customers with "consultation needs." These storefronts are complementary to direct sales and are mainly run by contracted agents. ALICO operated some 210 shops as of June 2008 and AFLAC operated some 600 shops as of August 2008.

One innovative company to look at in the brokerage channel is Advance Create, which pioneered the model of brokerage shops. From its inception as a single-room start-up in Osaka in 1995, to the end of 2003, Advance Create's business was lopsidedly dependent on one old-fashioned approach, a flyer-based, mail-order channel, the so-called "posting" method. Then, starting from 2004, the broker revamped its sales model by introducing insurance brokerage shops, located at high-traffic locations such as shopping centers and open to "walk-ins" at late hours and on weekends. Advance Create's life insurance consultants customize insurance packages by picking products out of a portfolio of some 40 insurance companies. This represents a major deviation from the traditional "push-based" approach where insurance agents contact potential clients unsolicited. The company's scale and impact has remained modest though. By March 2008, Advance Create had 69 shops in 26 prefectures across the country. For the year ending September 2007, Advance Create earned US$79 million in annualized new premium, approximately half of which originated from the brokerage shops.

Another interesting distribution model is shopassurance, which started in the 1980s and has seen mixed success. Shopassurance refers to the in-store insurance counters located in retail stores such as hypermarkets. For example, Ito-Yokado, one of the major mega-supermarket chains in Japan, owns an agent business with branches located within its supermarkets, selling the products of more than 10 life insurance companies. This model is not a straightforward success though.

ORIX Life launched direct channel sales in 1997 to sell its low-premium, no-frills, traditional insurance to retail customers. By cutting costs for agencies, it was able to offer discounts of 20–30 percent on premiums for direct channel products. For the 12 months ending March 2007, total premium income, including sales by direct and agency channels, was US$1.1 billion. Another innovative insurer is Sompo Japan Life Insurance Co., which has two subsidiaries: Sompo Japan Himawari Life and Sompo Japan DIY Life. It markets life insurance products using non-face-to-face methods, such as mail order, telephone sales, and internet sales. Its core products are various forms of one-year, term-life insurance, which allow customers to review their insurance needs according to their life stage by adding riders for various types of cover, such as hospitalization, cancer, and income replacement insurance. These products are very popular with customers who want to design their own insurance products. In 2002, Sompo DIY Life started offering one-year, term-life insurance called "*Kumitate Kit*" (assembly, or DIY, kit in Japanese) on the internet. Customers can input their needs and calculate the premium amount online. In November 2007, the company launched yet another product, a ready-made, one-year, term-life insurance called "Simple Select."

Meanwhile, the October 2007 privatization of Japan Post is seen as a significant event by many industry insiders. Japan Post's holding company, bank, and insurance company plan to launch public offerings in the near future, thus creating pressure for these entities to boost their revenue sources. This has opened up some 20,000 postal branches as channels for private insurers to sell products[18] that Japan Post Insurance does not itself carry. For example, AFLAC has been selected to be the exclusive supplier of cancer insurance through the postal system, significantly boosting AFLAC's distribution network.

In all, these new developments in distribution channels are creating strains for the traditional tied-agency model. The number of tied agents dwindled from over 300,000 in 2003 to less than 250,000 in 2007.

However, tied agents should not be written off just yet. Their competitiveness and survival depend on how well they respond to the challenge and transform themselves. Tied agencies are still the largest channel and are likely to remain so for the foreseeable future, and players with superior sales forces will continue to have a significant advantage in the market. For sure, the traditional, housewife-sales approach, based on strong customer relationships, is under pressure but like most things in Japan, will only change gradually. Its final demise should not be expected any time soon.

Meanwhile, agent networks with financial planners who tend to be better educated and often, male, have the upper hand in selling investment products. They are much more effective in serving the needs of increasingly affluent Japanese consumers than the traditional sales ladies. These more investment-focused agents have remained relatively small scale though. A good example of this is SONY–Prudential (US), a joint venture, started in the early 1980s and dissolved in the late 1980s as SONY and Prudential (US) parted ways to pursue their separate ventures. It captured significant market share by introducing the revolutionary concept of insurance agents as "life planners." Their success illustrates the point that in mature markets such as Japan, the agent channel will have to upgrade itself with the market and adopt a more professional approach.

Rewards for Innovative Players with Perseverance

Throughout Japan's life insurance history, innovations in products or channels have bumped the market upwards. Foreign players came to dominate the variable annuities and medical insurance submarkets, which have been the fastest-growing sectors in recent years. In 2006, AFLAC, ALICO, and AXA were the top three players in the healthcare sector by number of policies, while The Hartford, Metlife, and ING led the market for variable annuities.

We have already seen how SONY and Prudential (US) cracked the stagnant life insurance market by meeting Japanese consumers' demands for consultative selling. Even after the break-up of their partnership in 1987, each side of the joint venture continued to grow using a financial advisory model. The number of SONY Life Planners exceeded 3,700 in 2007, and by 2006, SONY logged in a US$5.4 billion in premium income while Prudential (US) reaped US$3.6 billion. Prudential (US) also acquired Aoba Life in 2005.

Another innovator in the Japanese market is the American insurer The Hartford which built a significant share of the variable annuity market over a period of 10 years. The company entered the market in 2000, when assets under management were less than US$1 billion and there were only five players. By 2006, The Hartford had a 22 percent share of a US$137 billion in-force, sum assured pool and was ranked first in terms of in-force policy amount for variable annuities. The Hartford was able to break into the variable annuity market by securing its sales channel through banks, paying high commissions to agents, providing the right training, and developing innovative products such as balanced-funds-backed variable annuities. However, other followers have quickly imitated The Hartford's approach. Most notably, Tokio Marine & Nichido Financial Life Insurance (see Box 4C) overtook The Hartford as the sixth-largest player in Japan by gross premium in 2006, through beating The Hartford at its own game.

4C—Tokio Marine & Nichido Financial Life Insurance: A rapidly growing newcomer

Tokio Marine & Nichido Financial is the result of Millea Group's acquisition of Skandia Life's Japan business in 2004. Millea Group itself is the product of two large P&C insurers, Tokio Marine and Nichido Fire.

The firm has made significant strides in the market since its establishment. By 2006, it had raked in almost US$10 billion in premium and became the sixth-largest life insurer in Japan, in terms of premium income. It was in 18th place just the year before.

Tokio Marine & Nichido Financial succeeded by expanding in the new bancassurance channel and by developing innovative products. It signed a business alliance with Mitsubishi Tokyo Finance Group (MTFG) in September 2004, not just for sales, but also for product development to better fulfill bank customers' needs. At the same time, it expanded sales partnerships with banks, signing up 30 partnerships by August 2005, and 67 by August 2006. New products were also launched with features popular with individuals, such as principal-guaranteed annuity, short-term products, special contracts that may be added or removed to the main contract during the investment period, and investment themes that change based on targets reached.

The success of this newcomer is proof again that with the right strategy and timing, it is possible for newcomers to break into the Japanese market and gain significant presence.

In individual health insurance, ALICO (an AIG subsidiary), and AFLAC grew by offering newly developed products through the right channels. ALICO was the first to offer medical insurance in 1976, and poured large amounts of money into advertising and promotion to build brand awareness. AFLAC was the first to launch cancer insurance in Japan, in 1974, and as a result, its Japanese business grew to be larger than its business in the US.

It is important to note that in all these success stories, the players viewed the Japan business as a long-term investment. Japan is notorious for its high start-up costs and time to reach a break-even point. It took SONY and Prudential (US) 13 years to reach break-even point after the joint venture was established. Similarly, AFLAC took eight years to break even.

Most other players also took around nine years to reach this threshold, as it takes time to build proprietary distribution channels from scratch.

Given the time it takes to start earning profits with a greenfield approach, acquiring incumbent companies may be an attractive alternative. But acquisitions have not proved easy to manage, especially in Japan with its distinctive corporate culture. In addition, there are not many high-performing local insurers available for sale, and prices are often high. Failure cases are plentiful. For example, the purchase of Kyoei by Prudential (US) and the AXA merger with Nippon Dantai were disappointing investments. Both companies' gross premium actually declined during their first four years of new ownership. Players who are most likely to make acquisitions work are those who have introduced distinctive products and new distribution models. An example of this is Manulife which bought Daihyaku and launched a variable annuities product using its expertise gained in the North American market. It also developed the bancassurance channel for sales. As a result, the company's gross premium shot up more than six times in a short span of four years.

The Future Outlook

If we were to fast forward Japan's insurance market to 2020, the market landscape would differ greatly from today, given the forces presently at work. A dramatic shift will occur in product and revenue mix as retirement, medical, and investment products outgrow the rest of the market. Similarly, channels will evolve such that the traditional tied-agent sales force will most likely be smaller and much more professional compared to today, and an even larger portion of sales will come from other channels, including banks, brokers, and other direct channels.

With the growing power of bancassurance and variable annuities, attackers—both foreign and local—will most likely gain a more significant share. Whether local incumbents will be able to adapt to the new business opportunities or remain rooted in traditional products remains to be seen, but without massive, drastic changes in their operations and distribution, the market share of large domestic incumbents will probably continue to shrink. The top five incumbents' share of private life insurance premium was down to 52 percent in 2006 from 68 percent in 2000. It is not inconceivable that the share of these incumbents could be down to one-third in 10–15 years time.

New powerful players will emerge based on their strength in third-party channels, integrated propositions in areas such as retirement, or business models based on lower cost delivery. Not only will these take a large share of the top line, but they are likely to be more profitable than traditional players. With leaner operations, lower commissions, and cross-selling synergies, margins from these players would be more attractive than those from traditional insurance models.

What is clear is that there are still many opportunities to be captured, by the right players, in the largest Asian market. The basic facts have not changed—Japan remains a very difficult market to enter and it does not have the same growth rates as the rest of Asia. But the sheer size of the market and the emerging growth opportunities make it worthwhile, or even necessary, for those with large Asian ambitions and long-term horizons to secure a position in Japan. In fact, given the fundamental trends driving the Japanese life insurance landscape over the next several years, there may be no better time to make a big move in this market.

	South Korea	Taiwan	Hong Kong	S'pore
Macroeconomic				
GDP (US$ billions)	963	388	207	169
GDP per capita (US$)	19,673	16,974	29,858	38,065
PPP GDP per capita (US$)	19,116	28,525	43,376	41,345
Inst. assets under management (US$ bns)	326	137	174	n/a
PFA (US$ billions)	939	741	314	299
Foreign reserve (US$ billions)	244	267	133	150
Socioeconomic				
Population (millions)	49	23	7	4
# of households (thousands)	17,550	7,260	2,226	1,039
Median household income (US$)	25,630	25,180	39,080	60,990
# of households earning >US$10k p.a.	16,000	7,082	1,945	1,031
% of households earning >US$10k p.a.	95%	98%	87%	99%
Urbanization (% of population)	65%	n/a	100%	100%
% of population older than 65 in 2005	9%	n/a	12%	8%
% of population older than 65 in 2025	20%	n/a	26%	26%
Life insurance				
GWP (US$ billions)	85	50	20	13
Life insurance penetration	9%	13%	10%	7%
Life insurance density (US$ billions)	108	68	31	18
Investment-linked %	23%	37%	39%	42%
Bancassurance %	40%	34%	38%	19%
# of life insurers	22	31	66	13
# of foreign life insurers	8	16	82	10
Foreign share %	19%	38%	71%	59%
Year foreign entry allowed	1986	1987	n/a	1931
Life insurance assets (US$ billions)	318	265	64	73

Note–all figures for 2007 unless otherwise stated

President Wu Chia-lu looked across the table at the young man sitting opposite him. "Are you sure you want to do this?" he asked. The head on the other side nodded in agreement. Wu continued, "I want you to go home first, and think about this carefully for a few days. If you still haven't changed your mind, then you can come to work. Law graduates from National Taipei University like you usually don't want to join our insurance industry." The year was 1964, and Frank Cheng was applying for a job at Shin Kong Life Insurance, a small subsidiary of the large Shin Kong conglomerate that made its fortune in garments and textile.

Frank ended up joining Shin Kong, and witnessed the growth of the tiny company into the second-largest insurance company in Taiwan with over US$30 billion in assets and over 12,000 full-time sales agents by 2008. He ended his career as the President of Shin Kong Financial Holdings, and devoted his professional life to building the life insurance company. During his memorial service, Wu (who became the vice-chairman of the Shin Kong Financial Holding Company) fondly remembered all the ups and downs that Frank led the company through, which in many ways reflected the economic ups and downs of Taiwan. Compared to the 1960s, when attracting people to work in the industry was difficult, the challenges faced by Shin Kong today are quite different. Competing in a much more mature market, Shin Kong has expanded beyond domestic life insurance, starting overseas operations in China, and investing over 35 percent of its assets overseas.

The Shin Kong story provides a glimpse into the development of the Asian Tigers—Taiwan, Singapore, Hong Kong, and South Korea. With their roots in manufacturing, few would have imagined the spectacular rise of life insurance in these economies. For many of the local conglomerates, their life insurance subsidiaries started off almost as an afterthought. Things have progressed quite a bit since then. During the 1980s, the Asian Tigers were the manufacturing powerhouses of Asia, but they have now ceded that title to other, lower cost markets, including China, India, and Vietnam. Meanwhile, the Asian Tiger economies have moved towards higher value opportunities, including financial services. These are maturing economies where consumers are increasingly sophisticated and the commercial land-scape is becoming ever more competitive.

Indeed, at first sight there appears to be little scope for growth because these markets have such high levels of life insurance penetration. But appearances are deceptive because, as the prosperity of the Asian Tiger nations continues and savings accumulate, there is plenty of scope for growth in the life markets. Not only are consumers saving more, they are also looking for new ways of preserving their wealth and they need greater protection.

Before looking at how insurers can benefit from opportunities here let us pause and consider the extent to which the economies of the four Asian Tigers boomed in the 1990s on the back of a relatively cheap labor force and an export-focused economic development model. From 1980 to 1990 these economies enjoyed real gross domestic product (GDP) growth of between 10 and 17 percent, then, from 1990 to 2007 they grew by 6–10 pecent. Collectively, the Asian Tigers accounted for 3 percent of world GDP in 2007. That year, the median annual household incomes in South Korea, Taiwan, Hong Kong, and Singapore were approximately US$24,000, US$26,000, US$37,000, and US$47,000 respectively.[1] Earnings at this level well exceed those elsewhere in Asia with the exception of Japan.

Meanwhile, life insurance premium as a percentage of GDP shot up from below 2 percent in 1980 to 7–13 percent in 2007, across these markets. In 2007, the four Tigers accounted for 55 percent of all life insurance premiums in Asia ex-Japan. A McKinsey 2007 proprietary consumer survey of personal finances among middle and higher income consumers in these markets indicated that life insurance ownership ranged from 67 to 83 percent. Yet all four markets have expanded at compound annual growth rates ranging from 8 to 19 percent between 2002 and 2007. While their growth rates and potential market sizes may be less impressive than the emerging markets of China and India, these are still significant growth markets. Expansion will likely slow down though: in the next five years these markets are expected to grow in the high single digits or low teens at best.

The combination of slowing economic growth, high market penetration, and the entrenched positions of the leading players, will mean that new contenders, and even established players, will need to adapt and innovate if they are to expand.

Three common themes run through these Tiger markets: First, these markets all have a high insurance penetration compared to the rest of Asia; second, the competitive landscape is quite mature, forcing entrants to find innovative niches to enter; third, foreign players have been quite successful given the lack of regulatory barriers, even dominating certain segments in these markets.

Additionally, despite their commonalities, the Asian Tigers have many differences in terms of sociopolitical environment, regulation, cultural background, and geographic limitations. As such, the life insurance markets, despite their similarities, have also developed in different ways and present different challenges to players today. These will be elaborated at the end of the chapter.

High Market Penetration

We saw in Chapter 2 that the Asian Tigers have very high market penetration. Taiwan was the most penetrated market in 2007 globally, with life insurance premium equal to 13 percent of Taiwan's GDP. Hong Kong has life market penetration equivalent to 9.8 percent, second to Taiwan, while South Korea's was 8.8 percent. Even the least penetrated of the four, Singapore, accrued 7.5 percent of its GDP in life insurance premium, significantly more than China (2 percent) and Vietnam (0.8 percent).

The high penetration of these markets has a lot to do with their long history and the large number of insurance agents in them, given that life insurance is largely a "push" product. For example, in Hong Kong, there are around 30,000 licensed agents, which, in an adult population of 5.3 million, works out to one agent per 175 adults. In contrast, in the US, there is only one agent per 670 adults. With this ratio of insurance agents it is no wonder that many consumers in these markets view insurance as a priority savings product.

As a result, growth will have to come from a deepening of the same customer base. Both the levels of protection, as well as the investment portion, have plenty of growth potential. For example, while Hong Kong's per capita sum assured in 2006 was about US$51,000, sum assured against death was only US$39,000. Similarly, in Singapore, the sum assured was US$80,000 per capita, but against death the sum assured was only US$46,000. This compares with death assurance in the United States at US$63,000 per capita.[2] More importantly, these markets have some of the highest savings rates in the world, which means that there is an enormous amount of money accumulated in the financial system, mostly sitting in bank deposits. Diverting some of these savings into insurance products will be one of the key themes for many years to come. In fact, it is not surprising to see some of these markets with a higher insurance penetration per capita than the mature markets of the US and Europe.

The challenges to the insurers are significant though: life insurance for many years has been characterized by high agent churn and aggressive push tactics. If insurers are to gain a larger wallet share of their customers' financial assets, they will need to develop a much higher quality agent force with a more consultative and long-term approach.

Stable Competitive Landscape

Compared to today's fast-growing markets in the rest of Asia, these Tiger markets are quite mature, with a relatively stable competitive landscape. For example, the rankings of players have not changed much in recent years. In each of these markets, the top three players have maintained a 40–60 percent share of the market over the past few years. The overall numbers do not tell the whole story though—we will see below that there are many underlying changes in these markets that are creating pressure on the incumbents. This is particularly significant in South Korea, where the incumbents have been rapidly losing market share to both smaller foreign players and local attackers.

Nonetheless, compared with the rest of Asia, these markets present a very different proposition to would-be entrants. Newcomers must take a very long-term view, because it is unlikely that a newcomer can organically grow a meaningful market position in these markets over a short period. The dominant channel is still the tied-agency force, which the existing players have built up over many years. Entrants will have to consider alternative business models, such as innovation in alternative channels, or establishing a highly specialized agency force. Some of these innovations have already taken place, especially in South Korea, and across the markets, the opening up of bancassurance has led to new players capturing market share through leveraging the branch distribution network.

A Sizeable Foreign Presence

Unlike the markets discussed in earlier chapters—China, India, and Japan—the Asian Tigers have been much more open to foreign entrants. Hong Kong has never been closed to foreign ownership of life companies. Except for a brief period in the 1980s and 1990s when it underwent a brief closed-door policy, Singapore has always been, by and large, an open market. Taiwan and South Korea opened their doors to foreign life insurers in 1987 and 1986 respectively.

Although the South Korean market opened to foreigners in 1986, overseas companies have only recently begun to take advantage of the deregulation trend to boost their market share of first-year premium from 9 percent in 2001 to 24 percent in 2006. They did so through the bancassurance channel, variable (investment-linked) products, and a more professional sales force (see Box 5A). Despite only having been introduced in 2003, bancassurance accounted for half of all 2006 first-year premium in South Korea, or US$2.3 billion. Foreign insurers sold 55 percent of that amount. At the same time, foreign players also capitalized on the opportunity opened by the deregulation of variable products. In 2006, foreign players collectively held nearly 30 percent of the market for investment-linked products, up from 2 percent in 2001. Indeed, these products account for 26 percent of foreign companies' premiums, compared to 15 percent for local companies. Finally, foreign players were also able to capture share by targeting high-net-worth and affluent markets through a professional sales force.

5A—How foreign players rapidly penetrated the South Korean market

A South Korean-based product development manager of a foreign insurer said that a key advantage for his company was the ability "to design sophisticated products by leveraging superior financial technology from more mature markets."

The ability "to make swift decisions in launching new products by using experience gained in other leading markets (for example, Hong Kong, Taiwan, US)" was cited as the foreign advantage by a vice president of strategy from a domestic insurer.

Foreign insurers were the first to roll out new, attractive products in the South Korean marketplace. MetLife introduced variable universal life insurance in 2003. AIG pioneered "equity-linked annuity" policies in South Korea. And Prudential (UK)'s Asia arm, PCA, brought in the "SI" product which guaranteed to pay a minimum (2 percent per annum) interest rate per year on top of the prevailing interest rate. Allianz introduced a "market-value-adjusted product," which pays out according to the US Treasury Bill return rate. These products are by no means new in the insurance field, but they were certainly novel to the South Korean consumer.

More importantly, foreign insurers also recruited a younger, better educated sales force. They are described as financial advisors, giving them higher status and thus attracting a better caliber of employees. Around 60 percent of foreign company sales forces have a college education compared with only 20 percent of the local "Big 3" sales forces which are dominated by part-time housewives. Also, 60 percent of the foreign insurers' sales forces are under the age of 40, compared to 40 percent for the Big 3 (see Figure 5.1). And foreign companies pay better: 64 percent of agents named a domestic firm when asked which company pays worst, according to a McKinsey agent survey. In contrast, 76 percent named a foreign company when asked who provides the best training. According to the Financial Supervisory Service, agents in foreign insurance companies receive, on average, US$2,500 more per month in compensation, due to either higher productivity or more generous commission structures.

The deregulation of bancassurance in 2002 gave foreign insurers a new channel via which to push their products. This channel, as in the rest of Asia, developed rapidly after deregulation. In 2006, nearly 80 percent of premium for the foreign players was sold through the bank channel. In contrast, 62 percent of the Big 3's 2006 first-year premium was derived from tied agents.

(continued)

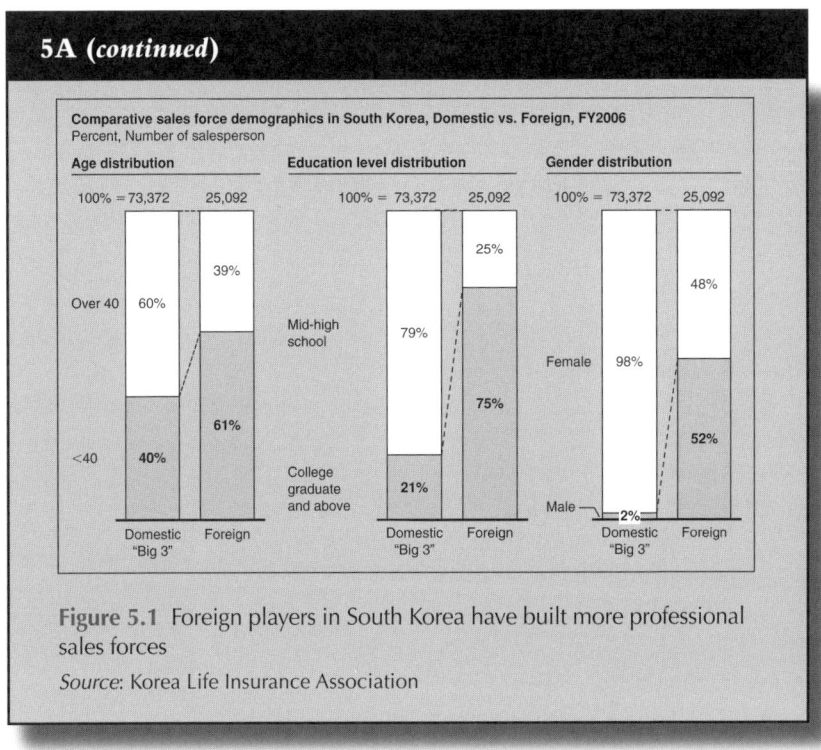

5A (continued)

Comparative sales force demographics in South Korea, Domestic vs. Foreign, FY2006
Percent, Number of salesperson

Figure 5.1 Foreign players in South Korea have built more professional sales forces
Source: Korea Life Insurance Association

It is important to note that there is also a third group of players in South Korea—small, domestic insurers—who accounted for 24 percent of first-year premium in 2006. Between 2001 and 2006, these players gained share in every single market category other than retirement. Without the baggage of a legacy sales force these players were more able to capture new sales channels. Companies such as Kumho and Dongbu acquired 75–85 percent of 2006 first-year premium through bancassurance. Meanwhile, Mirae Asset Group and Dongyang, who pursued tied-agency, brokerage, and bancassurance channels derived about 20 percent of their first-year premium through brokerage sales in 2006.

In Taiwan, foreign players accounted for 38 percent of 2007 gross premium. In interviews, 64 percent of insurance agents indicated that their customers prefer buying from a foreign firm due to its perceived higher trustworthiness. The majority of agents themselves, prefer working for a foreign company although the larger domestic firms—Cathay Life and Shin Kong—were also highly regarded. The four firms most often cited favorably were AIG, ING, Cathay Life and Shin Kong—a down-the-middle split between local and foreign companies. The 2008 financial crisis will likely change this dynamic though, with the sale of ING's Taiwan business to Fubon as well as the uncertainty over the future ownership of AIG's subsidiary Nanshan.

Hong Kong is probably the most extreme case in Asia in that it has no truly homegrown life insurance players—all of the major players are multinational firms. While over the years there have been a few local upstarts, once they grew to a certain size they were sold to a large foreign player eager to get a piece of the action in this vibrant market—Protective Life was sold to MassMutual in 2000; Pacific Century Insurance, another local start-up, was sold to Fortis in 2007.

Of the top five life insurers in Singapore, three are foreign-owned. It is possible that the foreign players could have gained more market share from Singaporean local companies were it not for occasional interventions by the government to protect local insurers, which included a closed-door policy in the 1980s and 1990s.

Market Snapshots

South Korea

The South Korean market is highly saturated and competitive, dominated by large local incumbents. Nevertheless, the South Korean market saw 10 percent compound annual growth between 2002 and 2007, despite an almost fully saturated market, with household penetration of 90 percent and life insurance premium equivalent to 8.8 percent of GDP—third only to Taiwan and Hong Kong in Asia.

One of the major demand trends in this market is the growth of investment and retirement products driven by the aging population. A 2007 McKinsey survey shows that most people in South Korea feel they are not sufficiently prepared for retirement and that existing products do not meet their needs. Meanwhile, the impending introduction of the Capital Market Consolidation Act (CMCA), which comes into force in 2009, has spurred considerable excitement and made consumers more comfortable about buying investment products (see Box 5B).

5B—South Korea moves to loosen restrictions on the finance industry

The proposed Capital Market Consolidation Act (CMCA) represents the first wave of regulatory initiatives to consolidate South Korea's financial industry. The Act relates to the financial investment services sector, which includes securities and futures companies, merchant banks, asset-management and trust companies, etc. Its aim is to consolidate all these companies into one type of financial institution: financial investment companies (FICs)—the South Korean counterpart of investment banks.

Under the current regulatory framework, financial investment services are divided into five groups and operations across segments are restricted. The CMCA is designed to bring about two major changes. First, it reclassifies financial investment services into six categories by economic nature: dealing, arranging, asset management, discretionary and non-discretionary investment advisory services, and trust services. This shifts the regulation framework from institutional regulation to functional regulation, meaning that the same regulation would be applied to the same financial function regardless of the type of financial institution providing the service. Second, the CMCA proposes to remove the boundaries between different financial investment services by allowing FICs to conduct all six categories of businesses. The restriction on mixed operation would be substituted by Chinese walls, or information barriers, between business segments.

The CMCA may lead to a shake-up in the financial investment services sector. In the short-to-mid term it is likely to prompt a wave of consolidation, giving rise to much stronger players. For example, in January 2008, Woori Finance Holdings, South Korea's largest financial holding group, teamed up with Aviva, the UK's largest life insurance group, to acquire a 91.65 percent stake in South Korea's LIG Life Insurance for US$146 million.

Furthermore, the government is rumored to be considering a second wave of reform that will bring down the division between securities houses and insurance companies. If this happens it will further accelerate the consolidation started by the first wave.

In terms of the competitive landscape, South Korea is the only Tiger nation to have seen its dominant players significantly challenged by newcomers who have been able to wedge their way into the market. The incumbents have traditionally relied on the legacy housewife-dominated agent distribution system for decades, influenced by the Japanese model.

Over the past few years, foreign companies and smaller local attackers were able to develop a more professional sales force or new channels that were better able to sell the newer investment products and consequently grabbed market share. This has not gone unnoticed by the Big 3 South Korean players—Samsung Life, Kyobo, and Korea Life—who have been fighting back to avoid losing an even greater proportion of market share. However, given their legacy sales force models, they will have tremendous difficulties in professionalizing their sales forces and introducing more sophisticated products.

The housewife sales force simply lacks the capability to sell more sophisticated products. Over the years, they have accumulated a large customer base on the basis of their strong local relationships. The Big 3 appreciate the need to both downsize and professionalize their agency forces but the transition is very difficult. While they understand the long-term imperative of doing this, they worry about diminished market share during the transition process. The pain of this trade-off has even led to some reversal of downsizing programs, pitting the reformers against the traditionalists.

Meanwhile, market share losses for these incumbents have been significant. In 2002, the Big 3 accounted for 77 percent of first-year premium; by 2007, their combined premium share dwindled to 44 percent by first-year premium. The Big 3 lost share in almost every single product category, from whole life to variable (see Figure 5.2).

Even in the miniscule group-life segment, where 2006 premium was only US$1.3 billion, the Big 3 slipped from having 94 percent of the market to 87 percent. How did this happen? The large incumbents kept to their historical strengths—traditional whole-life and term-life insurance via housewives channels, while the market had moved towards variable products, the bancassurance channel, and a more professionalized sales force. Variable products and bancassurance were introduced to the marketplace in 2001 and 2002 respectively (see Box 5A). The growth has been very significant. By 2007, variable products accounted for 23 percent of gross premium and pure endowment accounted for 19 percent.

So who gained market share? Primarily smaller players, many of whom were foreign entrants. For example, the market share of ING grew from 1.4 percent to 5.9 percent between 2001 and 2006. And a handful of local players, such as Shinhan, which grew its market share from 1.8 percent to 3.3 percent during this period.

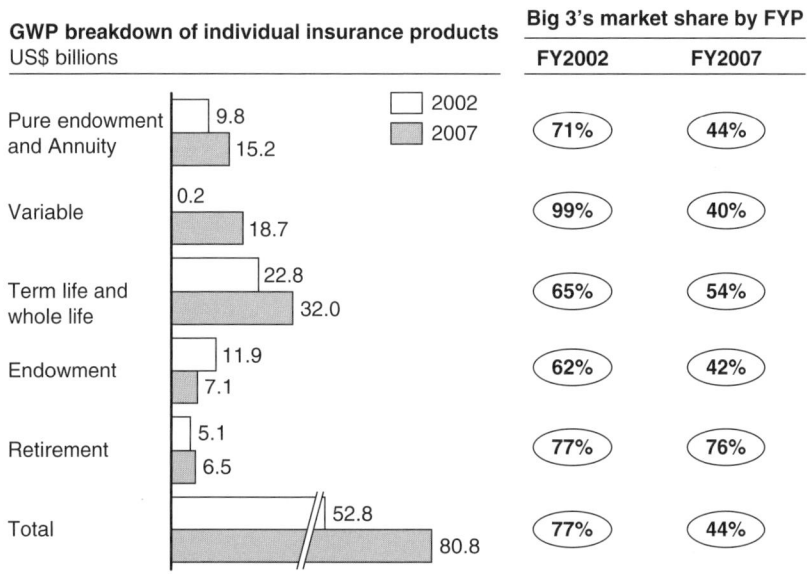

Figure 5.2 South Korea's Big 3 lost market share to attackers
Source: FSS

As such, one of the keys to the future of the South Korea life insurance industry lies in the growth of the smaller, more aggressive new players, who brought investment-linked products to the market and introduced distribution through banks. This distribution channel accounted for almost 50 percent of first-year premiums in 2006. The economic revival after the credit crisis and collapse of the dot-com bubble helped the South Korean life insurance market take off after 2003, growing by 10 percent annually after four years of near-zero growth from 1999 to 2003.

In addition to bancassurance, South Korea, like Japan, is pioneering interesting new distribution channels, of which the prime example is home-shopping TV sales, (life insurance is sold on television by an agent, with the support of call centers). Another innovative example is Mirae Asset Group—this up-and-coming player was the first to combine life assurance with investment centers and is positioning itself to lead the wave of professional financial planning (see Box 5C).

5C—Mirae leads the way in sales innovation

The distribution model of the Mirae Asset Group is highly innovative, although it remains unclear whether its efforts will be as successful as the initial marketing hype. The financial conglomerate attempts to cross-sell its products from its subsidiaries Mirae Asset Life and Mirae Asset Securities through shared retail outlets known as "Financial Plazas."

A Financial Plaza is designed to allow Mirae life insurance agents to sell asset-management products. They approach potential buyers through self-generated leads or those provided by call centers and try to persuade customers to come to the Financial Plaza where a professional mutual fund salesperson will introduce them to, and sell them, investment products. The Financial Plaza model results from regulations that specify fund sales can only be made at physical locations and prohibits insurance agents from selling mutual funds. By using its Financial Plaza, Mirae is working its way around these restrictions to create a new retail sales platform.

By the end of 2006, Mirae had established 47 Financial Plazas in middle-class locations throughout South Korea. Most of them are located on the second floor, or above, of retail complexes. This suggests that they are not looking for walk-in customers but those who have been targeted in advance. Each of these outlets has two to four tellers selling simple asset-management products to customers, spending about 20–30 minutes on each. A branch manager is on hand to provide in-depth financial planning advisory services.

Neither the direct store format nor cross-selling mutual funds through life insurers is a common practice in South Korea. Industry-wide, less than 3 percent of mutual-fund sales are through insurers. Mirae Asset Life is a pioneer in both. Already, around 11 percent of Mirae Asset Group's mutual-fund sales are through Mirae Asset Life, as compared to the industry average of less than 3 percent.

While Mirae has had early success in experimenting with new distribution channels, Samsung Life's challenges could not be more different. The life insurance subsidiary of South Korea's biggest *chaebol*, Samsung Life, has been grappling with the problems of change after decades of dominance (Box 5D). In many ways, Samsung Life is also representative of the Asia incumbents who are confronting a changing competitive landscape of life insurance.

5D—Samsung Life: Coping with change

South Korea's Big 3 insurers are interesting and unusual entities. Being subsidiaries to some of the largest *chaebols* (large, family-controlled, government-assisted corporations) endow these life insurers with a strong brand identity, but also constrain their ability to innovate because when making changes they are always mindful of the need to protect the entire family of related entities. Samsung Life provides the best example of these, in that the parent's size and strength brings both benefits and constraints to the largest insurer in South Korea. In addition, the company faces problems restructuring its massive, agent sales force both because of fears over the loss of market share and because, as South Korea's largest company, it is constantly in the spotlight and has enormous social responsibilities to its employees.

Samsung Life was established in 1957 under the name, Dongbang Life insurance. It became an affiliate of the Samsung Group six years later, and was renamed Samsung Life Insurance in 1989. The insurer commanded a market share of over 30 percent in South Korea in 2006. It sells individual and group life insurance as well as retail finance products through a distribution network of more than 1,000 branches and more than 30,000 salespeople.

The Samsung Group, the company's parent, is the largest South Korean corporation with a market capitalization of US$158 billion as of December 2007. Founded, and still largely controlled, by the Lee family, its business spans consumer electronics, heavy industries, and financial services. In 2005, Samsung overtook SONY as the world's top consumer electronics brand and became part of the Top 20 global brands overall.

The life insurance arm benefits from Samsung Group's brand equity and political influence in the country. As one of the most prestigious brands in South Korea, the Samsung Group attracts much of the country's best talent, many of whom hold prestigious degrees or equivalent qualifications. Local employees are highly loyal to the company, working very long hours and over weekends until retirement. Many South Koreans consider Samsung a source of national pride, and the company has powerful influence in political, media, and cultural circles.

However, any investment decisions taken by Samsung Life could have repercussions for the rest of the Samsung family. This is a conservative company with an acute awareness of its social obligations. No wonder then that the managers at the insurance subsidiary have been cautious about any change in their business lines.

As long as the market maintains an appetite for investment products foreign players are likely to continue gaining share. While domestic players will be able to replicate the foreigners' product offerings, the international companies have advantages that make them better able to market these products (for example, international experience and superior sales forces) which are unlikely to disappear in the near term. As in other Asian markets, the foreign players have been successful in attracting younger and more qualified sales forces. It is extremely challenging for domestic companies to acquire college graduates as members of their sales forces due to an image as "housewives" oriented and a lower compensation level.

Besides investments, the pension market also provides an attractive opportunity in South Korea. Aside from Japan, no Asian nation is aging as fast as South Korea. The government is committed to pension reform and many private pension schemes are being established. This will attract a great number of companies keen to enter this market, including insurers and asset managers. Contenders for market share will have to build sales forces with the credibility to sell these plans and they will need the right products. Armed with these attributes the companies need to position themselves as a retirement brand.

So what does the future hold for South Korean players? Part of the answer lies in the future sales of investment-linked products and the fast-developing retirement market. If investment products were to fall out of favor, foreign insurers could be faced with a slowdown in sales, given the small proportion of traditional products in their current mix of offerings. This may not be fatal, however, since the life insurance business has been through these cycles many times before. The quality of the sales forces will determine the speed at which they can adapt to different equity market environments and switch to other more conservative products.

Will incumbents fight back or at least halt the erosion of market share with new products and distribution methods? They need to do something, having faced five years of erosion by newer players who, like themselves, are operating in a market that is showing a slower rate of growth. It is difficult to be bullish about the Big 3 incumbents. Slowed by decades of inertia and legacy issues, they have yet to aggressively launch fundamental reform programs to halt the slow decay of their market share. While they cannot be written off (it is probable that one or two out of the group will be successful in their transformation), as a group, they will continue to witness a decline in their traditional dominance of the industry.

Overall though, the fundamental growth prospects in the South Korea market remain positive. It is estimated that premiums will expand by 5 percent annually until 2012. While the market is on a slightly slower growth trajectory than before, the prospects remain quite attractive for many of the attackers in the market. This is a market poised for drastic change—in 10 years, it will not be surprising at all to see the competitive landscape quite different from the one we see today. The winners will be those that can continue to best serve the increasingly sophisticated and aging customers.

Taiwan

On the surface the Taiwan market looks uninteresting: Taiwan is mired in a relatively low level of economic growth, especially compared to neighboring markets, and there has been a degree of negative sentiment around for years. In addition, the economy has been susceptible to swings in the local political environment. But this has also been a very high growth market over the past few years. Going forward, the factors that drove high growth rate remain intact: the island still enjoys a high savings rate, it has a large number of wealthy potential customers and a significant pool of untapped assets sitting in bank deposits. However, like many other Asian investors, it should be noted that investors in Taiwan have a reputation for seeking short-term gains and a high propensity for quickly switching their investment portfolios.

From 2002 to 2007 the Taiwan life insurance market grew at a compound annual growth rate of 18 percent, despite slow GDP growth during this period that averaged 4 percent. Regulatory changes in the Taiwanese banking industry have fuelled change in the Taiwan life insurance landscape. The period following the Asian financial crisis of 1997 produced financial reform in the shape of the Financial Holding Company (FHC) Act of 2001. The FHC Act allowed financial institutions to consolidate all their companies by forming a holding company that could include subsidiaries from all financial service sectors, including insurance. This Act, coupled with the government's stated intention to consolidate the financial sector, has led the largest financial players to establish their own FHCs, often with large banking and insurance subsidiaries. For example, the largest local insurers, Cathay Life and Shin Kong, have both made significant banking acquisitions over the past few years. The FHC Act is also prompting many banking players to consider setting up their own life insurance subsidiaries, which may have the potential of creating largely captive bancassurance channels.

As in all other Asian markets, bancassurance deregulation has propelled further growth in the Taiwanese industry. First-year premium generated through bancassurance grew at a compound annual rate of 42 percent between 2002 and 2007. During the same period, sales through agencies also grew 18 percent annually, suggesting that bancassurance *created* new business, rather than just diverting customers away from agencies.

In 2007, life insurance premium was equivalent to 13 percent of Taiwan's GDP, placing Taiwan at the top of the table globally. It is often surprising to insurance executives to see this number for Taiwan. However, insurance expense per capita was only US$2,218, ranking behind both Hong Kong and South Korea. Despite the large penetration of insurance into the population, there remain plenty of growth opportunities for protection and investments products.

Although projected population growth is negligible, an aging and wealthier demographic is expected to help drive the life and retirement market. Though not as significant as South Korea, Taiwan is aging as well. For example, Taiwan's median age shifted from 27 in 1990 to 34.9 in 2007; 0.3 million Taiwanese are expected to retire each year from now until 2025.

Despite deregulation of investment-linked insurance and bancassurance channels, the Taiwanese market remains an "old boys club" dominated by a few players with similar sales forces and similar market strategies (Box 5E). By the third quarter of 2007, the top three insurers in Taiwan—Cathay Life, Shin Kong, and AIG Nanshan—held nearly 50 percent of the gross premiums in the market; the remainder of the market is quite fragmented with 25-odd players holding as little as 0.1 percent market share. This looks remarkably similar to 2002, when the top three's combined market share was 50 percent (see Figure 5.3). In the rapidly changing Asian market context, the competitive landscape in Taiwan has seen little movement in recent years. The only change to the landscape has been the introduction of bancassurance in 2000 and attempts by companies to position themselves to gain a share of this business. This may change after the financial crisis of 2008. Fubon's acquisition of ING's Taiwan business will create another local giant, and AIG's potential divestiture of Nanshan may introduce another player to the market.

Due to the introduction of bancassurance, as well as the FHC Act, the top two local insurers, Cathay Life and Shin Kong, have expanded their business into integrated financial holding companies by buying local banks.

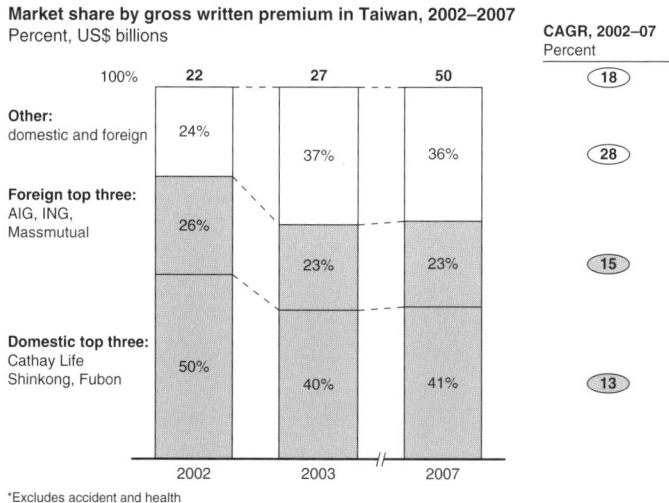

*Excludes accident and health

Figure 5.3 Market dynamics stabilizing in Taiwan
Source: Taiwan Insurance Institute

Meanwhile, deregulation has paved the way for smaller local players, such as Fubon, to grow their life insurance business by distributing over their captive banking channel. Fubon's gross premium market share grew from 4 percent to 6 percent between 2002 and 2007. This reform also helped some foreign entrants who used their size and know-how from other markets. For example, from 2002 to 2007, Prudential (UK) and Allianz increased their share of the market from 2.2 percent and 1.1 percent respectively to 2.6 percent and 4.9 percent. However, despite the growth in volume, the economics of the bancassurance product are quite marginal. Most of the bancassurance products sold today remain very simple deposit-alternative products with competitive interest rates.

In addition to marginal economics, it is unclear whether these smaller players will continue to gain market share after the initial growth from bancassurance. Newcomers are experiencing difficulties in capturing more than 5 percent of the market. Prudential (UK) for example, grew at a compound annual rate of 35 percent between 2002 and 2004 through a rapid expansion of its sales force. However, between 2004 and 2007, it only grew 7.1 percent, which is lower than the market average rate of 7.7 percent.

This is because the Taiwanese incumbents do not have a business model that is drastically different to that of the new players (for example, their housewife agent model is much less entrenched), unlike South Korea where there is a big gap in the operating style of new and old players. Taiwanese incumbents have adapted to the market changes by readjusting their sales forces and launching new products. In this way, they have managed to leverage their size and their brand names to maintain their market dominance. Furthermore, they have also used their immense bargaining power with asset-management houses for better fees on investment-linked products, and succeeded in cross-selling products within their financial holding company entities (for example, selling through their captive bank channels). As a result the loss in the dominant players' market share appears to have halted since 2003 and the incumbents continue to be market leaders.

However those investing in the Taiwan life insurance market must be wary of certain unique market challenges in Taiwan.

First, the short-term orientation of its investors and the instability of Taiwan's economic environment create high volatility in product trends, making it very difficult to predict product volumes. For example, investment-linked annuity policy sales went from −53 percent growth in 2004–05 to 91 percent in 2005–06. Even the most experienced executives in Taiwan say that they have no real way of telling at the beginning of the year whether their annual budgets and projections of product mix are realistic or not.

Second, given the mature and undifferentiated nature of the market, the life insurance sector, like the rest of the Taiwanese financial sector, is notorious for its thin margins. For example, Taiwanese banks have some of the lowest margins and returns on equity (ROE) in the region. In this market, price competition often becomes the only source of differentiation, and market-share ranking (in terms of volume) is often the key indicator of success. As a result, over the past few years, many insurers (mostly local) have come up with marginally profitable or even unprofitable products in order to grow market share. This has often led to price wars, especially with the simpler bancassurance products and other single-premium, interest-sensitive products where pricing is much more transparent compared to traditional products.

Third, there is a lack of depth in the domestic capital market, which poses a significant challenge for insurers. The 10-year bond yield in Taiwan has hovered between 2 and 3 percent over the past few years, consistently one of the lowest in Asia. Furthermore, there is a shortage of long-term investment assets, as the limited stocks of long-term government bonds are already held by the insurers and are rarely traded. The lack of long-term, local-currency-denominated assets has led to a large mismatch in assets and liabilities for the insurers (for example, the traditional life contracts are obligations of up to 20 years with some guaranteed interest rate). This problem is exacerbated by many of these insurers having issued policies during the late 1990s that had high guaranteed interest rates. This has given rise to the "negative yield" situation—while insurers promised 6–8 percent returns to many of their long-term customers, they are only able to generate a 4–5 percent return through their investments today, with current long-term government rates at 2–3 percent. There are essentially two ways to get around this problem. Either these insurers inject significant capital and limit their future downside today, or they try to grow and invest out of this problem. The massive size of these liabilities makes it impossible for most of these family-owned insurers to recapitalize, and as a result, they have no choice but to grow out of this dilemma. There is no free lunch in the investment world though, so in following the latter route these insurers have to take on more risk on their investments in order to generate higher returns. The regulator has also loosened many of the investment restrictions for the insurers to help them do this—for example, the latest regulation in 2007 allows life insurers to raise their current investments abroad from 35 percent to 45 percent as a share of total assets, which will make Taiwan insurers the only life insurers in the world with almost half of their assets invested in non-local currency assets (excluding the markets that have fixed exchange rates). The liberal stance on investments is a double-edged sword. On the one hand, it opens up more investment opportunities for the insurers to enhance their investment yield, but on the other hand, it imposes significant challenges for insurers to manage their risk in terms of new products, exchange rates, and others across a larger range of international asset classes. Not managing these risks properly will lead to disastrous outcomes for the insurers and their customers. For example, the 2008 financial crisis and meltdown in global equity and fixed-income markets have been a major crisis for Taiwanese insurers, who are very exposed to US high-yield and global equities.

Another theme for the large local Taiwanese insurers is regional expansion. Nearly all incumbent Taiwanese players—Cathay Life, Shin Kong, Fubon—have expressed an intention to expand into China. Although none has gained meaningful market share to date (Cathay Life is the only one with any real presence in China through its joint venture with China Eastern Airlines and Shin Kong has an insurance joint venture with Hainan Airlines), success in the massive Chinese market could significantly strengthen the financial strength and prospects of these companies.

5E—Cathay Life and Fubon: A tale of two brothers

Like the South Korean *chaebols*, powerful families in Taiwan also own large, diverse businesses, including the life insurers Cathay Life, Shin Kong, and Fubon. Their founders are legendary figures whose rags-to-riches stories are part of Taiwan's success. Among these, one family, in particular, has featured prominently in the island's life insurance history.

In 1962, brothers Tsai Wan-chun, Tsai Wan-lin and Tsai Wan-tsai, sons of peasant farmers, co-founded Cathay Life with Lin Ding-li. Prior to that date the Tsai brothers were already successful entrepreneurs with a soy sauce business, but they saw an opportunity in the insurance industry as the Taiwanese economy was taking off. The business turned into a success, and by the mid-1970s, the company was already a thriving conglomerate with diverse interests in banking, real estate, and plastics. In 1975, Lin Ding-li left Cathay Life; and in 1979, after suffering a stroke, Tsai Wan-chun proposed splitting the family business. Tsai Wan-lin got Cathay Life and three other businesses, while Tsai Wan-tsai took over the P&C business.

Tsai Wan-lin continued to grow his business, making Cathay Life the market leader of the life insurance industry. With more than 9.6 million policies in force, a significant percentage of all Taiwanese are Cathay Life customers. In 2007, Cathay Life recorded US$12.7 billion in premium and boasted a 24 percent market share. In 1995 Forbes ranked Tsai Wan-lin as the world's sixth richest man and the richest Chinese. Tsai Wan-lin died in 2004, but his son, Hong-tu, continued the family tradition of wealth and topped the list of richest Taiwanese in a Forbes 2007 survey.

Meanwhile, Tsai Wan-tsai grew his P&C business into today's Fubon Financial, a conglomerate with securities, banking, and insurance businesses. Fubon Life, established in 1993, was a latecomer to the market, but it quickly gained share, holding about 5 percent of the market by 2007 with it's acquisition of ING's business in 2008, Fubon will join the ranks of Taiwan life insurance heavyweights. Tsai Wan-tsai was ranked the fourth richest Chinese by *Forbes'* 2007 survey.

After the break-up of the original Cathay Life, the brothers' relationships became strained. In particular, an embezzlement scandal in the 1980s, involving their nephew, Tsai Wan-chun's son, further deepened the tension. Nevertheless, there is no doubt that with the two families each still holding tight control over Cathay Life and Fubon, the Tsai brothers are an integral part of the life insurance industry in Taiwan.

There is still a significant upside in Taiwan for those who can navigate this unique market. The local insurers are aggressively moving into China and also expanding into the domestic banking industry. A few of the foreign players have been generating a significant portion of their Asian profits from Taiwan and many more see this as a market where they have raised ambitions in the short term. This remains one of the Asian markets where customers have accumulated significant wealth and are relatively rich.

Hong Kong

With a stable political and socioeconomic environment, the Hong Kong Special Administrative Region has always been one of the most profitable markets in Asia. In the years 2002 to 2007, life insurance premium grew at a moderate 19 percent. Hong Kong remains secure in its role as a major financial center as well as a favored location for the regional headquarters of multinational insurance companies (see Box 5F). Arguably, it also has the most sophisticated consumers and insurance agents in the region. All this stems from a long history of foreign life insurance companies operating in Hong Kong, who continue to dominate the market.

Hong Kong has proved not only to be a highly regarded center for regional operation but has also become a talent pool extending its influence all over Asia, and most prominently in China. Many top Hong Kong executives have been headhunted to run insurance businesses in China. For example, Dominic Leung, who ran Prudential (UK)'s greater China business and has been in the industry for over 25 years, joined Ping An in 2004, becoming the first non-mainlander to take the reins of a life insurance company in China. Similarly, Patrick Poon, who headed ING Asia, left to chair the Operations Committee at China Pacific in 2007.

Relative to the size of the population and its economy, it is remarkable how much this one small territory can contribute to the insurance business—for example, Hong Kong accounted for 13 percent of Prudential (UK) 2007 Asian annualized premiums.

The more recent growth of Hong Kong's life insurance market is attributable to the opening of new market segments by bancassurance and increased demand for investment-linked products.

5F—Hong Kong: The Asian base for multinational insurers

Traditionally, Hong Kong and Singapore, with their advanced infrastructures and sophisticated financial and banking systems, were the two destinations commonly chosen as regional headquarters by global life insurers. In recent years, Hong Kong has emerged as the pre-eminent of the two, due to the increasing focus on north Asia, particularly China. China's accession to the World Trade Organization (WTO) has strengthened Hong Kong's position as the regional gateway to Asia. Besides Prudential (UK), players such as AIG, New York Life, and Standard Life are all using Hong Kong to spearhead their operations in China. There were 177 direct insurers in Hong Kong as of March 2008: 47 life only players, 111 general insurance only players, and 19 composite players with business in both life and general insurance.

A major consideration is the availability of skilled human resources, not only in insurance, but also in IT, accounting, and legal. Such resources are especially scarce in China, and Hong Kong has become a critical contributor in providing these resources for both local and international insurers' mainland China business. Howard Green, director of investor relations at Prudential Corporation Asia, says "Ultimate success in mainland China will depend on a number of factors, but people, especially those experienced in the insurance industry and having the entrepreneurial flair to build a new business in a new market, are critical. With its geographic proximity, plus cultural ties and sound industry already in place, Hong Kong is a good source of these skills."[3]

Prudential (UK), known sometimes as Prudential Corporation Asia (PCA) in this region is a player with a strong Asian focus. In 2007, around 45 percent of its annualized premium equivalent (APE) was generated out of Asia and many analysts see the Asian part of Prudential (UK)'s business as the key driver of its market value. Prudential (UK)'s business in Asia, with regional headquarters in Hong Kong and operations in 12 markets across the region, is the largest life insurance operation by a European insurer. This strong Asian franchise was handsomely rewarded by Prudential (UK)'s capital market valuation, with an average trailing price earnings ratio of around 18 throughout 2007, the highest among the top 10 listed global life insurers.

Bancassurance accounted for 38 percent of the market in 2006 by attracting consumers who had not previously bought insurance. Hong Kong has the strongest bancassurance presence in Asia, and some of the strongest bancassurance capabilities. Most of the large banks have established their own life insurance companies—for example, HSBC, Hang Seng, and Bank of China (HK), all have their own life subsidiaries. This has prevented independent life insurers from capturing share in the bancassurance market, with the exception of Prudential (UK) which has a strong bancassurance partner in Standard Chartered, one of the major banks in Hong Kong.

Investment-linked life insurance premium grew from US$1.57 billion in 2002 to US$7.90 billion in 2007, representing a 40 percent hike in market growth during this period. This has been aided by one of the most advanced sales forces in the region where insurance agents have been upgrading themselves to become wealth managers in the broader sense. In 2007, about 550 insurance professionals—life and general—held the highly regarded Certified Financial Planners (CFP) qualification; this represents approximately 20 percent of the total pool of CFP certificate holders. CFP is just one example; there are many other certification programs that have attracted Hong Kong agents to improve their qualifications to serve as wealth planners. Although, upon closer scrutiny, many of these so-called wealth planners still have much room for improvement, Hong Kong is emerging as an example of best practice in professional agency forces for other markets in Asia.

Undeniably, these eye-popping numbers have been supported by an extremely favorable investment market since 2003. Going forward, it is likely that the Hong Kong market will experience a slight slowdown in growth rates from the previous extraordinary pace; however, growth should remain healthy at around 9 percent due to a number of factors.

First, Hong Kong's economy, backed by its proximity to the Chinese mainland, is expected to continue expanding, bringing increased wealth to the population. Real GDP is expected to grow at 5.2 percent from 2007 to 2012, the highest among the Asian Tigers.

Second, bancassurance continues to play a big role in the market. Major banks, such as HSBC, have made insurance a key component of their growth strategy, especially for the mass-market segment. A consumer survey indicates that despite a relatively high premium penetration as a percent of GDP, only 67 percent of Hong Kong residents hold a life insurance policy. This is a lower rate than the other Tigers. For example, 83 percent of Taiwanese are estimated to hold some form of life insurance policy.

Third, there is a fundamental demand from Hong Kong consumers for wealth management, as they seek avenues to invest their money.

One additional factor fueling the growth of the Hong Kong market is an upsurge of life insurance policies sold to mainlanders. It is estimated that they accounted for 5 percent of new insurance policies sold in the first half of 2007. It is important to note that this is a significant but gray market because under the current currency regime there are many rules on how mainland Chinese can move their assets overseas. Some insurers have banned this practice in fear of violating these regulations.

Given the financial center status of Hong Kong, it is probably the most mature and sophisticated market in Asia. The market today is dominated by a few large players but also has a healthy set of smaller competitors. The three dominant players with a tied-agency sales force are AIA, Manulife, and Prudential (UK) who accounted for an estimated 30 percent of the market in 2007. The dramatic development of bancassurance has produced significant growth by the bank players, led by HSBC, Hang Seng (majority owned by HSBC), and the Bank of China, enabling them to grab approximately 19 percent of the market through their life insurance subsidiaries. It is important to note that most of the large banks have established wholly owned subsidiaries to produce life insurance products, effectively shutting out the largest bancassurance channels for the insurers. But as is the case in many other markets, this is not so much a "lost" market share by the traditional life insurers; rather, the banks have expanded the pie of life insurance through opening up their distribution and selling their own products.

Unlike other Asian markets, there is no large indigenous local player in Hong Kong. This is an international market, and given its British colonial past, there really is no distinction between local and overseas life insurers.

Hong Kong will remain a very significant and relevant market for most insurers. For players already in the market, this will remain a profitable market with healthy but not economically destructive competition. While there is little prospect of major change among the players in terms of market share, the Hong Kong market will continue to be an important profit generator and a center for multinational insurers to launch their regional activities.

Singapore

In many ways Singapore is similar to Hong Kong in the life insurance market. It too hosts a significant regional financial center and growth in its domestic market is driven by an expansion of wealth management and bancassurance.

The differences lie in the extent to which the government views Singapore insurance as an important national industry and actively supports it, compared to the more laissez-faire stance taken by Hong Kong regulators. For example, the insurance cooperative NTUC Income has strong ties with the government (see Box 5G). In the 1980s, the government tried to adopt a closed-door policy in order to prevent "unhealthy" competition, favoring local players over foreign ones. However, the plan backfired; the policy only reduced the competitiveness of the market and benefitted the foreign insurers who were grandfathered in and able to leverage their know-how from other markets to beat the local players. Meanwhile, industry growth was stunted, as there was little motivation for players to develop new products and channels. Foreign-owned insurers ended up holding more than half the market share in both the life and general insurance business. In 2000, the government reopened the industry to foreign ownership, with its new policy of developing Singapore as an insurance hub for the region. Incentives such as rent and training subsidies were established to attract foreign firms, and the Monetary Authority of Singapore (MAS) has confirmed that it intends to support training initiatives to build the talent pool. The impact of this policy is so far unclear. Singapore faces a very formidable competitor in Hong Kong which is at a much more advanced stage of serving as a regional center. At present, the number of life and general insurers in Hong Kong still far outnumbers those in Singapore. In 2007, Singapore had 55 direct insurers,[4] as opposed to Hong Kong's 178.

5G—NTUC Income and the Government of Singapore

NTUC Income is a local insurance player that emerged from the national umbrella trade union. Serving the public interest is a stated priority.

NTUC Income is one of nine cooperatives under the National Trades Union Congress (NTUC). The NTUC, the sole trade union confederation in Singapore, was created in 1961 and backed the People's Action Party (PAP) in its successful drive for self-government. Relations between the PAP and NTUC are very close, and have often resulted in members holding office in both organizations simultaneously. For example, Ong Teng Cheong, the first directly elected President of Singapore, was both the NTUC secretary general and deputy prime minister in the late 1980s and early 1990s. The PAP has been the only ruling party of Singapore since the island nation's independence in 1965. As of 2008, the NTUC has 62 trade unions and 7 associations affiliated to it and, in addition, includes 9 cooperatives and 6 affiliated organizations.

In 1970, the union established NTUC Income in response to a growing need for affordable insurance. The cooperative began by selling low premium insurance to union members, co-paid by the unions and the workers themselves. By employing union members as part-time agents to sell products to fellow members, NTUC Income was able to build its customer base quickly and affordably. Today, the cooperative has developed into one of Singapore's top five insurers, offering life, general, and health insurance. It has over 1.8 million policyholders and earned approximately US$1.6 billion in premium for the fiscal year ending December 2007.

Given its continued affiliation with the NTUC and the government, NTUC Income retains a high level of social commitment. Its senior management continually stresses that profit maximization is not a top priority. Rather, it aims to: improve product and service quality, meet the insurance needs of members, redistribute profits back to policyholders, and improve the lives of customers. Initiatives include job creation, product innovation, fund-raising for the union, and support for the arts. In recent years, NTUC Income has hired older, retrenched workers and fresh graduates in support of government policy. It has also introduced Singapore's first reverse mortgages for the elderly, and supported a variety of fund-raising efforts such as training programs and bursaries.

Besides its indirect involvement in NTUC Income, the government has played a central role in promoting insurance ownership. The Central Provident Fund (CPF), started in 1955, is a mandatory savings plan and social security scheme that helps working Singaporeans save for retirement, home ownership, healthcare expenses, life insurance, and wealth management. From 1997, citizens were allowed to put a portion of their CPF funds in specified unit trusts, insurance policies, and certain types of securities. The net effect of this was that insurance premiums increased as CPF funds could be used to pay for insurance premiums (as well as investment in certain approved products).

The government has clearly signalled its continued support for the CPF scheme, which is a major driver of insurance premiums in Singapore. Approximately 64 percent of 2007 new business premiums were subscribed to CPF accounts. There was a premium surge in 2001 when the government allowed investment in "special CPF accounts." This resulted in a leap of first-year premiums from US$6.5 billion in 2000 to US$10.4 billion in 2001, an increase of US$3.8 billion. The government has also focused on public education. For example, the MAS hosts the MoneySense program, which includes a Web site, brochures, workshop, and even a game show to educate the public on financial matters.

In terms of the competitive landscape, similar to Hong Kong, the Singapore market is also highly mature. Although entry to the Singaporean market is open to any company, final approval of the central bank is required, and regulations frequently favor established players. Consequently, the top three players—AIA, Great Eastern, and Prudential (UK)—accounted for 60 percent of gross individual premium in 2007 and the top players have been in the market for an average of 71 years.

The Singaporean insurance market grew at a compound annual growth rate of 8 percent during 2002–07, driven by strong fundaments. Government incentives and moderate penetration indicate that the Singapore market represents an attractive growth opportunity going forward. With life insurance premium accounting for 7.5 percent of GDP, and a per capita life insurance premium of US$2,889 in 2007, Singapore has potential for further penetration. The population is projected to grow at 1.4 percent per annum from 2007 to 2012, mainly as a result of government-encouraged immigration. Real GDP growth is in line with that of other Asian Tigers; the economy is expected to expand by an average of 4.8 percent during this period.

In addition, insurance has been a beneficiary of the flow of capital to Singapore. The development of Singapore as a regional financial center has attracted significant flows of capital from across Southeast Asia and even from as far as India. Insurance is not the only financial services industry to benefit from these capital flows—the asset-management and private banking markets have grown at extraordinary rates of over 20 percent in the past few years.

The Future: Solid Growth with Increasing Professionalization and Sophistication

These four markets will remain some of the most important profit-generating markets in Asia in the short term, despite the vast attention paid to the rapidly growing markets of China and India. For many of the pan-Asia foreign players, these are some of the most important markets that fall in the "sweet spot"—markets that have the necessary scale to generate meaningful profit numbers without significant regulatory restrictions.

The nature of the growth opportunity, going forward, will be quite different. Growth in the upcoming years will be in more sophisticated products through more professional channels. Most players are vying to launch newer, more competitive products to lure consumers—such as accident and health riders, interest-sensitive annuities, and more open-architecture-type, investment-linked products. There is no turning back for these trends. Investment-linked products will continue to be important, even though their popularity may be tested during down markets. For example, South Koreans today view investment-linked products as an alternative to mutual funds and often trade them as such. In Taiwan, investment-linked life insurance, first approved by the government in 2000, expanded to account for 36.8 percent of all premiums by 2007.

The agents in these markets will also continue their path towards becoming professional financial advisors. This is most evident in Hong Kong and Singapore where there has been an ongoing trend towards professionalization through a financial advisory approach rather than product-pushing. Of course, this will take time as agents change their behavior—in fact, it is likely that the older generation of product-pushing agents will never be able to transform fully into financial advisors. But with a consistent churn in agents and an across-the-industry focus on quality, professionalization will happen sooner rather than later. While South Korea and Taiwan are a few years behind Hong Kong and Singapore in this development, the rapid displacement of the housewives sales force by the younger investment advisors is already underway.

Industry predictions of the demise of the agent channel are exaggerated. The life insurance agency force is still a unique channel in product distribution, where the sale takes place at the customer's home. As long as the agency force keeps up with the times, this lifeline of most of the large life insurers will remain intact. This is not to say that innovation in other channels is not important. Some of these channel experiments in South Korea, as discussed earlier in the chapter, indicate how such a strategy can lead to very promising penetration in certain segments.

Lastly, it is important to note the differences as well as similarities in these markets; the themes for each of these four markets are actually quite different. In South Korea, the ongoing theme will pit the foreign players and smaller attackers against the local incumbents. For the time being, the attackers are continuing to make inroads into the market share of the local incumbents. In Taiwan, a more homogeneous market of local incumbents and foreign players has led to stabilized competitive dynamics, but the challenge remains in overcoming legacy issues such as high guaranteed policies, navigating the difficult investment environment, and ongoing professionalization of the agent channel. In Hong Kong, the ongoing journey towards a much more financial advisory approach has begun, and this market, in many ways, serves as the harbinger of what is to come for the rest of Asia. In Singapore, the development of the city-state as a regional financial hub and government support have largely influenced, and will continue to support, the growth of the industry.

Southeast Asia: Back on a Growth Trajectory

6

	Malaysia	Thailand	Indonesia	Vietnam	Philippines
Macroeconomic					
GDP (US$ billions)	194	252	421	72	161
GDP per capita (US$)	7,301	3,911	1,819	819	1,830
PPP GDP per capita (US$)	15,313	11,144	4,885	4,018	4,922
Inst. assets under management (US$ bns)	18	10	n/a	n/a	0
PFA (US$ billions)	194	132	70	0	0
Foreign reserve (US$ billions)	91	73	40	13	25
Socioeconomic					
Population (millions)	26	65	225	85	84
# of households (thousands)	5,678	17,500	59,650	25,600	17,480
Median household income (US$)	10,100	4,680	2,420	1,230	2,410
# of households earning >US$10k p.a.	2,823	2,968	3,440	341	934
% of households earning >US$10k p.a.	50%	17%	6%	1%	5%
Urbanization (% of population)	68%	33%	49%	27%	63%
% of population older than 65 in 2005	5%	7%	5%	5%	4%
% of population older than 65 in 2025	11%	15%	10%	10%	9%
Life insurance					
GWP (US$ billions)	7	6	5	1	2
Life insurance penetration	3%	2%	1%	1%	1%
Life insurance density (US$ billions)	10	10	13	2	4
Investment-linked %	49%	n/a	31%	0%	74%
Bancassurance %	n/a	28%	25%	n/a	n/a
# of life insurers	16	24	46	7	36
# of foreign life insurers	13	12	16	7	8
Foreign share %	55%	65%	56%	65%	74%
Year foreign entry allowed	1924	1938	1975	1999	1895
Life insurance assets (US$ billions)	31	24	n/a	n/a	9

Note–all figures for 2007 unless otherwise stated

"What keeps me going are my clients. All my clients became my friends; and that's what makes me stronger." Lili Lim, an insurance agent in Jakarta, has been in the Indonesia insurance business for over 10 years, experiencing market-specific ups and downs such as the 1997 Asian financial crisis and the 1998 Indonesian government political crisis along the way.

The first couple of months of the financial crisis, Lili recalled, were indeed difficult, as many policyholders lapsed on their US dollar-pegged insurance contracts. However, some Indonesians also cashed in their US dollar accounts and signed new contracts. The economy, and the insurance business, eventually picked up and that incident is but a memory to Lili. Since the financial crisis, the Indonesian industry has moved away from US dollar contracts to local currency policies.

Similarly, Lili lightly dismissed the 1998 government political crisis. "Of course I was afraid then, but I realized that being in Indonesia, and doing my job, were really important to me." The insurance agent had temporarily moved to the United States for two months, but eventually returned to Indonesia and her profession.

To Lili, selling insurance is more than earning a commission; it also allows her to be her own boss and help others around her in financial matters. In this emerging market, most people are only starting to understand basic financial products. Among her friends, she is far better informed in finance. Reflecting on the opportunity, the Jakarta-based agent noted that "Most Indonesians don't know the benefits of insurance. People know it is good, but they don't know *what* about it is good. If I educate them on what these products do for them in the future, then at least the family's financials would be better." The agent recounted the story of a 29-year-old father, who suffered a sudden, acute sickness and was rushed to the hospital. That day, Lili accompanied the young wife to the hospital and submitted the claims for the operation. Today, 10 years later, the man is alive and healthy, and half of the sum assured from the policy Lili sold them still remains. The family maintains close contact with Lili. "It was the first time I felt that I could really help a family escape an otherwise terrible fate," noted the agent.

Lili's story is typical of those in Southeast Asia—Indonesia, Malaysia, the Philippines, Thailand, and Vietnam. These markets are known for their volatility but also their resilience. They are rapidly transforming markets where new developments in products and geographic expansion to the hinterlands are shifting the competitive landscape. Although foreign insurers dominate these markets, the domestic players have increased in strength over the last few years.

The combined markets of Indonesia, Malaysia, the Philippines, Thailand, and Vietnam have a population of some 486 million, which adds up to 43 percent of India or 37 percent of China; their estimated gross written premium (GWP) was slightly less than US$20 billion in 2007, compared to India's US$52 billion and China's US$68 billion. And Southeast Asia's markets are particularly open to foreign entrants—in fact multinational corporations (MNCs) are market leaders in many of them.

Growth rates are just as impressive as the rest of Asia. We expect the region to grow at around 15 percent, doubling its aggregate market premium to US$39 billion by 2012.

But Southeast Asia is hardly a homogeneous market. Instead, it is a region divided by language, culture and, of course, different levels of development (see Figure 6.1). The markets in Thailand and Malaysia are more mature, with more developed channels and better educated consumers. The competitive landscape is relatively stable and rather difficult for new entrants. The Philippines is a relatively small market, with US$1.8 billion gross premium in 2007. Prospects for growth in the next five years are bright at a projected growth rate of 15 percent per year, but the market is gradually becoming more difficult for the foreign players with tightening regulations. Vietnam and Indonesia rank high among Southeast Asian countries in terms of expansion prospects, with an expected growth rate of some 25 percent per year in the next five years. This could mean that Indonesia will become the biggest market within the region. Meanwhile, Vietnam is often referred to as "the next China," as its economy opened up roughly 10 years after China and has since followed its development footsteps—although it has been facing some economic disarray lately. We describe in further detail below the last two markets, which are among the most eagerly sought after in recent years.

Vietnam

Of the five markets we have analyzed for this chapter, Vietnam stands out as being in the start-up phase. Its rags-to-riches story also highlights the volatility that often accompanies developing economies.

Vietnam's economic reform program (*doi mo*) only started in 1986, under a "market economy with socialist orientation" model that has similarities to China's model. In the 10 years between 1997 and 2007,

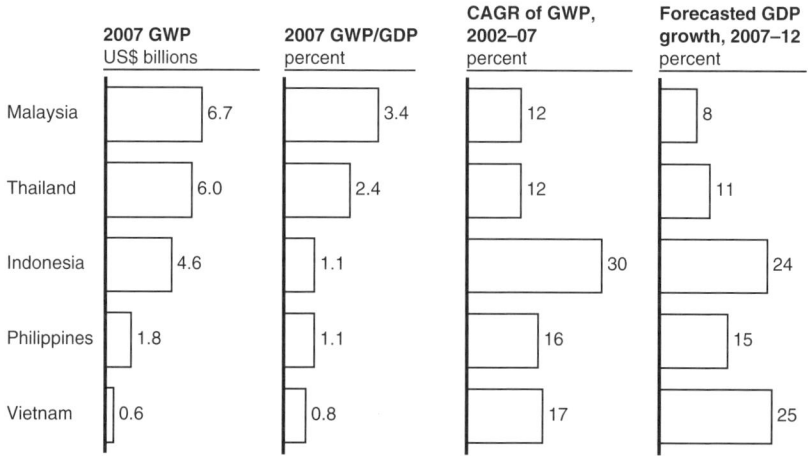

Figure 6.1 The rapid growth of Southeast Asian markets
Source: Sigma; McKinsey analysis

Vietnam's nominal gross domestic product (GDP) grew at a 10 percent compounded annual rate. The government has set an aggressive target of doubling the size of the country's economy over the period 2000–10. A stable political environment and the government's willingness to integrate with ASEAN and the global economy have attracted lots of interest from foreign investors. Vietnam joined the World Trade Organization (WTO) in January 2007. Foreign direct investment inflows in 2006 reached US$12 billion, with a growth rate of 32 percent per annum for the period 2002–06. Foreign investments almost doubled to US$20.3 billion in 2007 (12 months after Vietnam joined the WTO).

Vietnam's life insurance market is still small in size in comparison to its Southeast Asian peers. However, many industry insiders consider the market a tremendous growth opportunity. This is supported by macro-economic fundamentals. Life insurance penetration today is extremely low—it was just under 1 percent of GDP in 2007 and market development is at a very nascent stage with most players still selling simple endowment products. Today, five players in the market take up over 97 percent of market share. The local incumbent, Bao Viet, had seen its share eroded while foreign entrants, Prudential (UK) and Manulife, have taken much of that business. But the competitive landscape has, by no means, settled down. For example, a newcomer, ACE, was able to establish around 2 percent market share within one year of entering the market, and we predict that a lot more MNCs, and some leading Asian life insurers (for example, the Taiwanese and Chinese insurers), will enter Vietnam over the next few years.

Some of the market dynamics are quite reminiscent of the development of many other Asian markets. In a high-interest-rate environment, Vietnamese insurers have been offering policies with high interest guarantees of 7–8 percent, which is similar to many Asian markets in the late 1990s. The booming stock market has often led to unrealistic return expectations from retail investors, and increased pressure on life insurers to offer products with competitive returns. In November 2007, the Ministry of Finance approved the sale of investment-linked products, after much lobbying from insurers.

Not everything is plain sailing for Vietnam, however. With continued high inflation and slowed economic growth, the economy started to run into troubled waters in early 2008. Vietnam's GDP slowed down to 6.5 percent growth in the first half of 2008, a much slower pace of growth than the 8.5 percent registered for 2007. In June 2008, inflation hit 26.8 percent as oil and food prices continued to skyrocket. Government initiatives to contain inflation further slowed down the economy. Consequently, investor confidence dipped and the Ho Chi Minh stock exchange halved between March 2007 and March 2008.

Vietnam is entering a challenging period, and many investors have, since 2008, reconsidered their former enthusiasm for the country. Whether or not Vietnam can rebound on this setback will depend on the government's ability to keep its industry humming along at the current pace without further significant hiccups. Fortunately, the long-term fundamentals are sound in Vietnam: the country is not heavily indebted, and export growth is strong. The biggest constraint to growth is the state of its infrastructure. Basic elements, such as roads and power, remain a concern, and despite efforts, Vietnam still remains among the 60 most difficult countries to do business in.[1] Large investments and government initiatives are required to further develop its economy. Many steps have been initiated to improve the business infrastructure in Vietnam, but it is still not an easy place to do business. The gap between ideas and execution remains wide.

But despite the recent problems, Vietnam remains a "little China" in the eyes of many long-term investors—and the life insurance industry should be no exception here. The fundamentals are very strong and the long-term growth prospects for the insurance industry, plus the openness to foreign investors, make this country a highly attractive market for potential entrants.

Indonesia

The life insurance market in Indonesia enjoyed a strong annual growth rate of over 30 percent during 2002–07. This growth was evident across all product lines, but most noticeably in investment-linked products, which alone accounted for 42 percent of gross premium growth. The proportion of investment-linked premiums in total gross premium increased from 9 percent in 2002 to 31 percent in 2007.

Indonesia is a relatively consolidated market dominated by foreign players. In 2006, the top seven players accounted for about 58 percent of the market in gross premium; four of the top seven—AIG, Prudential (UK), Manulife, and Allianz—were multinational insurers.

Growth prospects remain bright; we forecast gross premiums could expand by 25 percent annually from 2007 to 2012, driven by continued economic growth and high market potential as indicated by a current low premium penetration at 1.1 percent of GDP.

Growth is also expected to come from the development of *Sharia*-compliant *takaful* insurance, which allows life companies to tap into the 200-million strong Muslim population of the most populous Muslim country in the world. Penetration of Islamic banking and *takaful* is still low compared to neighboring Malaysia. At the moment this is a small market segment, accounting for just over 1 percent of Indonesia's gross life premium but it grew 34 percent annually from 2001 to 2006, compared with a 25 percent growth rate in the overall life market. To sustain this growth, government support is needed to increase transparency and develop the Islamic banking system, as well as increase the service quality of *takaful* players so that they are competitive with conventional insurance offerings. Islamic insurance is not limited to local insurers. Multinational players such as Allianz, Manulife, and Prudential (UK) are also committed to developing this market.

Despite the various peculiarities in each of the Southeast Asian markets, they have as much in common as they have differences. The three major themes across the region are:

- Growth opportunities via diversified product portfolios
- Increasing competition between foreign and local players
- Channel upgrades to reach more customer segments

While the large markets of China, Japan, and India are undoubtedly attracting more investments than Southeast Asia in absolute terms, the region is providing good value for those who can navigate the waters. Multinationals have traditionally dominated most of the markets in the region, which have been meaningful profit contributors for these players. However, it is important to note that most of these multinationals entered in a period when they had significant first-mover advantages. This dynamic is changing somewhat; while foreign incumbents have a tight stronghold, local players are becoming savvier. New players contemplating entry will encounter greater challenges than those that went before them.

Growth Opportunities via Diversified Product Portfolios

Between 2002 and 2007, the Southeast Asian life insurance markets grew at an astonishing average pace of 15.4 percent per annum. While fundamentals played an important part in this growth, life insurers' efforts to reach new customer segments also played a significant role. Increasingly, insurers are designing products catering to specific segments in Southeast Asia, from micro-insurance for rural areas to *takaful* insurance for the Muslim population in the region.

There is good reason to be optimistic about the fundamentals in this region. For a start, the economy grew between 5 and 8 percent per annum in real terms from 2002 to 2007, which is comparable to the growth rate in India at 8.3 percent and China at 8.8 percent. Despite increasing insurance sales, the current level of market penetration remains low at 1.8 percent of GDP. Furthermore, product awareness and understanding of life insurance benefits is still nascent among consumers. Consumers are increasingly making use of life products as savings vehicles and to capture taxation benefits, but protection coverage remains low.

The urban population has traditionally been the target customer segment for life insurers. Part of the challenge in the future will center on how to move beyond the large city centers into the more rural areas. To some extent, traditional tied agents, such as Lili Lim, had tapped the rural markets through personal relationships, traveling to rural areas regularly to visit their networks, but large-scale, systematic distribution to these segments will require changes in both distribution and product offerings. In this aspect, some players have been quick to move and gain market share. AIA, for example, is aggressively targeting rural markets in Thailand and has devised a new, single-premium insurance product. The new product, 1 Pay Life, which is targeted at farmers whose incomes may not be consistent, will provide lifetime coverage for 99 years on the payment of a one-time premium. The launch of this product coincides with the record margins being earned by farmers from the increase in rice prices and AIA is hoping to significantly increase the share of premium from rural areas from the 5 percent it accounted for in 2007. Another insurer joining the bandwagon is Muang Thai, which has started selling to lower income customers and is also active in rural areas. The insurer intends to recruit one agent per village—the agents themselves actually being from these villages. This can be quite important, since 60 percent of the Thai population lives in 70,000 villages spread across the country. The policies sold have a low face value and are no-frills products, so volume is key. For example, one product is designed purely to help finance cremation costs. In 2007, up to 20 percent of Muang Thai's clientele was from rural areas and this was their fastest-growing segment.

Meanwhile, an emerging middle class has driven insurers to create tailored products that bundle risk and savings. Thus, in Malaysia, insurers are offering retirement, education, *takaful*, and other product combinations. Prudential (UK), for example, launched PRUVantage, which is a combined traditional and investment-linked product that allocates a portion to a traditional, guaranteed-return account and the remainder to an investment-linked account. Another popular product in this region is the combined protection and education savings plan.

Finally, as mentioned in Chapter 2, the small but burgeoning Islamic finance sector will see increased penetration particularly among the significantly untapped Muslim population in Malaysia and Indonesia (see Box 2C).

Increasing Competition between Foreign and Local Players

A hallmark of the Southeast Asian market is the proliferation of foreign players. In all five markets, foreign players have more than 50 percent of market share, with a handful of leading multinationals—namely AIG, Prudential (UK), and Manulife—enjoying entrenched positions (see Figure 6.2). However, there are signs that domestic insurers in Southeast Asia are growing in sophistication and ambition. In all of these markets, there are one or two prominent domestic insurers—these include Thai Life in Thailand, Bao Viet in Vietnam, Bermasa Bumi-putera in Indonesia, and Great Eastern in Malaysia (see Box 6A). For

Percent market share by GWP in select Southeast Asian markets (year of data)

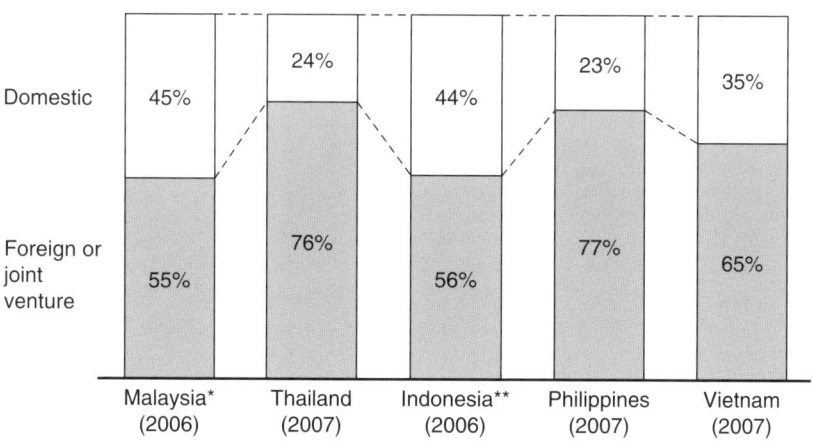

*Great Eastern is considered as a domestic insurance company
**Net premium

Figure 6.2 Foreign players are dominating share in Southeast Asian markets

Source: Bank Negara Malaysia; Thai Department of Insurance; Indonesia Ministry of Finance; Philippines Insurance 2006; Annual report of Vietnam Insurance Market 2006; literature search

foreign players seeking first-time entry into these markets, the golden period of "first-mover advantage" has gone. While foreign market share had increased over the past five years, the number of foreign insurers has held steady and in some cases declined. For example, there were 22 foreign insurers in Indonesia in 2001. By 2007, there were only 16. Similarly, in the Philippines, the figure dropped from 20 to 11.

6A—Great Eastern: Southeast Asia's GE

Great Eastern is technically a foreign company in Malaysia, but the Singapore-based company is deeply rooted in the country. Founded almost simultaneously in Malaysia and Singapore in 1908, it is the oldest and most established life insurer in these two countries. Great Eastern (Great Eastern and its sister company, OAC, taken together for Singapore) had 24 percent of the Singaporean market in 2007, and 24 percent of the Malaysian market in 2006. It was the market leader in both countries. While its ventures in neighboring countries have not yielded the same level of success (99 percent of its 2007 revenue was derived from these two countries), it has a geographic footprint across Asia, nevertheless, and appears to aspire to further expansion.

Currently, Great Eastern has branches in Brunei, Indonesia, Hanoi, Ho Chi Minh City, Shanghai, and Beijing, in additional to its home markets in Singapore and Malaysia. Since Singapore's Oversea-Chinese Banking Corporation (OCBC), owned by the same family, bought a majority stake in the insurer in 2004, Great Eastern has shown a bigger appetite for international growth. In 2006 it entered into a Chinese joint venture, and it increased its equity stake in a joint venture with an Indonesian partner. In 2007, it established a wholly owned subsidiary in Vietnam. Following OCBC's acquisition of a majority stake in 2004, the insurer terminated its distribution contract with HSBC and started to use its new parent's extensive network in the Asia-Pacific region, covering Indonesia, Thailand, Vietnam, China, Hong Kong, Taiwan, Brunei, Myanmar, Japan, South Korea, and Australia.

A combination of strong, transferable capabilities from home markets, local knowledge of Southeast Asia, and an extensive bancassurance network via its parent provides Great Eastern with some competitive advantages. However, there have been very few Asian players that have been able to translate success in home markets into other markets. While dominant in Malaysia and Singapore, Great Eastern is virtually unknown in northern Asia, and it remains to be seen whether it can leave its mark on these larger and much more competitive markets as well.

Foreign players who are well established in the region, namely AIG and Prudential (UK), often enjoy a market-leading position. AIG, for example, raked in a gross premium of US$3.6 billion from these five Southeast Asian markets for 2006, equivalent to 5.4 percent of the company's global GWP and 33 percent of its business in Asia. It is the market leader in two of the five countries, and ranks within the top five in all five markets (see Figure 6.3). For these players, Southeast Asia currently contributes more profits than the giant markets of China or India combined. The China market, for example, is significantly larger, but AIG—the top foreign player—only collected US$1.2 billion in premium, in 2007. In the same year, AIG collected premium amounting to US$2.3 billion in Thailand alone, where it has a whopping 39 percent market share. This dominance in the Southeast Asian markets has a lot to do with the multinationals' leverage of international expertise, a favorable regulatory environment towards foreigners, and their early entry with regard to market development.

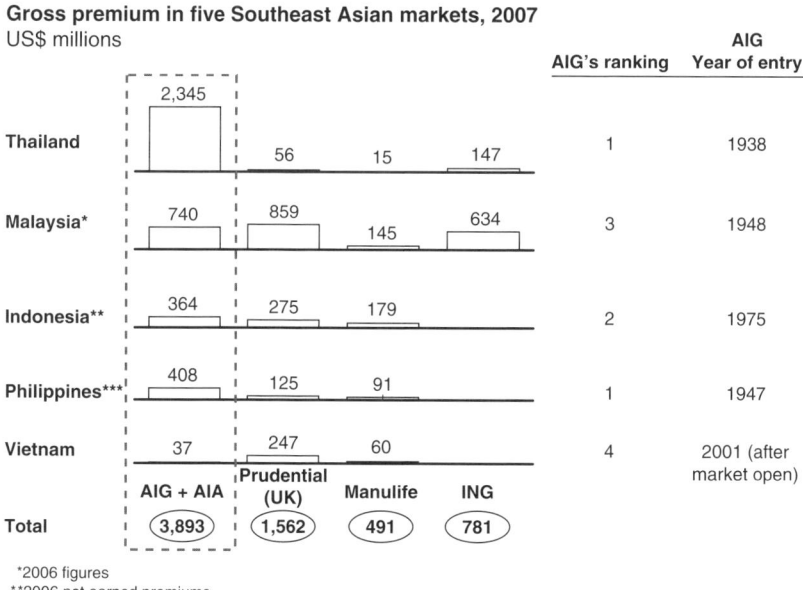

Gross premium in five Southeast Asian markets, 2007
US$ millions

	AIG + AIA	Prudential (UK)	Manulife	ING	AIG's ranking	AIG Year of entry
Thailand	2,345	56	15	147	1	1938
Malaysia*	740	859	145	634	3	1948
Indonesia**	364	275	179		2	1975
Philippines***	408	125	91		1	1947
Vietnam	37	247	60		4	2001 (after market open)
Total	**3,893**	**1,562**	**491**	**781**		

*2006 figures
**2006 net earned premiums
***Premium income

Figure 6.3 The leading players across the Southeast Asian markets
Source: Company websites; various insurance regulatory bodies

In these markets, insurance is often one of the first financial products bought by customers—a McKinsey consumer survey found life insurance consistently ranked within the top five most popular financial products held in the region. Traditional savings accounts always top the list with a penetration rate of over 90 percent, while debit cards are the other consistent product across the region. However, consumers are less knowledgeable on the risk/return profiles of different investment products. Foreign insurers have been able to take advantage of the developmental stage of these markets, and have created products that are designed to fit the needs of emerging-middle-class customers. For example, we had mentioned earlier Prudential (UK)'s combined protection and investment product, PRUVantage.

Indonesia provides a good example of the dominance of MNCs—two of the top four life insurers are multinationals, AIA and Prudential (UK). Foreign players outperformed the market by aggressively positioning themselves in the growth sector—investment-linked products. Figure 6.4 shows each company's percentage of net earned premium from investment-linked products. While

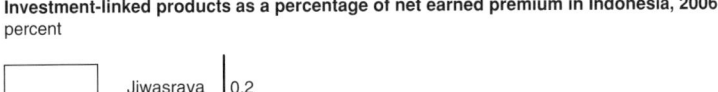

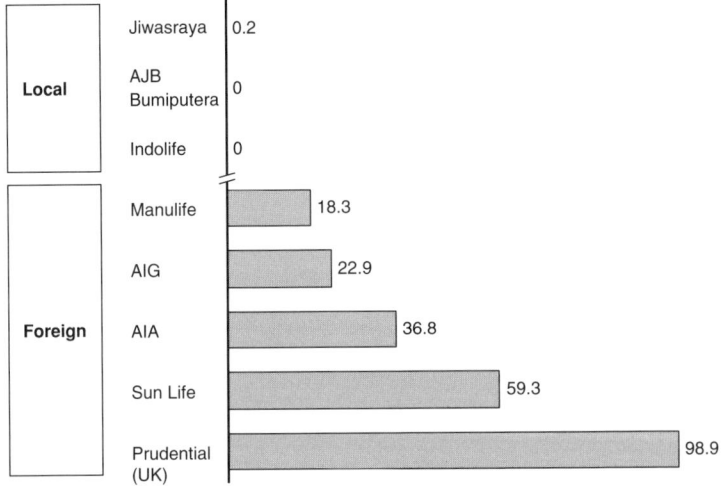

Figure 6.4 Foreign insurers sell more investment-linked products in Indonesia than their domestic peers

Source: Bureau of Insurance

foreign insurers have a significant proportion of their business in investment-linked sales, the three largest domestics have virtually none.

There are still some restrictions on foreign ownership in the Southeast Asian countries, albeit less than those in China and India. Vietnam allows for 100 percent foreign ownership of insurance companies; foreign ownership in Indonesia is only limited to 80 percent, and in Thailand and Malaysia, the limit is currently 49 percent.

Changing regulatory environments and consumer needs are moving these countries towards greater market involvement by local players. In the Philippines, for example, foreign players are allowed to own 100 percent of an insurance company, but asset restrictions favor local players (see Box 6B).

6B—Tightening regulations in the Philippines

The Philippines has been open to foreign players for over a century, and it is dominated by foreign companies who account for over 70 percent of gross premium. For those already in the game, it is a profitable and stable market. For example, AIG's Philippines American Life earned over US$400 million in premium income in 2007. France's AXA stood in second place with almost US$395 million.

However, recent regulatory changes in the market, aimed at consolidating and growing the industry, are likely to favor local players. A combination of four factors is forcing smaller insurers to sell their businesses: i) a new Department Order from 2006 that requires insurers to raise net worth fivefold in five years; ii) a large number of life insurers competing in a small market; iii) tight regulation on the investment activities of insurance companies; and iv) notoriously heavy tax burdens.

The implementation of the Department Order of 2006 clearly favored local companies, requiring existing local companies to hold a minimum net worth of US$12 million by 2011. Whereas, insurers with 40 percent foreign equity must have a net worth of US$14.5 million by the end of 2010; insurers with a 40–60 percent foreign stake must have a minimum capital of US$17 million by the same date; and insurers that are more than 60 percent foreign-owned must increase their net worth to US$24 million by the end of 2010.

As a result, weaker foreign players have been bought out by local enterprises. In 2007, a local family business, Yuchengo Group, bought out Nippon Life's Philippines operations and Allied Bank and Lucio Tan Group acquired New York Life Philippines.

Channel Upgrades to Reach More Customer Segments

As in other parts of Asia, agency distribution is still dominant in Southeast Asia, but bancassurance has been a big driver of recent growth. In Vietnam, Prudential (UK) made rapid progress by building a national network of 70 branches and customer service centers in 47 cities and towns through agreements with Vietnam Commercial Bank and Agribank. In Malaysia, first-year premium sold through banks went from 21 percent of the market in 2002 to 45 percent in 2005.

And the proliferation of bancassurance is allowing newer players to access the market through alternative channels. In both Malaysia and Thailand, local banks are becoming active in the insurance industry by partnering with foreign insurers in bancassurance deals. This includes Siam Commercial Bank in Thailand and Maybank in Malaysia, who partnered with New York Life and Fortis respectively.

The growth of bancassurance is also driven by more demanding customers who associate banks with higher trustworthiness and better advice. And what makes the trend for better distribution even more pronounced in Southeast Asia is the increasing need for customer segmentation. Urban customers are becoming more sophisticated and seeking improved service. Meanwhile, rural segments require cost-effective channels—such as bancassurance and other alternative channels—that are more capable of reaching these underserved regions. Unlike the more established markets in Asia, where the local incumbents have the legacy agency channels, in Southeast Asia, it is the multinationals that are faced with the urgent need to revamp their sales forces. But they have been quicker to react than incumbents in other Asian markets—insurers are stepping up their efforts to improve their existing channels and innovate in direct channels. In Malaysia, there has been a movement to introduce more quality into the sales force. Great Eastern launched the Life Planning Advisor program, while Allianz developed the Allianz Achievers Academy (AAA).

Meanwhile, innovative distribution strategies are also at work. Thailand has been in the vanguard of call center sales. Thai Life, Thai Cardif, Allianz, ACE, ING, and Prudential (UK) are some of the players developing telemarketing as an alternative channel. Of these companies, Prudential (UK) in particular relies heavily on call centers as a distribution channel—it accounted for 85 percent of their total sales in 2007. In contrast, in

6C—Text-message-based insurance distribution in the Philippines

It may come as a surprise to some, but when it comes to alternative distribution channels, the Philippines is a pioneer in text-message-based insurance selling. Text message insurance services come in two forms: either as customer service akin to phone-banking, or as an actual point of sale.

In the first instance, insurance companies partner with technology companies to provide a mobile platform for policyholders to check their policy due date, beneficiaries, amount due, and other information via a text message request. It also allows insurance companies to alert policyholders to when their policy is due and to broadcast announcements.

More interesting is the concept of text-message-based registration for insurance policies. In December 2006, Philam Life, the Philippine insurance subsidiary of AIG, introduced a micro-insurance product, Aksitext, which is packaged like a prepaid, mobile-phone card and can be activated via text message registration. This product, open to anyone aged between 18 and 65, costs less than a dollar and gives the buyer coverage against accidental death for 15 days.

This is just one of the initiatives promoted by the Philippines' Insurance Commission's plan to develop the country as the micro-insurance center of Asia. The commission aims to have 40 percent of Filipinos insured by 2010. As of December 2006, only 8 percent of Filipinos had insurance coverage.

Prudential (UK)'s other markets, only 4 percent of sales were derived from direct channels. Alternatively, insurers in the Philippines have exploited the wide usage of text messaging among young Filipinos in their sales and marketing drives (see Box 6C). Filipinos sent an average of 2,300 text messages per person in 2003, far more than in neighboring Southeast Asian countries and other regions, notably Europe and North America.

The Future: Reaching Scale

Looking forward, all multinational incumbents, local players, and foreign insurers seeking entry will need to focus on scale in Southeast Asia. Whereas a 5 percent market share in China or India is large enough to be attractive, it is not so for the smaller Southeast Asian markets. As the Philippines example illustrated, foreign players who did not reach adequate scale chose to exit rather than increase their investments. In this environment, the ability to leverage footprint across the region theoretically helps regional players to benefit from economies of scale. Many are now engaged in projects to upgrade and consolidate their operations in an attempt to reap more synergies; whether they will succeed only time will tell.

Meanwhile, with a single-country focus, local incumbents need to step up their competitiveness in alternative methods to make up for less scale. Players are leveraging their more extensive channel networks or local knowledge in certain products. For bank players, the natural strategy is to leverage their banking networks, while in Indonesia and Malaysia, *takaful* products could also provide a future growth engine.

For potential new players, there is an ongoing debate as to whether there is still room to enter into these markets. A lack of ability to reach scale may be an impediment. On the one hand, given the growth trajectory, there should be ample room for more competitors. Markets with strong fundamentals such as Indonesia and Vietnam should offer interesting opportunities. On the other hand, the increasing competitiveness and smaller scale of these markets renders them less attractive, especially vis-à-vis the long-term growth opportunities in China and India. Many companies eyeing the Southeast Asian markets are also deterred by the entrenched positions of the large multinationals that went before them, such as AIG, Prudential (UK), and Manulife.

In all, Southeast Asia looks set to remain a market in which multinationals will maintain a heavy presence alongside a few local heavyweights. Threatening newcomers will be few, but given the early development stage of these markets, there will be room for some new entrants. We predict that among the entrants there will be a mix of MNCs and a few, select Asian players. Competition is intensifying and domestic companies have recently turned up the heat on their large MNC rivals.

Southeast Asia may not be the largest market in Asia, but for players committed to a pan-Asian footprint, it deserves a close look. Furthermore, its openness to foreign players makes this region an interesting play. For those with the right strategy, these markets can be extremely profitable and added together, can be a meaningful part of an overall Asian portfolio.

Australia: Light at the End of the Tunnel?

	Australia
Macroeconomic	
GDP (US$ billions)	960
GDP per capita (US$)	44,091
PPP GDP per capita (US$)	37,757
Inst. assets under management (US$ bns)	0
PFA (US$ billions)	0
Foreign reserve (US$ billions)	62
Socioeconomic	
Population (millions)	21
# of households (thousands)	7,723
Median household income (US$)	49,420
# of households earning >US$10k p.a.	7,216
% of households earning >US$10k p.a.	93%
Urbanization (% of population)	89
% of population older than 65 in 2005	13%
% of population older than 65 in 2025	n/a
Life insurance	
GWP (US$ billions)	36
Life insurance penetration	4%
Life insurance density (US$ billions)	40
Investment-linked %	76%
Bancassurance %	n/a
# of life insurers	32
# of foreign life insurers	n/a
Foreign share %	27%
Year foreign entry allowed	1980s
Life insurance assets (US$ billions)	219

Note—all figures for 2007 unless otherwise stated

Despite its geographical proximity, the Australian life insurance industry bears little resemblance to the other markets discussed in this book. It is well established, having matured over the past 15 years, and remains relatively small, with US$31.2 billion of sales in 2007.[1] Australian insurers have not connected more with the rest of Asia due to a history of poor expansion outcomes and ongoing fears about regional fundamentals, including fallout from the Asian financial crisis of the late 1990s.

Although there are few growth prospects remaining in Australia, we are cautiously optimistic about the future of the industry. In particular, there are opportunities to more effectively extract value from the risk and savings needs of Australian consumers. For example, there are many unmet risk management needs that must be addressed, such as longevity and morbidity risk, that have been opaquely transferred from government to individuals over the last 20 years or so.

An Introduction to Life Insurance and Retirement Savings in Australia

A fundamental aspect of the Australian life insurance and retirement savings market is the extent to which risk and savings products have been unbundled. Although there are some products that combine both elements, they are a small minority of the total business and tend to take the form of an investment product with guarantees rather than an insurance policy with investment attributes.

The superannuation (retirement savings) industry has a legislated mandate to provide retirement savings for all working Australians and provides the vast majority of the retirement and savings infrastructure. This legislated mandate has seen the superannuation industry grow to US$1,036 billion in assets by 2007, making Australia the fourth-largest asset-management market globally. Furthermore, there have been recent discussions about increasing mandated superannuation contributions (potentially up to 15 percent, from 9 percent today), which would drive growth for at least the next 10–15 years. By contrast, the domestic life insurance market languishes in its shadows with US$224 billion in assets.[2] The Australian life insurance market is comprised of three very distinct segments:

- *Risk products*: These include term-life, temporary and permanent disability, and business continuity insurance covering both individual and group business. Annual sales are around US$1.5 billion. There is a negligible amount of whole-life products sold in Australia.
- *Annuities*: These are typically termed with residual, capital-value guarantees. There is a negligible volume of life annuities sold in Australia (around 1 percent). Annual sales are around US$6.0 billion.
- *Investment products*: These include conventional, individual, and group investment accounts and investment-linked business. Annual sales are around US$23.8 billion.

Figure 7.1 outlines the sales volumes and trends over time for each of these segments.

Compared to the rest of Asia, the growth numbers here are weak; overall premium has grown at only 2 percent annually from 2002 to 2007. The only highlight has been that risk products grew by around 12 percent—although a large part of this growth has been driven by stepped premiums that carry their own risks (see Box 7B). By comparison, annuities and investment products have shown little growth. In fact,

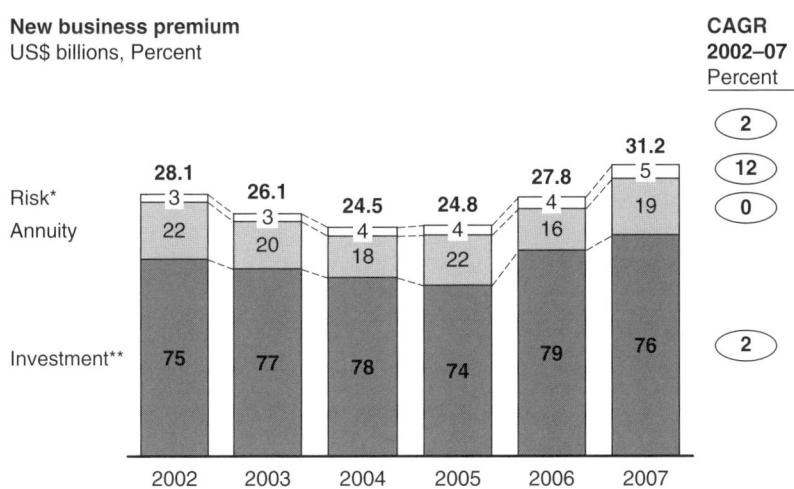

*Risk products include term life, total and permanent disability, trauma and business expense
**Investment products include conventional, individual, and group investment account and investment-linked business

Figure 7.1 Risk products growing fast from a small base
Source: Plan for Life 2007

annuities have yet to clearly demonstrate their value proposition against traditional, allocated pensions. Therefore, new sales have predominantly been in the term-annuity space with relatively few players offering guaranteed or lifetime annuities. Moreover, little product innovation has taken place in recent years.

Despite their size in terms of sales, the annuity and investment segments are relatively modest profit contributors, as a percent of sales, compared to risk products. They are distributed in similar ways to the majority of asset-management and retirement products in Australia—via wholesale or independent retail distribution channels (that is, independent or tied financial-planning forces). Our focus is primarily on risk products.

Distribution of individual risk products in Australia is primarily through aligned and nonaligned dealer groups (see Figure 7.2). These groups include, for example, Commonwealth Bank Financial Planners, AMP, and Genesys Financial Advisors (now owned by AXA). However, many of the bank-owned life insurers are enhancing their cross-selling of insurance products through the bank channel to maximize the value

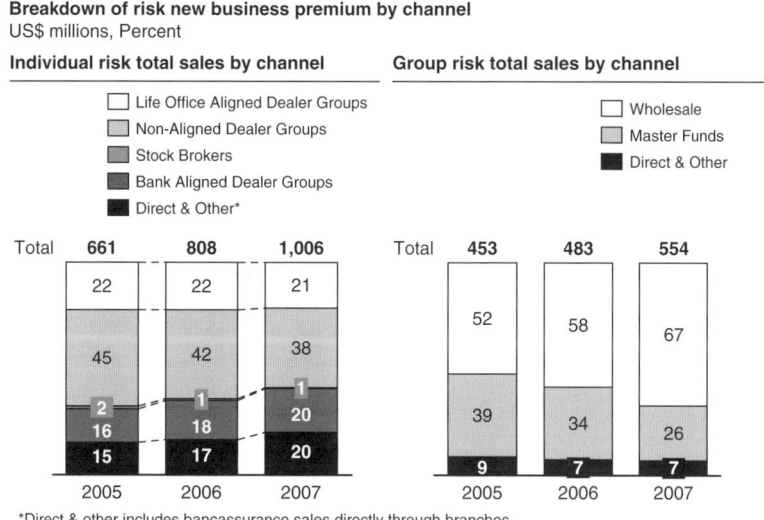

Figure 7.2 Inrisk product banks and wholesale channels are taking market share
Source: Plan for Life 2007

of their proprietary distribution channels (see "Direct & other" figures in Figure 7.2). This channel has grown relatively quickly in recent years as a result. Group risk product sales are mostly done via the "whole-sale" channel. The wholesale channel covers premiums associated with stand-alone corporate, government sector, and industry superannuation group risk schemes.

Figure 7.3 presents the 2007 market shares for each of the players in the Australian market for the different risk products in terms of in-force premium. CommInsure (a subsidiary of the Commonwealth Bank of Australia), NAB/MLC (a subsidiary of the National Australia Bank), and ING Australia have leading positions in nearly all five products. A number of other players, notably Tower and AXA, have leading positions in specific products. Compared to other parts of Asia Pacific, the competitive dynamics in Australia has been much more stable. With the exception of a small number of acquisitions and joint ventures (for example, the acquisition of Asteron by Suncorp in March 2007 and the tie-up between ANZ and ING in 2002), this landscape has remained remarkably similar over the past several years.

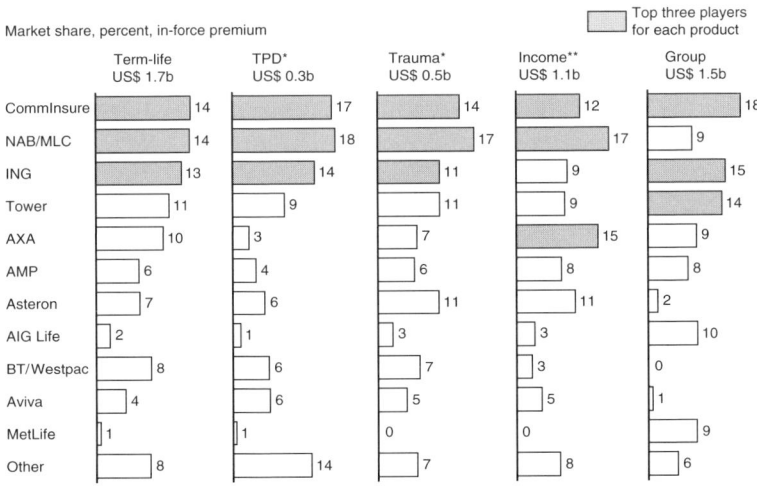

Market share, percent, in-force premium

Top three players for each product

	Term-life US$ 1.7b	TPD* US$ 0.3b	Trauma* US$ 0.5b	Income** US$ 1.1b	Group US$ 1.5b
CommInsure	14	17	14	12	18
NAB/MLC	14	18	17	17	9
ING	13	14	11	9	15
Tower	11	9	11	9	14
AXA	10	3	7	15	9
AMP	6	4	6	8	8
Asteron	7	6	11	11	2
AIG Life	2	1	3	3	10
BT/Westpac	8	6	7	3	0
Aviva	4	6	5	5	1
MetLife	1	1	0	0	9
Other	8	14	7	8	6

*Total and permanent disability primarily sold as rider, around 55 percent of trauma sold as rider
**Income insurance includes income protection and business expense insurance

Figure 7.3 The top three players dominate most risk categories

Source: Plan for Life 2007; McKinsey & Company

The Development of the Australian Life Insurance Industry

Three major trends, each of which has been the result of government intervention, have shaped today's Australian life insurance and retirement savings landscape: (i) the introduction of superannuation and the unbundling of risk and savings products; (ii) deregulation and the emergence of bancassurance models; and (iii) demutualization and changing business models.

The Introduction of Superannuation and the Unbundling of Risk and Savings Products

With the emergence of superannuation (see Box 7A) onto the Australian financial landscape, risk and savings products effectively became unbundled. Compared to the rest of Asia Pacific, where there is still significant opaqueness in product structures and, therefore, high embedded margins in life policies, Australia presents the opposite picture.

To understand this, one must appreciate a bit of history. Superannuation schemes were introduced in Australia after World War II as a way of providing for servicemen in retirement. During the 1960s, these schemes emerged as major competitors to the traditional savings and risk management products of life insurers. By the end of the 1960s, superannuation had taken over from traditional products as the way Australians thought about savings and retirement.

To address this new form of competition, Australian insurers responded through innovation in product design. In particular, during the 1970s, they started to unbundle traditional life insurance products into separate risk and savings products. There were a number of reasons for this. Unbundling produced products made them much easier for retail consumers to understand. The new products could then compete directly with those from the superannuation industry. Furthermore, it allowed investors the opportunity to better tailor their product portfolio and have greater control over decisions, such as where their funds were invested.

Also, government intervention has completely changed the face of the insurance industry through concessionary tax treatments and the introduction of compulsory superannuation contributions in 1992. Compulsory superannuation quickly enlarged the size of the industry to such an extent that it is now a fundamental element in the Australian financial system. Many Asian governments have studied the superannuation scheme, and a few countries have actually put mandatory systems in place, such as the Central Provident Fund (CPF) in Singapore and the Mandatory Provident Fund (MPF) in Hong Kong. However, the extent to which superannuation took off in Australia and "crowded out" retail financial products is truly unique. None of the markets we describe in this book has anything close to the 360-kilo gorilla that superannuation has become in Australia.

7A—Superannuation in Australia

The impact of superannuation schemes in Australia is an interesting study in the effect of government intervention on a nation's financial system.

Retirement savings in Australia are funded through three channels: government-funded pensions, government-mandated savings by the individual and their employer (superannuation), and discretionary personal savings. In the 1980s, upon realizing that pensions were not going to sustain a steadily growing and aging population, the Australian government heavily promoted superannuation as the primary means of providing for retirement.

The primacy of the superannuation system was established through compulsory contributions and tax concessions. Since 1992—the year the superannuation guarantee scheme was first introduced—employers have been required to pay a minimum percentage of an employee's salary into a superannuation fund. This fund could only be accessed at death, retirement, or upon reaching a "preservation age" (currently 55) to ensure that it is used for income in retirement. Minimum contributions were initially mandated at 3 percent of salary, though they have since been raised to 9 percent, with discussions for further revisions to 15 percent currently taking place. The ages at which contributions can be made have also steadily increased, to encourage employees to work—and save—for longer.

The incentive for contributing to these funds lies in the concessionary tax status afforded to them. Both contributions and investment earnings are taxed at 15 percent (compared to a maximum marginal tax rate of

(continued)

7A (*continued*)

45 percent). Superannuation funds are thus a major point of contact between consumers and the financial services industry. As a result, many financial products are offered through this vehicle to benefit from the tax advantages—from classes of investment-linked funds to pure risk products.

Looking forward, the current Labor government appears to favor superannuation as the primary means for funding retirement, by continuing to refine the "savings infrastructure" of the scheme built over the past 15 years. As a result, it seems unlikely that there will be a major shift towards funding retirement savings through retail risk management products—such as life annuities, longevity options, and longevity insurance—without major pressure applied by the industry.

Deregulation and the Emergence of Bancassurance Models

Since the deregulation of the Australian financial sector, the major banks' desire to develop bancassurance models has played an important role in shaping the life insurance industry. A large percentage (63%) of the Australian banking sector is shared between its top four banks—Commonwealth Bank of Australia (CBA), Westpac, National Australia Bank (NAB), and Australia and New Zealand Banking Group (ANZ). However, prior to the 1980s these colossi of the local market were not able to offer insurance products as a result of strict domestic regulation. For a period of 35 years, the Australian banking sector was one of the most heavily regulated in the world, as the government operated through the banks to implement monetary policy. While the tight regulation did not directly affect life insurers, it did prevent banks and other financial institutions from entering the industry.

Deregulation of the financial sector began in 1983 following a government-sponsored, broad-based review of the financial sector (known as the Campbell inquiry). The banks quickly took the opportunity to enter the insurance market, starting with NAB in 1985 and swiftly followed by the others in the subsequent years. Deregulation also led to other new entrants; the number of registered life insurers grew from 45 in 1980 to 58 in 1990. Since then, a consolidation has occurred, with the number dropping to 37 by 2008.

Once the banks had established a foothold in the insurance market, they quickly gained market share on the back of strong brand recognition and extensive retail distribution networks. By 1990, bank-owned life companies held 9 percent of the Australian insurance market. By 2000, this had grown to 44 percent, though much of this growth has been through acquisition. The competition presented by the bancassurance model placed new capital demands on existing life insurers as they sought to develop products to compete in new areas. This eventually led to the shift away from the "mutual" structure of life insurers during the 1990s.

Overall, the introduction of the bancassurance model has linked captive distribution channels and encouraged significant cross-selling between traditional banking and insurance products, reshaping the face of the industry.

Demutualization and Changing Business Models

Traditionally, a handful of mutual life companies accounted for the majority of assets in the industry. In 1980, of the 47 registered life insurers, only four were mutually owned but they accounted for 69 percent of industry assets. However, since then all four mutuals have demutualised, starting with Capita (now MLC Life) in October 1990, National Mutual in September 1995, Colonial in December 1996, and ending with AMP in January 1998.

The goal of demutualization was to allow insurers to address the forces of banking deregulation and the more competitive environment faced by the insurers during the 1990s. Banking deregulation introduced a number of large, well-capitalized players into the market that were offering a full suite of financial services. The unbundling of insurance products brought insurers into direct competition with other financial service providers. The traditional information asymmetry considerations that inspired mutual structures seemed to no longer apply as data processing improved and the size of insurers grew. Intergenerational equity issues also began to arise as reserves were established from one generation's premiums yet paid out to another. Therefore, all four mutuals decided to raise capital through issuing ordinary shares in exchange for membership rights, and listed on the Australian stock exchange.

Demutualization quickly led to a period of turbulence for the newly listed public insurers as they faced the harsh realities of the market. They quickly broadened their product offerings and sought to become integrated financial services providers. However, many did not effectively manage the major organizational transformation required. With competition heating up, rationalization took place in the market. National Mutual was purchased by AXA in 1998 and MLC was acquired by NAB in 2000. In the same year, Colonial was acquired by CBA. Only AMP managed to maintain its independence.

The combined effects of the introduction of superannuation, deregulation of the banking sector, and demutualization of life insurers have created the Australian life insurance market of today. We will now shift from a historic perspective and discuss the changing customer needs and the opportunities in the market.

Increased Risk, Responsibility, and a Collective Failure to Respond

Despite the maturity of the market, Australians today are still very much underinsured against the list of ever-growing risks (for example, health and adequate retirement savings). Coupled with this has been a shift in the responsibility for managing these risks from the public and private sector to the individual. The result is effectively a "double whammy" for Australians. A range of factors, including poor consumer understanding, limited product innovation by life insurers, and a laissez-faire government approach have contributed to these risks not being effectively managed today.

Increased risk and responsibility

Over the past 20 years, four significant changes have increased the level of risk for Australians. First, Australians are more financially stretched than ever before, increasing their exposure to potential hardship following premature death, sickness, or accident. For example, in May 2008, mortgage repayments accounted for 29.1 percent of an average first-homebuyer's income—the highest percentage on record. Second, Australian mortality rates are decreasing and this trend looks likely to continue with advances in healthcare. This is particularly the case at older ages, which increases significantly the spending on healthcare in the twilight years. Third, retirees face longer retirement periods than at any other time in history, increasing the chances that they outlive their retirement savings. As seen in much of the developed world, longer life spans are being compounded by increasingly earlier retirements. Since the 1970s, the Organization for Economic Co-operation and Development (OECD) rate of labor participation by males aged 60–64 has dropped from 60–90 percent to 20–50 percent. Fourth, as in many mature markets, due to the aging "baby boom" generation, fewer workers are supporting a greater number of individuals in retirement. This reduces significantly the ability for the government to provide an effective safety net.

At the same time, the responsibility for managing these risks—particularly in retirement—has shifted from the government and the private sector to the individual. Superannuation-defined benefit schemes, which provide consumers with a guaranteed benefit at retirement, are being phased out. In their place are the defined-contribution schemes that provide only an accumulation benefit, leaving consumers with exposure to investment and longevity risks that may leave them with insufficient savings in retirement. Also, in retirement the preference has been for allocated rather than lifetime annuities. This is a result of their relative simplicity, strong investment returns in recent years, and the fact that consumers are generally unwilling to cede any residual savings they may have on death to insurance companies (as is generally required in lifetime annuities). Alongside this, the government pension provides only 25 percent of the male total average weekly earnings, all of which means that consumers are more exposed to longevity, morbidity, and market risk in retirement.

The result of these increased risks and the shifts in responsibility will have a real impact on many Australians. Approximately one-third of the population have no coverage, one-third are only covered through their superannuation fund, and only the remaining third have voluntary coverage. More surprisingly, two-thirds of Australians are fully aware that their level of insurance coverage is either inadequate or nonexistent. They simply choose to do little about it. This fact of underinsurance is well known and every year or so a new report is released revealing its extent. One of the drivers is the generally optimistic attitude of Australians. For example, in 2007, AXA released its Protection Report which asked respondents whether they think something bad (for example, serious illness) may happen to them. Out of 11 developed

Things we think may happen to us—survey results*—rank of likelihood

Serious illness	Serious car accident	Unemployment	Work accidents	Serious financial problems
1. France	1. France	1. Germany	1. France	1. France
2. Japan	2. Germany	2. France	2. Switzerland	2. Germany
3. Switzerland	3. Switzerland	3. Hong Kong	3. Germany	3. Belgium
4. Germany	4. Belgium	4. Japan	4. Japan	4. Italy
5. Belgium	5. Japan	5. Switzerland	5. Spain	5. Japan
6. Italy	6. Spain	6. Italy	6. Belgium	6. Switzerland
7. USA	7. Italy	7. UK	7. Italy	7. USA
8. UK	8. USA	8. Spain	8. USA	8. Hong Kong
9. Spain	9. UK	9. USA	9. UK	9. UK
10. Australia	10. Hong Kong	10. Belgium	10. Hong Kong	10. Spain
11. Hong Kong	11. Australia	11. Australia	11. Australia	11. Australia

*Survey covered respondents in France, Japan, Switzerland, Germany, Belgium, Italy, USA, UK, Spain, Australia, and Hong Kong

Figure 7.4 Australians are very optimistic
Source: AXA 2007 Protection Report

countries Australians came out as the most optimistic in four out of five areas, and as the second-most optimistic in the fifth (see Figure 7.4)![3]

Similarly, Australians are not effectively managing their longevity risk exposure through superannuation and the annuity market: 3.4 million Australians, or one-third of the workforce, are expected to suffer from inadequate income in retirement at current rates of saving.[4] On average those falling short will do so by US$3,125 a year (in today's terms). Even more worrying, of workers aged 45–55, 38 percent are expected to have insufficient retirement savings, suggesting that these shortcomings may start to materialize in the not-too-distant future.

A Collective Failure to Respond

There are a number of reasons why the Australian life insurance and annuity markets have not penetrated the retail customer base more effectively. These include inadequate product offerings, perceived attractiveness of alternatives, insufficient consumer education, and a laissez-faire government approach.

Inadequate Product Offerings

The current range of available products contains a number of gaps and does not satisfy the demands of both the retail and wholesale markets. In the annuity market there are very few products structured attractively to capture and manage the outflows from the superannuation industry. Currently, the market is split approximately evenly between term and residual capital value products. For example, very few lifetime annuity products are available.

There are also few integrated savings and risk mitigation products covering a number of risks—for example, longevity risk, market risk, and healthcare expense risk. As has been outlined, the past three decades have seen a disaggregation of the savings and risk management components of insurance products. This has made the products more accessible to consumers, but this simplistic disaggregation seems to have missed the opportunity to satisfy certain needs. For example, we believe that there is a demand for risk-management products—especially in retirement—that incorporate savings components to satisfy motives such as bequeathal among retirees.

Many retail risk-mitigation products are also not offered at attractive prices. This is primarily due to wholesale methods for managing risk. Longevity-linked products are a case in point, with some insurers declining to offer them at a competitive price as they see the risk as "toxic." These products will become increasingly attractive to both insurers and consumers when wholesale methods are available to transfer the risk, reducing the capital strain on insurers.

Perceived Attractiveness of Alternatives

A range of attractive alternatives to life insurance products has been available in the investment markets. In particular, pure savings funds have, with the exception of the financial year just ended, enjoyed excellent returns over the past 14 years as a result of strong equity markets. These vehicles are also relatively simple and provide greater consumer control over where their funds are invested than risk-only insurance products. As a result, many consumers have chosen to manage their financial health through conscientious saving rather than investing in risk-management products, consciously or unconsciously ignoring the shortcomings of this approach.

Insufficient Consumer Education

In keeping with the laconic "she'll be right mate" national persona, more than half the Australian population believe they "do not need insurance" and approximately half regard it as a "waste of money."[5] Closely linked to this is the extreme optimism of Australians about remaining healthy (see Figure 7.4). Despite this optimism, Australians have also neglected the risk that they will outlive their retirement savings, as seen in the US$6 billion of annuity sales in 2007, compared to superannuation outflows of US$56 billion.

Australians are also confused about how and when it is appropriate to purchase life insurance within a superannuation product wrapper. Currently, there are tax incentives in place which allow for life insurance premiums (under certain conditions and with some limits) to be paid from pretax dollars. However, superannuation trustees and administrators cannot legally offer advice. This, coupled with a tendency to avoid seeking financial advice and the problems of dual coverage, has led to investor confusion.

Efforts to improve consumer awareness and education have largely failed to hit the mark. Forty percent of Australians use no information to assist in their financial decision making and 56 percent of respondents said they felt they needed further education or information about financial matters. The top two sources of financial advice for Australians are family and friends, and accountants.[6] This has made Australians, relative to their mature market, less advanced in their understanding of financial matters. In a recent OECD survey, 67 percent of Australian respondents indicated that they understood the concept of compound interest, yet when they were asked to solve a problem using the concept only 28 percent had a good level of understanding.

Laissez-faire Government Approach

Finally, the government took an arm's-length approach in supporting the development of a private infrastructure for managing consumers' risk exposures. While the UK has made the purchase of life annuity products by retirees compulsory, Australia does not provide tax incentives for the products. In the 2006–07 federal budget, tax incentives for taking superannuation benefits as an annuity stream were removed. This was done by reducing all superannuation outflow taxes, which effectively equates the treatment of annuity and lump-sum benefits. Furthermore, default life insurance coverage levels within superannuation funds are extremely low. The standard level of coverage is two to three times income while recommended standards are up to 10 times. Surprisingly in Australia— a country with one of the world's most advanced retirement savings systems—post-retirement, risk-management policy and infrastructure are lagging behind significantly.

Opportunities Ahead

The nature of the opportunities for domestic incumbents and foreign entrants is markedly different in Australia to the rest of the Asia-Pacific region. Domestic incumbents must influence government and educate consumers to create and capture significant value from the management of savings, as well as retirement, morbidity, and longevity risks. In addition, there are a range of distribution, product, and cost innovations available to improve the attractiveness of the industry for participants. For foreign entrants, a pure-play, life insurance entry strategy seems unlikely to be financially attractive. A combination of a life and wealth play—focused on combining savings and risk-management skills—to meet the needs of the Australian "wealth builder" could be one attractive option. However, the Australian wealth-management market is extremely sophisticated and well-populated with few assets likely to be for sale. For example, with a few exceptions, most wealth-management franchises are core to the major Australian banks and unlikely to come up for sale.

Domestic Incumbents

We believe players already in the market should focus on two central issues: (i) reshaping the industry through influencing regulators and educating consumers; and (ii) innovating in distribution, product, and cost management.

Reshaping the Industry Through Influencing Regulators and Educating Consumers

Government intervention is the most direct way of rejuvenating the current life insurance and retirement savings industry. Given the impact of government regulation on the current life insurance and retirement savings industry any significant change to the industry will require government intervention to amend the relative incentives and benefits of different products. This intervention can be explicit, through providing incentives and tax concessions for investing in risk-transfer products; or implicit, through encouraging consumer education programs and rewarding innovation with supportive regulation. Achieving this requires the education of government bodies on the enormity of the latent risks already in the system, the advantages of private risk-management schemes, and the need to develop legislative support and tax concessions for these products. To make this happen, we believe that the life insurance industry in Australia needs to become more effective at creating industry-level lobbying. By comparison, the superannuation players have worked relatively effectively at an industry level.

In addition, consumer education is required on the level of risk exposures and the types of products available. For example, retirees need to be convinced that life annuities are not simply a "gamble" on their own life expectancy where they may see life savings forfeited to insurance companies. Rather, they must be shown that by using life annuities to manage their retirement savings, based on expected rather than maximum lifetimes, their yearly pension income can be substantially increased, improving their quality of life.

Innovating in Distribution, Product, and Cost Management

Distribution Innovation—The emergence of real, online approval has been the major innovation in distribution in the Australian life insurance industry. Historically, Australians have bought the majority of their insurance as part of their mandated, retirement-savings plan, or for a small percentage of relatively wealthy Australians, via financial advisors. Recently, high-quality, online coverage options are beginning to emerge, increasing the ease of access for ordinary Australians. This online approval functionality is also being rolled out to third-party intermediaries (such as financial planners) in the hope that it will increase sales of the product given the quick turnaround time for approval. ING Direct recently launched an online approved product allowing the customer to buy up to US$450,000 of coverage in 10 minutes. Allianz have launched a similar product allowing coverage of up to US$1 million. This market is still young with great potential for growth. In particular, offshoring or outsourcing the underwriting and claims processing for these types of policies has the potential to yield significant cost savings.

Beyond online approval, innovation is also needed in the delivery of effective advice, without directly linking advice and sales. The current model places excessive reliance on the role of intermediaries and commission-based sales. Establishing independent advisory services would provide a solution to this, as would the delivery of advice through the workplace. Such services could be funded through service fees, industry-sponsored funds set up for this purpose, or in the case of the latter, through salary packages. This would help to dispel consumer confusion and misinformation around available insurance products. It would also encourage product innovation among insurers as consumers become able to make more informed financial decisions.

Product Innovation—Many industry participants see product innovation as the key to creating and capturing new growth opportunities in the Australian life insurance industry. For example, Simon Swanson, the managing director of Australia's largest life insurer, CommInsure, sees three main opportunities in the life insurance market (see Box 7B).

But product innovation should not stop at the creation of new risk products. For annuities, there is also significant scope for innovation in the structured payout market, which has large potential given the gap between the US$56 billion of superannuation outflows and the US$6 billion of annuity sales in 2007.[7] As we have seen above, Australians are not prepared for the risks they will be exposed to in retirement. In particular, they are not prepared for longevity and morbidity risks such as home care, nursing, and prescription medicines.

While there has been resistance against annuities due to their high capital cost and the forfeiting of residual value in the event of early mortality, there may be other options. Such alternatives may include reverse mortgages (popular due to the high concentration of Australian wealth in primary residences), longevity insurance, and retail longevity options.

There is also scope for innovation in the market for hybrid products, which integrate savings and risk-transfer components. Potential products that have seen success in other markets, such as in the US, include variable annuities with guaranteed minimum balances and wrap accounts that allow investors to move funds between investment and risk-management products, allowing a greater level of control. Due to the central role of agents in the sales of insurance products, hybrid products—that include both savings and risk-management functions and retain the need for ongoing financial advice (to maintain agent commissions)—should prove popular.

Finally, the wholesale risk-management market is also in need of further innovation. However, this is likely going to be driven by innovation in countries with more developed retail insurance and annuity markets. Interesting developments are already happening. For example, the UK bulk purchase annuity businesses (such as Paternoster) provide a viable way for transferring longevity risk exposures to specialist risk managers. Longevity and mortality bonds, forwards, and options are also areas of active research and development on the international stage, which may in the future provide new methods for managing wholesale risk exposures.

7B—Major issues and opportunities in the Australian life insurance industry

Simon Swanson, the managing director of Australia's largest life insurer, CommInsure, sees four major issues currently affecting the Australian life insurance market:

- **Stepped premiums**—These rise in line with an insured person's age. Of the 10 percent nominal premium growth in the industry, approximately half is attributed to stepped premiums. In periods of low inflation, these premiums will increase the likelihood of lapses.
- **Improved health technology**—Advances in health technology have meant that minor ailments are more identifiable and thus more likely to trigger trauma policy claims (for example, the detection of minor heart attacks). Better treatment of sicknesses is also lengthening the tail of health insurance claims.
- **Income protection insurance**—Inaccurate pricing and reserving in what is a growing class of policies—especially those based on mental trauma—will present significant opportunities for insurers who can get it right.
- **Changing distribution models**—The emergence of online-approved life policies and the potential for better leveraging of bank channels and existing advisory services is causing the industry to rethink its methods of distribution.

Alongside these issues, three key opportunities will become increasingly important for players in the Australian insurance market:

- **Capital-guaranteed products**—The use of life insurers' balance sheets to provide capital-guaranteed products that balance investment-market exposure without accepting excessive risks.
- **Longevity-risk products**—The promotion of retail, income-stream products that manage longevity risk, and the funding of them through innovations in wholesale, insurance-linked securities.
- **Morbidity and old-age products**—Catering to the demand for health and morbidity insurance from an aging population who face longer lives and extended reliance on the medical system.

Cost Innovation—In the Australian market, cost efficiency and effectiveness remain an area of critical importance. For many players, the major constraint to creating more efficient and flexible cost bases is a legacy of archaic and overlapping systems.

Distribution cost savings involve pursuing the development of online approval and revisiting the use of existing channels. Alongside the convenience and data-mining advantages of real online approval, it also presents significant cost savings through reduced overheads and the capacity to outsource back-office operations. In the UK, Prudential has utilized its joint venture with ICICI to supplement its advanced online distribution channel with outsourced back-office operations in India.

The emergence of online underwriting programs has the potential to provide a window into the once opaque art of insurance underwriting. Greater transparency in underwriting standards may lead to more standardized underwriting practices. This will then provide scope for competitive advantage in those players able to maintain distinctive underwriting practices.

Wholesale risk-management developments will provide the ability to more efficiently manage risk exposures through the transfer and hedging of mortality, morbidity, and longevity risks. If effectively structured, these have the potential to reduce the level of required capital. These reductions could then either be translated either into more attractive profit margins or be passed on to policyholders through reduced premiums.

Foreign Entrants

Given the modest size of the market, the large number of existing, sophisticated foreign players (for example, AXA, ING, and MetLife), and the consolidation that has already taken place in the industry, a pure-play life insurance entry into the Australian market is not likely to be attractive at this stage.

A combined life and wealth strategy that brings together risk- and wealth-management skills is a plausible proposition. However, creating an end-to-end presence in the wealth-management space is unlikely to be achievable due to the critical importance of platforms in accessing distribution. Platforms bring together multiple product manufacturers to wrap products for retail investors and financial intermediaries. There are currently six scale platforms in Australia and the opportunity to create or acquire a platform is low. The likely implication is that new entrants would need to focus on a play in either the distribution or manufacturing ends of the value chain. A number of players (for example, AXA) have been focusing on rolling up independent financial advisors. The industry is fragmented; it comprises around 16,000 planners but the five largest groups only account for around 30 percent of planners. However, rolling up planner groups is a complex and risky process. Holding onto individual planners during the roll-up process is risky, and driving economies of scale and preferential distribution through the network are equally challenging.

In summary, the nature and size of the Australian life insurance market is unlikely to justify a pure-play organic entry. The wealth-management market is extremely sophisticated, well-populated, and has a critical choke point around platforms with few significant assets likely to be for sale. However, the consumer and regulatory drivers for the industry are attractive, highlighting the opportunity of creating an innovative new model that can connect directly with planners and disrupt the current platform-based status quo.

The Next Decade: What it Takes to Win in Asia ⑧

When viewed from 10,000 meters, the pace of change in life insurance in Asia can appear almost glacial. Most of the large players have been dominant for a very long time, and the market-share rankings in most countries barely shift from year to year. However, there are many forces that are about to change the industry fundamentally. In fact, life insurance in Asia is reaching an inflection point, where the industry, in the next 5–10 years, will likely witness some very dramatic changes that will make it look very different from the one in 2008.

Key Success Factors

Asia is entering a new phase of development following a period of extraordinary growth. While the overall growth drivers in Asia remain very strong for the next 5–10 years, competition is increasing significantly, margins are beginning to erode, and local and foreign players alike will have to build superior skills in distribution, product innovation, operations, and investment management to be able to sustain current levels of value creation. We see five key success factors to win in Asia over the next decade:

- Building a sustainable agent force
- Creating value in bancassurance and alternative channels
- Upgrading the business model to combat intensifying competition
- Capturing the pan-Asian opportunity
- Sustaining margin pressure

Building a Sustainable Agent Force

Over the last decade, most of the enormous value in life insurance in Asia has been created through the agent channel. Bancassurance only started to take off in the early 2000s and, in most markets, has much slimmer margins. However, the model of the past—building vast but low-qualified agent forces with a "landgrab mentality"—is unlikely to lead to success in the next decade. In fact, we believe that some of the massive agency sales forces that have provided the core growth engine of life insurance distribution in Asia are likely to reach their maximum size and will slowly begin to erode. This is already happening in Japan and South Korea, as the housewives sales forces gradually scale down in number and influence. While the pace of this development will differ from country to country, the sizes of the agency forces will not grow indefinitely at the current growth rates. At some point, even in a country as large as China, we anticipate the growth of the agency forces will "max out" and move into the next phase, which will be characterized by consolidation, upgrade of capabilities, and management of quality. In many countries, reform of these sales forces is already underway and the process will accelerate as, for example, most of the unproductive and part-time sales agents leave the business. Over the next several years, the nature of the competition will change from size to quality, and this will pose serious challenges to many insurers who will not be able to manage the transition.

It is well known that the massive sales forces of large Asian insurers suffer from problems such as low productivity, high agent turnover (up to 80 percent annually in countries like China and India), and, in extreme cases, mis-selling. On the other hand, there is no doubt that these sales forces are also tremendous assets for those who have been able to build them, since their distribution power is unmatched. In the past, these sales forces have carried insurance companies through upturns and downturns, and the loyalty and strong bonds between the agents and these incumbents are legendary. Nevertheless, the traditional sales model, relying on a large number of low-quality sales agents, is starting to show cracks due to three interlinked factors.

First, there is an emerging segment of mass affluent consumers in Asia that are demanding a better level of service, which includes better under-standing of products and customer needs, as well as more professional advice. These mass affluent customers are typically not well-served by the agency forces of the incumbents, since the education levels and sophistication of the agents are quite different from those of their customers.

Second, the growing complexity of products, particularly in the investment-linked area, is creating difficulties for the traditional sales forces. For example, the push tactics of the mass sales force can create mis-selling practices as agents understate the risks of the investments. While there are signs that insurers are finding ways to control mis-selling, their agents are not the most natural investment advice-providers.

Third, a lot of these agency forces are aging. While the relationships the sales forces have with their customers remain strong, aging sales forces are quite difficult to motivate and manage. For example, many agents are almost semi-retired, living off their existing customer portfolios. For these agents, and their managers, who have spent the last two decades pursuing the same mass market with a push-driven business model, one can imagine how difficult it is to inject more professional skills. Compared to some of the latecomers—in particular foreign players—with their younger and more professional sales forces, it is easy to see why, in many markets, the incumbents are losing momentum.

Indeed, across Asia most of the incumbents are losing market share. Life Insurance Corporation (LIC) of India's gross written premium (GWP) market share in India plummeted from nearly 100 percent in 2000 to 82 percent in 2006. This trend is even more pronounced in the larger cities where competition is fiercer. For example, in China, China Life's GWP market share in Shanghai dropped from 29 percent to 22 percent between 2000 and 2007 (see Figure 8.1). Furthermore, measuring by gross premium masks the effect somewhat. These incumbents may still have a large market share overall, but in terms of new business, they are losing momentum rapidly. For example, by GWP, the market share of South Korea's Big 3 dropped from 76 to 57 percent between 2002 and 2007, but by first-year premiums (FYP), their share dropped even further—from 77 percent to 44 percent.[1]

Restructuring of the Sales Force

We see rejuvenating sales forces as the number one priority for most established insurance companies in Asia, in particular the local incumbents.

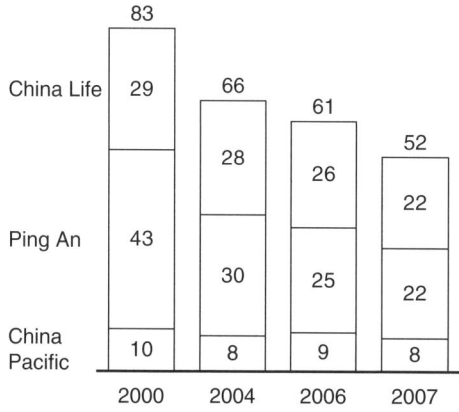

Figure 8.1 The incumbents are losing market share in large Chinese cities
Source: CIRC

However, it is also probably the most difficult endeavor for them, since this involves facing up to a lot of legacy issues, and potentially challenging some highly engrained cultural values at these companies. The pace of these changes reflects the resolve of the top management.

There are some encouraging signs. A few of the large incumbents have started to hire new, better-educated agents and provide them with improved training while gradually eliminating unproductive sales people. Some of the bigger players in Japan and South Korea have started to cut down the size of their housewife agency sales forces.

One of the biggest challenges in building a more sustainable agent channel is to standardize the way it operates. Sometimes these sales forces, especially in countries with large geographical spreads, look so different from region to region that they give the impression that they belong to different companies! This is due to the fact that during the ramp-up period, the entrepreneurial branch managers each dictated the direction and culture of the sales force in their region. However, without standardization and a sharing of best practices across the organization, it is very difficult to improve beyond the initial buildup. These sales forces are also extremely vulnerable to the turnover of their founding managers. Tough decisions will have to be made as standardization takes away some of the local flavor. In extreme cases, it may even involve removing some of the founding managers and agency leaders in order to direct change.

A restructuring program typically is designed around four key elements: (i) best practice agency management, (ii) improving the quality of recruiting; (iii) systematic improvements in agent productivity; and (iv) an overhaul of the incentive system. This kind of program has been proven many times in mature markets, but nowhere at the scale of some of the Asian sales forces. Implementing such a program in rapid growth markets, for hundreds of thousands of agents, is a unique challenge.

Part of the restructuring involves more rigorous management of the agents. Since agents are paid entirely on commission, it has long been the tradition to "leave them alone." However, in order to upgrade the agents' skills and improve their productivity, it is important to start managing these agents in a more systematic and professional manner. For example, even the simple task of getting the agents to show up more frequently for reviews and morning meetings runs into fierce resistance. This often brings into conflict the "old guard" versus the "reformers." Given the large resistance of the agents to change, their behavior, and the management's fear of alienating the top producers, a lot of change programs never get off the ground.

Improvements in the sales force model also entails finding better recruitment methods and abandoning the practice of simply recruiting large numbers (which used to mean employing anyone who walked through the door). Finding better qualified agents also involves fundamental reassessment of compensation (especially base compensation), as well as training in the initial ramp-up period.

Furthermore, as the quality of agents improves and productivity rises, there is a counter process of reducing the number of unproductive, part-time agents, many of whom rarely sell anything and have other jobs. In many cases, up to a third of the overall agents could be part-timers, which creates a significant challenge since in absolute terms, their contribution is still quite substantial.

Finally, the incentive system is often purely top line and growth focused—with little incentive for pulling the improvement levers laid out above—and does not reflect the profitability margins of individual products. Given the high share of variable pay and the enormous responsiveness of agent forces to changes in the commission structure, this is a highly sensitive topic. The risk of getting it wrong, thereby endangering growth and losing top producers, has led many companies to shy away from touching the commission system. Yet, without this any substantial progress in the transformation program is unlikely. In fact, we see a lot of commission systems that continue to reward agents who sell large amounts of barely profitable products.

Revamping the sales forces will take years to implement. Radical change is probably unrealistic—what is required is continuous improvement that becomes part of company culture. There are no silver bullets for upgrading a large sales force and the process is extremely painful as difficult decisions need to be taken on legacy issues. It may even involve a temporary dip in revenues. The likely winners are those players who adopt a long-term perspective to ensure the sales forces that have served them so well in the past continue to be a strength of their strategy for the future.

Developing the Next Generation of Agents

The restructuring of legacy sales forces is likely to be a long-term exercise and the traditional sales forces will largely remain focused on the mass market. Therefore, to capture the fast-growing, affluent-customer segment, a new approach is required. New sales forces that can target this segment with a more professional advisory approach and with a larger arsenal of financial products are likely to emerge and grow very fast. This requires recruiting agents with higher quality backgrounds and providing better infrastructure support.

An example of how this can be achieved comes from Germany where MLP has built a sales force that targets specific niches of affluent customers. For example, MLP recruits agents from specific professions, like doctors, who will then cater mainly to doctors and others in the medical field. By having a sales force specialized in the same profession, MLP has managed to capture a large market share within these highly valuable segments since its sales force has the unique credibility and capabilities to understand and connect with their target segments. This model has been very successful, and provides a good example of how to develop a more professional and highly targeted sales force.

We anticipate that a few insurers in Asia will be successful in developing much higher quality, advisory sales forces that will be able to penetrate deeply into the more affluent customer base. While the scale of such sales forces will be small compared to the traditional, mass market agency forces, the quality, and thus value, of such sales forces will be significantly higher. As such, one can anticipate much greater diversity of life insurers as they each develop their niches in various customer and product segments.

The affluent segment opens up an opportunity for newcomers to the market who cannot, and probably should not, replicate the model of the large local incumbents if they want to be among the winners in Asian life insurance markets at the end of the next decade. But even some of the large local companies should take a close look at this opportunity and consider setting up a separate channel to capture the affluent customers in a more systematic way. As the incumbents restructure their legacy sales forces, creating new, high-quality, agency forces alongside could be an effective shortcut to addressing the fast-growing affluent segment. This is not easy though, since the buildup of such targeted sales forces is slow and their financial impact is insignificant in the beginning, thereby making it very difficult to get the proper attention during the development stage. Channel conflicts will surface with existing sales forces that also have some agents serving affluent customers. Long term though, this initiative may well be one of the most important investments an incumbent insurer can make today.

Creating Value in Bancassurance and Alternative Channels

Bancassurance has grown from almost zero in the year 2000 to a range of 30–50 percent share in most Asian markets. However, insurance companies have found it increasingly hard to generate value in this channel that is proportionate to the top line. Banks have been able to negotiate very competitive commissions across Asia, and products are mostly very simple, single-premium, investment products that offer little differentiation in the market beyond price. Life insurers and banks often have arm's length relationships where the life company is barely more than a capacity provider. Banks have mostly focused on converting their customers' deposits into simple savings products that have a more attractive interest rate—and hence, the product has generated strong customer demand. In this scenario it is very difficult for the life company to add a lot of value to what the banks are doing; since the banks are adding all the value, the low share of the profits to the insurer is probably justified. But, as we described in the second chapter, we believe that in most Asian markets, banks will soon have collected the low-hanging fruit and growth in these types of products will max out—if they don't change their model. This should create an interesting opportunity for life insurers to create a second generation bancassurance model—with much closer relationships between insurer and bank, selling more complex, higher margin products that allow life companies to generate a lot more value in this channel.

Banks across Asia are discovering the retail and wealth-management opportunity. While in markets such as China, corporate lending has been the key profit driver for banks, the retail and wealth-management businesses are catching up fast. We predict that in China the retail and wealth-management business will grow from 29 percent of financial services profits, in 2007, to 59 percent by 2015. To capture this opportunity, banks are building client advisory and sales skills in their often vast branch networks. The pace of this development varies by market—and it will, of course, take time in markets such as China and India with their huge institutions and relatively weak starting positions. But eventually this development will enable banks to advise their customers much more holistically on financial products—including more sophisticated insurance products. From a life insurance perspective, the key to unlock this potential will be to build much more integrated business models with the banks. Experience in Europe has shown that bancassurance is really successful when products are bundled based on customer preferences, life insurance is integrated into the banks' incentive systems, processes are tightly integrated, and the insurer delivers value-added support in the form of tailored marketing materials, training, and customer relationship management.

We are seeing some initial signs of banks and life insurance companies moving in this direction. For example, Prudential (UK) and Standard Chartered have built a much more integrated business model in Hong Kong.

We believe we will see a lot more of this in the next decade—including more joint ventures between banks and foreign insurers who have built the relevant skills in other markets and can leverage them in Asia. This will change the nature of the bancassurance opportunity and create a win-win situation—for those players who manage to find the right banking partners and build and apply the required skills in the local market context.

Compared to bancassurance all the alternative channels are still miniscule in size. But they are growing fast—and if the mature markets in Europe and North America are any indication these channels will continue to capture market share. While for most players this is still a niche opportunity, we believe that this is an area worth exploring. We already see retailers selling life insurance products in countries like Japan and South Korea—and increasingly India. Brokers and independent agents are also on the rise. They usually have a higher credibility with customers given their independence from single producers and can capitalize on the increasing affluence and sophistication of customers across Asia who are demanding higher quality advice. As described in the chapter on South Korea, the Mirae Asset Group approach of using investment centers to sell financial products is one example of this. In China, CNInsure is an independent agent company listed on the NASDAQ. And even the direct channel—that is, selling life insurance through call centers and the Internet—is building some scale. In China, Ping An and MetLife have been pioneers in this field with encouraging results. Although still at an early stage, the prospect of building a nationwide call center network with tens of thousands of sales representatives is very real and can be extremely compelling if done properly.

Experience from Western markets shows that the prize in these channels goes to players that build a specific business and support system and tailor products to these channels' needs. Some of the multinationals in Asia should be able to leverage their experience but we also see some of the leading local companies, such as Ping An in China, conquering this space.

Upgrading the Business Model to Combat Intensifying Competition

Growth has been the key value driver in life insurance in Asia in the past decade and is likely to remain so—but the basis of competition is changing. In the past, insurers achieved high growth using a "landgrab model"—being one of the first into many regions and segments. However, this model is beginning to run out of steam. There is hardly any uncovered territory in Asia and competition from local and foreign companies is increasingly fierce. Maintaining rapid value creation going forward, therefore, requires players to be able to outcompete the competition through superior business models. These require higher quality skills along the value chain, not just in distribution but also in product innovation, IT and operations, and investment and risk management. And it will also require them to significantly strengthen their management bench.

Winning Through Product Innovation

We have already talked about the shift across Asia from traditional life products to investment-linked vehicles, along with the need to tailor products much more to the needs of individual channels and customer segments. All this requires an upgrade of product development capabilities at life insurers across Asia.

First, life insurers need to link product development much more closely to channels and customer segments, systematically understanding their specific needs better and incorporating their insights into the product development process. For example, Prudential (UK) has been very successful in South Korea with products that are linked to specific investment themes that hit the nerve of the market—such as a Vietnam fund incorporated into a investment-linked policy in 2007 (although given the volatility in these emerging markets these products obviously have a highly speculative element and can pose large risks mis-selling).

Second, many life insurers need to upgrade their skills in understanding the value creation of individual products and product components. The more complex products are becoming more important and it will be vital to fully understand their economic impact. For example, in South Korea many life companies are selling riders with such additional protection elements as health insurance—but without the data and experience to price these riders adequately. And more often than not, it is unclear if the additional benefit is worth the cost from the customer perspective.

Many life insurers today have no clear understanding of the exact value contributions of the different products they are selling and the channels they are using to sell them. Revisiting the product portfolio through a "value lens," pruning less profitable products, and adjusting product features to enhance value contributions, (for example, through riders or longer durations), are often sources for major improvements in the value of new business. Analyzing the channels with regard to their value contributions, adjusting commissions to align with product profitability, and defining clear targets for value improvements by channel are also major value drivers. We often hear the argument that this is a clear trade-off between profitability and growth—but frequently companies are claiming this without having a full understanding of the value drivers they could leverage in the product and channel composition. This is not about closing channels or product families, but about the transparency of economics and the alignment of value creation and incentives. Better understanding leads to a multitude of little changes that add up to significant value creation over time.

Third, life insurers need to think through the organizational implications of product innovation. Many global insurers have begun to drive the actuaries out of their ivory tower and marry the product development with a strong product-management function. This integrates marketing, channel management, and actuarial skills. It also allows for more rapid reaction to changes in market trends and for constant re-evaluation of the product portfolio in terms of sales effectiveness and value creation. However, many Asian life insurers have yet to build up the talent pool and the cultural readiness to adopt these types of organizational changes.

Revolutionizing IT and Operations

The life insurance industry around the world is not well known for world class IT and operations skills. This is often a neglected function that suffers from a dependency on legacy systems and that is not recognized as a source for value creation. Asia is no exception—but we believe this might change. First, in the vast markets of China and India, IT and operations play a crucial role in allowing continued fast growth by running massive distribution networks across enormous countries, delivering customer and agent service to the most remote places, and tapping into rural opportunities. The large local players in these markets have begun to realize that they need very strong IT and operations functions to gain full control over their networks and to guarantee customer satisfaction (and lower churn rates) across geographies. Most of the time, they realize quickly that gradual improvement is not sufficient to address these challenges. Some players in these markets will jump directly to state-of-the-art IT and operations models to cope with the enormous challenges resulting from their size and growth. Ping An in China has already embarked on this journey of revolutionizing IT and operations by centralizing the back-office functions in a nationwide operating center and by centrally building and managing customer service and call centers. Second, as more insurance companies operate across Asia they are looking at ways to create synergies across the region. This is a huge challenge given the different regulations, languages, and maturity of the various markets. But the case is compelling for the few players who have sufficient scale to build some key functions centrally that will allow for more control and quality. AIG is the natural leader in this field, given their footprint across the region. They have already begun to operate some back-office functions across Asia and are continuing down this path. Others will follow.

Third, IT and operations are, of course, key enablers to control cost. While most life insurers have not focused on this topic in the past, given the priority to grow the top line during the landgrab stage, this is likely to change with increasing margin pressure. In particular, in markets where growth rates are coming down, fierce competition requires tight cost management to maintain margins. In a similar fashion to Western life companies only a few years ago, many Asian life insurers measure operational efficiency by cost ratios only. This is a highly misleading indicator, and best practice globally has moved to more industrial measures like unit cost. Given that centralization, or even regionalization, of operations, streamlining of processes, and effective operations management take time to achieve, the leading life insurers of tomorrow have to start to address these issues today.

Professionalizing Investment and Risk Management

Investment management is a critical pillar of the insurance business, and one that is particularly important for large incumbents who have significant assets under management. The stakes are high. If they get this right it can serve as a structural advantage; on the other hand, the risk of not getting this right can be fatal—Asian life insurers are under tremendous pressure due to the high cost of their liabilities and, thus, any mis-steps in investments can ruin the entire franchise.

Local incumbents have traditionally viewed investment management as an afterthought. For decades, in many companies, the investment function has been organized as a department under finance. This is because for a long time, in most Asian markets, investment options have been rather limited by regulation and an immature capital market. Hence, the investing of insurance assets has been rather straightforward, mostly involving fixed deposits, government bonds, and in some cases, large real-estate holdings. During long periods when interest rates were high, this investment strategy served the incumbents well. However, the situation has changed considerably in recent years.

First, many insurers have issued long-term, high-guaranteed products in periods when interest rates reached heady levels (mostly during the late 1990s). However, during that period, there were not as many long-term assets, such as 20-year government bonds, to invest in—most insurers held their assets for a significantly shorter duration, assets such as short-term government bonds and bank deposits. Therefore, as interest rates declined insurers were landed with a big problem—their investments yielded less than the cost of their liabilities. This negative spread is a very serious issue—as is well known, it has brought many Japanese life insurers to the brink of collapse. But this is not just a Japanese phenomenon. For example, the average liability of Taiwanese insurers was in the region of 6.5 percent in the late 1990s while returns on their own investments were around 4.5 percent resulting in a 2 percent gap. South Korean and Chinese insurers have similar legacy issues.

Second, regulators have loosened restrictions on insurers, allowing them to invest in a greater variety of domestic and foreign asset classes. Much of this deregulation is due to the realization of regulators that insurers needed to find ways to alleviate their negative spread problem and to generate attractive returns for policyholders in low-interest-rate periods. For example, in Taiwan the restrictions on investments in foreign markets have been raised from 5 percent of total investments in the 1990s to 45 percent in 2007. China now allows companies to invest in domestic equities and domestic alternative asset classes, particularly infrastructure products. And in 2006, the Qualified Domestic Institutional Investor (QDII) scheme was launched allowing Chinese insurers to invest part of their assets overseas (see Box 8A).

8A—China's QDII

The Qualified Domestic Institutional Investor (QDII) scheme was established to facilitate offshore investment by Chinese citizens and corporations through qualified financial institutions. The aim was to reduce the pressure on China's foreign reserves buildup and provide a means to diversify the investment portfolios of both households and corporate entities beyond Chinese assets. QDII is part of the process of liberalizing China's capital accounts.

The scheme was announced in April 2006, with the first product authorized in June. QDII had an approved investment quota of around US$40 billion at the end of 2007. This quota is allocated to banks, asset managers, and insurance companies.

The banks and asset managers comprise the QDII's retail sector and give these institutions a means of investing offshore on behalf of their clients. Even more experimental are the rules for insurance companies, which allow insurers to invest up to 15 percent of their assets offshore in the near future. This amounts to US$50 billion for the whole industry, based on the total of assets under management by Chinese insurers. The two largest players, China Life and Ping An, are both gearing up their investment offices to manage these new asset classes.

Despite all its fanfare, the QDII program got off to a slow start. The banks' quota utilization rate was low at around 30 percent, reflecting lack of interest in QDII products. This is not surprising, since the initial QDII products were primarily linked to conservative, US, fixed-income products. Due to the appreciation of the RMB versus the US$, dollar-denominated, fixed-income investments are not attractive.

QDII equity products offered by mutual funds also face a timing issue because the funds were deployed offshore around the time of the subprime crisis and a subsequent meltdown in the global financial market. The four mutual funds that "went abroad" in 2007 all sustained heavy losses in net value, falling by as much as 60–70 percent by the end of 2008. For Chinese investors investing for the first time abroad this proved to be a very unpleasant introduction to global investment. The insurers did not fare much better—many of their QDII assets, invested in overseas equities, have suffered losses, which are magnified by the steadily appreciating RMB.

Despite this bumpy start, the long-term prospects for QDII remain bright. Once the overhang of local currency appreciation has run its course and local stock markets cool down, institutions will start to understand the virtues of a more diversified investment strategy.

The pressure of the negative spread and the opportunity to diversify investments into new asset classes are creating an urgent need for Asian insurers to professionalize their investment management function. The urgency is not only in investment management, but also in risk management, since investing in these new asset classes brings a lot more volatility to the insurer.

There are three ways for Asian life insurers to make their investment management function more professional in the short term.

First and foremost, they need to upgrade their investment management talent. This sounds obvious until one realizes the extent of the culture changes that need to happen in an incumbent insurer. Investment management is a very talent-intensive business, which is not something that insurers are good at managing (retail insurance is much more about size and scale). In particular, domestic insurers have a very tough time attracting the best investment talent since they are competing with local and foreign fund management houses as well as hedge funds. Part of the problem is the pay scale—many Asian life insurers have adopted a very rigid compensation structure and hierarchy over the years, and their approach to investment management falls within that construct. Compared with the much more flexible and professional environment that fund houses provide, it is not surprising that insurers are far behind in this war for talent. One insurance executive mentioned to us that he had to go through layers and layers of paperwork just to hire one portfolio manager, and there were so many constraints and so much bureaucracy that the new hire just gave up and went to a foreign fund-management company. The asset-management pay structure has also increased substantially in recent years, and presents a shock for most local insurers. In the past, investing was a low-cost activity, where the life insurers would find investment professionals to place their assets into long-term government bonds or they simply negotiated bank deposits. However, as the insurers venture out towards hiring professionals to manage more international asset classes, they are finding that salary expectations are often significantly more than the company's culture and bureaucracy can absorb.

Second, with the right talent in place, life insurers in Asia will need to significantly upgrade investment, asset liability management (ALM), and risk-management processes by learning from best practices. Despite all the peculiarities of the Asian markets (for example, lack of deep fixed-income markets, a legacy of high-guaranteed policies, structural mismatch of assets and liabilities), there is no excuse for not adopting some of the best practice tools that are used by many of the leading global players. Life insurers in many mature markets have learned the hard way that excessive risk-taking can endanger the very existence of the company. Asian life insurers are well advised to learn from those examples and build the analytical tools required to assess the economic value that is created with more risky investment strategies. The accounting-based, absolute-return number that most insurers focus on—even if required to service liabilities from high-guaranteed, interest rate products in the in-force book—is not a good measure to determine value in the investment function.

Using modern analytical tools to derive investment decisions from a rigorous strategic asset allocation is key to improving investment decisions. Many consulting firms and insurance IT vendors can provide the tools and processes that can be adapted to local Asian market situations. While localization of these tools is a significant effort, it is a necessary process that can involve quite a bit of learning for the local insurer. Controlling risks and increasing risk-adjusted returns can be facilitated in a number of ways including ALM, strategic asset allocation (the science of allocating the asset base to different asset classes), stock picking, and running a professional and systematic investment process. Having a proper risk-management process is also critical. The combination of chasing returns to minimize losses on the negative spread and investing in unfamiliar foreign asset classes can be lethal in terms of risk management. For example, a few of the Asian life insurers invested in subprime assets, which led to significant write-offs and subsequent capital calls. Another significant risk is currency exposure—with substantial volatility in currency markets, investing in foreign asset classes can lead to a myriad of new exposures that are very complex to manage. The foreign currency exposures of many assets cannot be easily hedged, and there are also market circumstances where the hedging costs are prohibitively expensive and will take away any incremental gain from the investments. For these incumbent insurers, hiring a proper chief risk officer could be one of their most worthwhile investments at the start of their journey toward upgrading skills and practices in investment and risk management.

The risk of not getting this right is huge. From Japan to South Korea to Taiwan, the contribution of investment management to total returns is higher than it has ever been, and, subsequently, risks have also increased significantly. For example, in October 2008, Yamato Life in Japan filed for bankruptcy after significant losses from its securities holdings. Life insurers have a disproportionate value at stake due to the large sizes of their portfolios, and it is imperative that they upgrade this area as quickly as possible.

Some insurers, once they have successfully professionalized their investment management function, may consider taking the next step— separating the asset-management unit into its own profit center and expanding into third-party asset management. Many European and US insurers have made asset management an important, independent part of their business. Global insurers such as Allianz, AXA, and Prudential (UK) have sizeable asset-management businesses with assets under management (AUM) in the hundreds of billions of dollars. A significant part of this business comes from third-party institutions and retail investors. Some of the players in Asia have started on this trend. In China, Ping An and China Life are seeking to replicate the Western development and have started to build their own asset-management businesses. In January 2007, China Life announced a partnership with Franklin Templeton to form a joint venture in Hong Kong for its overseas asset-management business. Ping An announced a joint venture with Singapore's UOB to create a new domestic funds business in China, and paid US$154 million for a 9 percent stake in Value Partners, one of Hong Kong's leading asset managers in November 2007.

Building a brand in the third-party, asset-management business will take time and a track record. On the retail side insurers need to develop distribution channels with banks and other distributors (for example, securities brokers) in order to reach customers. In most Asian countries, banks dominate mutual fund distribution; a strong distribution team that can work closely with banks will be one of the critical factors for success. It typically takes over five years to achieve the required scale when building a third-party, asset-management business (meaning that as a percentage of total assets, third-party assets need to reach 20 percent or more), and insurers embarking on this road should ready themselves to learn quite different skills in order to compete. Acquisitions may be a way to accelerate this process; indeed most leading global insurers with sizeable asset-management businesses have at some point relied on acquisitions to grow. For example,

Allianz bought PIMCO in the US, while AXA bought Sanford Bernstein's asset-management businesses and Rosenberg, a well-regarded, quantitative asset manager.

Strengthening the Management Bench

The insurance industry has underinvested in management talent for decades. This contrasts sharply with the banking business. Until very recently, no insurance company would have shown up on a list of preferred employers at top business schools. Furthermore, compensation was generally less attractive than in other parts of the financial services industry. This is driven partially by the retail nature of the business with a strong focus on mass operations—but it has clearly become an issue for the industry at large, and Asia is no exception. The most aggressive players have already begun to change—globally and in Asia—and have identified talent as a key success factor for further growth and value creation.

In many Asian markets the situation is aggravated by the fact that the insurance industry is still very young and, therefore, lacking a whole generation of managers with more than 5–10 years of experience, notably in India and China. But even here the winners are already pulling away from the pack. Ping An of China now has 74 expats within their top 100 executives—mostly, but not all, with a Chinese background. And ICICI–Prudential is attracting top talent in India, capitalizing on the strong brand and image of the group and a sense of national pride.

The key to developing and attracting top talent to life insurance companies is taking a holistic approach. Compensation, although important, is certainly not the only element, and in the eyes of young managers also not the most crucial. For example, graduates from top business schools regularly cite attractive career opportunities and corporate culture as more important than compensation. According to a Hill & Knowlton study, which surveyed 527 MBA students at 12 top-ranked international business schools, 95 percent of the students ranked career opportunities as "extremely" or "very important" factors in selecting an employer, while 86 percent of them ranked corporate culture as equally important.[2] Life insurers should look at best practices from other industries to upgrade their human resources and talent management functions. Companies such as GE demonstrate that hiring the best, giving them great responsibility early on, and actively managing their professional development through systematic training, career paths, and mentoring is key to building a strong management bench. This is particularly important in Asia where management talent is scarce, and a culture of poaching people from competitors often starts a downward spiral of overpayment and frequent job hopping. Building a strong management bench will be a key success factor in life insurance in Asia for the next decade.

We believe that this challenge—the need to upgrade and professionalize all key functions of the business system—gives the multinationals a substantial competitive advantage. In general, MNCs have put a higher emphasis on quality than many of the purely growth-focused local players. This has sometimes limited their growth ambitions in the last decade, but increasingly, should become a strength going forward. Furthermore, they have the option to adapt best practices they have learned from their mature home markets, as well as their operations in Asia, to the Asian marketplace (as we have already described in chapter two). Over the next several years, we may even see some of these multinational insurers deriving more value from their Asian operations than from their home markets. From nascent markets, such as India and China, to the maturing markets of South Korea and Taiwan, to the "post-mature" Japan market, we can expect to see some MNCs significantly raising their game to gain market share from the local incumbents.

Capturing the Pan-Asian Opportunity

Almost all multinationals are already playing a multicountry game in Asia—but most of them are still operating in just a handful of these countries, leaving significant opportunities on the table to broaden their footprint. Meanwhile, most of the Asian incumbents are still confined to their home markets, with no, or just a few, businesses outside their country of origin. We believe this will begin to change: we will see some of the more adventurous Asian players branch out of their home country to capture opportunities in new markets. While some of them will see neighboring Asian markets as the next stepping stone, some of the players will aim even further and enter the Western markets. Given the difficulties of going global, it is unlikely that all of these moves will be successful. However, it is also important to note that many of these Asian insurers have significantly upgraded their management capabilities in the past decade, and riding on the strength of their successful domestic business, there will surely be a few winners who will be able to force their way into the global elite. In fact, a few Asian players have already risen to the top of the global elite by value, including China Life, Nippon Life, Meiji Yasuda, Ping An, and Millea.[3] We see three main ingredients in a successful recipe to capture the pan-Asian opportunity.

Market Prioritization

As described in earlier chapters, Asian markets have very different characteristics and, therefore, very different risk-return profiles from an investment perspective. From "high-risk, high-return markets" such as China and India (markets with enormous long-term growth potential but high regulatory constraints and tough competition), to Japan with its enormous size but little growth, to some of the Southeast Asian markets which offer free entry to foreign insurers but are relatively small in size, the landscape could not be more diverse. Hence, an entry into these markets has very different capital requirements, break-even scenarios, and skills needed to become successful. For MNCs and Asian life insurers who want to expand in the region, it is very important to understand these trade-offs and requirements before making an investment. For example, we have too often seen Western companies entering China with huge growth expectations, only to be disappointed by the required time horizon and the slow pace of development in the short term. Similarly, we have seen several MNCs entering India through joint ventures, only to witness themselves becoming a very passive partner with little value added to the local venture. Also, previous attempts by many Asian players to expand in the region (mostly from Japan and South Korea), have been met with disappointment. Therefore, fully understanding the realities on the ground, identifying the right entry options and expansion plans on a market-by-market basis, and utilizing the experience and skills learned from other markets in the local context are vital to building a successful pan-Asian footprint.

Organic Growth or Acquisitions?

We are often asked whether an organic expansion or an acquisition is the best entry model in Asia—and obviously there is no single answer. First, it depends on the market. In general, acquisitions are the preferred option in the more mature markets where organic expansion is very difficult for latecomers and will take a long time. In the high-growth markets on the other hand, such as China and India, and also Vietnam, organic growth is a more likely vehicle for success.

Second, it depends on the availability of acquisition targets—which are generally scarce in Asia. Against the backdrop of high industry growth, consolidation in most markets might still be many years away. And valuations continue to be very high—despite the recent volatility in equity markets. On the other hand, life insurers in many Asian markets are still suffering from high-interest-rate guarantees on their in-force books and are, subsequently, taking on a lot of risk on the investment side (Taiwanese insurers are a good example). This dramatically increases their exposure to market volatility and might open up opportunities. The acquisition of ING's Taiwan business by Fubon is a prime example of such opportunistic acquisitions.

Third, timing is an important factor for consideration. Given the lack of availability of attractive targets, we often find strategies successful where life insurers start building a business organically and use this as a bridgehead to prepare for future acquisitions. This has the advantage of building a network within the industry—rather than just relying on investment bankers—by establishing relationships with local regulators and building a local management bench that will be required in case of a later acquisition anyway.

Finally, players should be very clear about their acquisition objectives: Is this "to get a toe in the water" or is it a transformational deal? In many markets in Asia, there are some small local, and also foreign, companies that might be up for grabs for the right price. The logic for such a deal is not so much the attractiveness of the target itself, but the timing of entry for players who have decided to enter the market. Buying into an existing company can often accelerate the start of operations in a specific life market, and the value is mostly derived from obtaining a license and accelerating the business plan rather than from the existing franchise. At the other end of the spectrum is the possibility of making a transformational move. Local Asian companies who want to branch out of their local markets should consider a substantial acquisition. Given that their home management teams may lack the experience of operating in foreign markets, a major acquisition of a player with a good management team could be a transformational move to internationalize the company. Often, taking some minority stakes to get to know the target better is a good way to start this journey. We have not seen any examples yet for this kind of bold move in the Asian insurance industry, but the aspirations of many of the local Asian players suggest it is likely that over the next several years we will see some of these transformational deals.

Regardless of whether organic or inorganic measures are employed to build a pan-Asian footprint, winning players will be those who systematically build on their strengths while expanding. Whether this is a particular skill in channel management, (for example, agent management, experience in bancassurance), or know-how in direct-response models, or product know-how—such as The Hartford with its variable annuities that led to a market-leading position in Japan—building on existing strengths is a good recipe for success.

Cultural Adaptation

One of the key challenges for a successful expansion is managing cultural differences. This is as true for local Asian companies expanding across the continent as for multinationals. In particular, Asian companies from markets such as China, South Korea, and Japan find it very hard to operate successfully outside their own territory. Why is this? First, there is a language problem. Many top executives, not to speak of the more junior levels, are not comfortable in English, which makes an international expansion much more difficult. Second, the business culture in these markets is substantially different from international practices in many aspects. The communication style, the organization model, and the decision-making processes are highly idiosyncratic—they are grounded in the cultural and historical context of these countries, but very hard to apply in other markets. Third, many companies in these markets have no history of making foreigners successful in their own organizations—which is a major obstacle when setting up an international operation. But this does not mean that it is impossible to change. In all three of these markets there have been initial moves from the leading incumbent players to set up businesses outside their home markets. For example, Dai-ichi in Japan has decided to demutualize and to deploy more capital in other Asian markets; in South Korea, Samsung Life has started to build businesses in China and other markets; in Taiwan, Shin Kong has begun hiring non-Taiwanese for its top executive team and has started to expand into China and Vietnam; and Ping An of China has acquired stakes in foreign companies while building the most international management team in the region, with three-quarters of the top 100 having a foreign passport—many of them have an ethnic Chinese background, but not all.

Compared to the Asian incumbents, multinational life insurers have much more experience in building international operations. Nevertheless, many of them have struggled to adapt to the Asian environment. This has much to do with the cultural differences described above. Many MNCs also struggle with building a local management team. It is a common perception within MNCs that they can trust Western managers more—in particular, those from the same country of origin—which, true or not, is often an obstacle to putting the best management talent on the ground to do the job. Furthermore, many MNCs find it hard to adjust to the highly entrepreneurial environment in high-growth markets such as India or China. In India for example, almost all private life companies set up since deregulation in 2000 are foreign–local joint ventures. But in most of them the Indian partner took over full control and currently runs the operation. The foreign partners were often unable to put the required management talent on the ground to manage the enormous entrepreneurial task of building huge agent forces, numbering hundreds of thousands, in only a few years. Some blame the 26 percent cap on foreign shareholdings for making it not worthwhile to the MNC partner to do all the work but only receive a quarter of the rewards. However, it is unlikely that this is the full story; there are successful examples such as BAJAJ–Allianz, where the German insurer is clearly in the driver's seat and has created one of the largest life insurance joint ventures in India.

One way for MNCs to improve the leadership and management of their local Asian operations is to set up a strong Asian headquarters. AIG and

Prudential (UK) have led the way here, with strong Asia CEOs running the Asia business from their respective Hong Kong headquarters. But many other multinationals have not created this management layer, and still have their various Asian country operations reporting directly to a global head office. This often slows down decision making, makes it difficult to build market insights and understanding at European or US headquarters level, and often leads to frustration on both sides. These MNCs should ask themselves if they are really the best owner of these Asian businesses in this kind of set up—and what is the group adding to the individual country operations? Strategic decisions on the expansion of the footprint across Asia, capital allocation across markets, product guidelines and margin requirements, centralization and regionalization of operations, and talent management are topics where a regional headquarters can add a lot of value—as long as this management layer has real market insights, still encourages local entrepreneurship, and stays close to decision-making in these fast-moving markets. The Asia CEOs of AIG and Prudential (UK) are both members of their global executive board and others will surely have to follow this pattern if they want to become successful pan-Asian players.

Sustaining Margin Pressure

We believe it is unlikely that the current high levels of profitability in Asia's life insurance business, relative to the more developed Western markets, will be sustainable in the long run. Competition is already eating away at profit margins and will continue to do so. This has been most visible in bancassurance, where the banks have squeezed the margins of the life insurers. On the other hand, in the agent channel and in more traditional life insurance, many of the features of life insurance products continue to be opaque to customers, so the compression of margins will most likely be a much slower process. While the margins of Asian life insurers will gradually decrease in the long term, in the context of global life insurance, this region will still be significantly superior in terms of profitability in the years to come.

What we do not anticipate in the next several years is major consolidation in the industry. Asia is still very much a growth market, and for many of the players, throwing in the towel and selling to competitors is not an option. In fact, the slowdown in their home markets has prompted many international players to double down on their Asian efforts. In the longer term— and it may be quite a long term—consolidation in the industry may happen, but no one should be waiting for consolidation to play their cards.

In this market context, life insurers across Asia—in particular, many of the local players—need to shift from a growth to a value paradigm. Many life companies are still mainly focused on growing the top line. This is only natural, since the current market valuations of these companies assume that 70–80 percent of their value will be from future growth expectations (see Figure 8.2). But even in markets such as China and India it is becoming increasingly clear that high growth alone is not sustainable in the long term, and is no guarantee for success. What investors are looking for are sustainable business models and long-term, value creation opportunities. To take a value perspective, life companies will need to adopt some of the initiatives described above, which include maximizing the product and channel economics, introducing a cost perspective into operations management, and rationalizing investment decisions from a risk perspective.

Analyst's sum-of-parts estimation of insurers' life business by geography
Sample of multinational insurers*

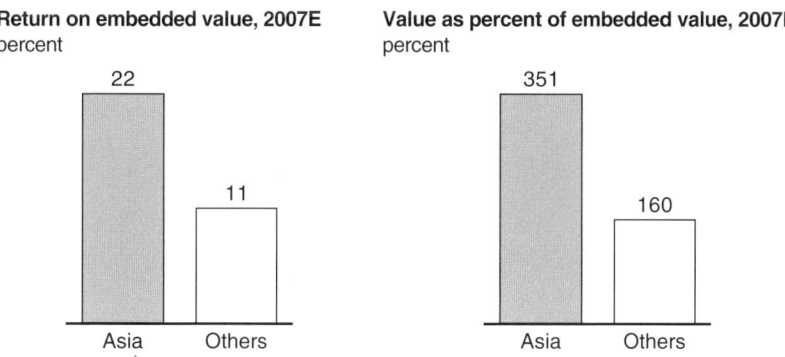

Return on embedded value, 2007E
percent

22 Asia
11 Others

Value as percent of embedded value, 2007E
percent

351 Asia
160 Others

*AEGON, Allianz, AXA, Prudential (UK)

Figure 8.2 Asian businesses are more profitable and highly valued
Source: Deutsche Bank analyst report

Challenges and Opportunities for Life Insurers in Asia

Above we have looked at the five key success factors for winning in Asia. The following section will describe the specific challenges and opportunities for life insurers in Asia. The strategy for every company will of course be different and each one's success will depend on its ability to leverage its natural strengths and adapt its competitive positioning to capture value creation opportunities. The nature of the response will very much depend on the starting point of the many players in the market. At the risk of over-generalizing, the starting point of life insurers in Asia can be roughly divided into four groups:

- *Large local incumbents*—Characterized by major market positions, first-mover advantage, close regulatory relationships and seen as national champions, these organizations usually have a large agency force with numbers in the tens or hundreds of thousands.
- *Smaller foreign and local players*—These are usually companies which are much smaller and nimbler than the large local incumbents, burdened with far fewer historical legacies, and have strengths in particular localities or product areas.
- *Well-established foreign multinational companies*—These are companies with long experience in Asia, usually the first overseas movers in local markets, well-positioned across several Asian markets, and operate a well-staffed Asia headquarters.
- *Emerging foreign multinational companies*—These are small latecomers to individual markets and typically have a limited footprint, focusing only on a few markets.

The following details the top strategic priorities for each of these types of players.

Large Local Incumbents

Most Asian markets are dominated by a handful of large local incumbents. These companies are very well established and often had a near, or actual, monopoly in the past. Their corporate culture and practices were nurtured in a time when they faced little competition. Among the many advantages they retain are: strong relations with a range of partners and official bodies, strong brand awareness, and large sales forces. Companies that fall into this category are China Life in China, Samsung Life and Kyobo in South Korea, Cathay Life and Shin Kong in Taiwan, LIC in India, and Nippon Life and Dai-ichi in Japan.

These local incumbents are increasingly being squeezed by more nimble foreign players and local competitors. As deregulation accelerates and competition intensifies, this pressure on the incumbents will continue to build up and a proactive response is needed. In general, we believe that these incumbent players have two broad priorities: transforming the core, and creating new growth horizons.

Transforming the Core

Many of Asia's local incumbent life insurers have enjoyed a quasi-monopoly, or at least a dominant market position, in the past. This has led to very large sales forces, but also to more bureaucratic and hierarchical organizations, slower decision-making, and often lower productivity. As a consequence, many of these incumbents have continually lost market share to smaller attackers and foreign entrants when their home markets were opened up. Many of them are now in need of a massive transformation program to protect their market position but—as outlined above—they need to perform a fundamental and extensive upgrade of their sales forces and create a more sustainable model. Furthermore, they need to systematically address weaknesses in other parts of the business system—for example, in IT, operations, and investment management. And they need to strengthen the management bench—renewing the top team and hiring and developing top talent at all levels of the organization.

Given the scale of these companies, this is an enormous task—but it can be done. We have found that a strong leader, a clear vision, a detailed road map, and a strong implementation setup are the ingredients required to succeed. This kind of transformation program usually takes three to five years and requires the whole organization and key stakeholders to be aligned behind the ultimate goals. There has yet to be an example of a completed transformation of an incumbent life insurer in Asia, but there are some encouraging signs. For example, Samsung Life has made remarkable progress in increasing the productivity of their housewife sales force. There are also success cases in other financial sectors, for example, the transformation of ICICI Bank into a market leader in India. We believe some of Asia's incumbent life insurers will follow this path and a few will regain their strength and market-dominating position. Just as many incumbents though, will not be so successful—it may be difficult to imagine now—but in 10 years time, it is possible that some of these incumbents may become marginal players in their own markets. This in turn will open up new opportunities for smaller attackers and foreign players.

Creating New Growth Horizons

Beyond improving the core, which inevitably takes years to complete (and is very much an ongoing effort), incumbent insurers in Asia need to rebuild momentum and develop new growth options. They can look at new channels or business models, other businesses in financial services, and other markets to expand into. The challenges involved in making this work are enormous and cannot be undertaken where there is risk of undermining the core business or removing the focus away from the required improvements stated above.

The Asian life insurance incumbents are still relying largely on their massive sales forces—which are simultaneously a strength and a weakness. Of course, the enormous selling power of these agent forces is a huge advantage that incumbents need to build on. At the same time, other channels, notably bancassurance, have grown much faster than the agent channel in general. The often lower qualifications of incumbents' agents, compared to some attackers in the market, tends to hinder them when they try to sell the faster growing products such as investment-linked or health insurance. Across the region, local incumbents have a much lower share in bancassurance and alternative channels than in the agent channel. This might be surprising at first glance, but can be explained by the difficulty in managing channel conflicts. The agent sales forces usually have substantial internal power in these organizations that allows them to push back at the development of competing channels. Furthermore, incumbents have been much slower to react to emerging trends than the smaller attackers in the market. Nonetheless, incumbents should be able to turn this around. They should leverage their strong relationships in the financial services market and their strong brand power to become market leaders in alternative distribution channels and bancassurance. By developing these channels parallel to their traditional sales forces, they also reduce the number of legacy issues they have to deal with and can set the aspiration of building best practice channel management capabilities. This might require them to hire the best talent and maybe even set up these new channels separate from the rest of the organization, to prevent channel conflicts.

Local incumbents should also look at new growth opportunities in related financial services. This might seem like a stretch given the enormous challenges in the core life business, but there are some obvious synergies within the financial sector that are worthy of consideration by large incumbent insurers. These have already been recognized by a number of local insurance companies who have expanded domestically into banking, for example, Cathay Life in Taiwan acquired the United World Chinese Commercial Bank (now Cathay United Bank) in 2001 and Ping An in China bought 89 percent of Shenzhen Commercial Bank (later renamed Ping An Bank) in 2006. On the surface, expansion into banking may look obvious. Analysts tout obvious synergies such as securing control over a captive bancassurance market, cross-selling and sharing information on the customer base, and creating back-office synergies. In practice though, synergies arising from insurance-bank combinations are very difficult to achieve. For example, the Allianz–Dresdner merger in Germany took many years to realize the expected distribution benefits, and the insurer eventually chose to break off the bank. Other mergers such as Travelers–Citigroup and Winterthur–Credit Suisse also demerged a few years later after it was found that the costs and complexity of integration outweighed the benefits. Another area of natural expansion into other financial services is asset management. Again, there are some obvious benefits with 80 percent of life insurance in Asia flowing into savings products. We have described the challenges and opportunities already, but again this is an area where incumbents can leverage their size and brand to create new growth horizons.

Meanwhile, some larger Asian life insurers are running out of expansion space in their domestic markets. This has led a number of companies to think about extending their reach into other Asian, and even global, markets. Many Taiwanese insurers, for example, have expanded into China, including Cathay Life, which formed a life insurance joint venture with China Eastern Airlines and Shin Kong, who has a joint venture with Hainan Airlines. Ping An dipped its toes into overseas markets by opening a branch office in Vietnam. The large Japanese insurers have also begun their journey towards a more international portfolio. Players like Nippon Life and Dai-ichi have already set up businesses in some Asian markets and have expressed their objective to raise revenues outside of Japan. For example, Dai-ichi, in July 2008, bought 24 percent of Ocean Life Insurance in Thailand, and in October 2008 completed its acquisition of its one–third stake in Tower Australia. So far, these have been relatively timid steps by the leading Asian incumbents, but they are likely to give rise to some much larger overseas steps as they become more comfortable with forays into these markets. Of course, not all of these will be successful moves—in fact the financial crisis in 2008 has made many acquisitions look very untimely—but from the vantage point of these incumbents, this could be a step that they can ill-afford not to take in the long term.

Smaller Foreign and Local Players

Chasing the large incumbents are the smaller foreign and local players. Most of these players have a much shorter history than the incumbents, and they have accumulated only single-digit market shares over several years. The strategic imperatives for these players depend on whether they are in more mature or nascent markets.

In many of the Asian markets the landgrab phase is over, and, consequently, smaller foreign and local players are likely to find it much more difficult to expand significantly beyond their current market position in a short period of time. Therefore, they need to choose whether to remain as fringe players with a similar model to the larger players or to find a niche they can dominate and potentially become much more profitable within that niche.

Across Asia, life insurance players are not very well differentiated. While the brands may differ in terms of history and recognition, the operating model and the target market are remarkably similar across all players. Most players today focus on the mass-market segment, and sell very similar products.

Smaller players can certainly survive in their current form for some time. Market growth is strong and there is still little pressure for consolidation. In fact, there seems to be relatively few scale benefits for the large players, and most of the smaller players have been able to enjoy healthy margins without experiencing the disadvantages arising their from their smaller size. With the largest players typically saddled with historical legacies and aging sales forces, there is little urgency for smaller players to change their business model radically. For these reasons, consolidation has not yet happened in these markets.

In fact, given their more nimble starting point, smaller players are better situated to capture the growth potential from these markets. The opportunity to create a differentiated branding and business model is large.

In mature markets, such as Japan, South Korea, and Taiwan, where customers are becoming more sophisticated and the competitors are well established, the niche for smaller companies is likely to be in distribution—for example, targeting high-touch, high-margin customers or innovating the operating model to deliver low-premium, low-margin products to the mass segment.

This is already evident in the more mature markets of South Korea and Japan where there is a growing proliferation of smaller, but highly successful, niche players. This includes ALICO's direct-channel strategy in Japan that mobilizes corporate agents to sell medical insurance, and ORIX Life's low-premium strategy, which uses the mail-order channel for low-margin policies. ALICO's market share jumped from 1 percent in 2000 to 4.8 percent in 2007.[4]

Most of these strategies involve pursuing niche distribution channels and developing different business models. This means acquiring different types of staff for specialized sales channels or focusing on niche products. As explained in previous chapters, Mirae Asset Life in South Korea was the first insurer to combine an insurance sales force with a deep focus on premium, asset-management products. Part of the strategy was to develop mini-retail investment centers in convenient locations alongside a roaming sales force that would bring potential clients to these centers for sales meetings. By the end of 2006, Mirae had established 47 so called "Financial Plazas" in convenient, middle-class locations throughout South Korea. Already, around 11 percent of Mirae Asset Group's mutual fund sales are through Mirae Asset Life, as compared to the industry average of less than 3 percent (see Box 5C).

Meanwhile, ING in South Korea provides an example of a player attacking the incumbents' housewife-dominated sales forces with agents who are mostly male, younger, and better educated and thus able to target a different customer base. And in Japan, Sompo Life successfully markets basic life insurance products using non-face-to-face methods. Its core product is a one-year, term-life insurance, which allows customers to review their insurance needs according to their life stage by adding riders for various types of cover, such as hospitalization, cancer, and income replacement insurance.

There are also the product specialists. For example, The Hartford, in Japan, concentrates solely on variable annuities and manages 22 percent of the total in-force sum assured, as of financial year 2006. Indeed it can be said that The Hartford created this market.

In less mature markets, the strategy for the smaller players can be quite different. In these markets, such as India and China, but also some of the Southeast Asian markets such as Vietnam or Indonesia, there is much more room for smaller players to participate in the natural growth of the market. These markets are still in landgrab mode, where the penetration of insurance to gross domestic product (GDP) is still low (2 percent in China and 4.3 percent in India). For smaller players in these markets, the business model need not necessarily be different from the large incumbents; instead, the focus should be on execution excellence and the development of a stronger management bench. Choosing the right channel mix and geographic focus is also important, as it is not feasible to expand nationwide without the proper management resources and for some foreign players, the proper licenses.

Execution excellence is key for the smaller players to succeed in these markets. But this is no small thing to achieve. Many of the smaller players in markets such as China and India have grown at breathtaking rates. They often struggle with a lack of management talent, poor operations, and a lack of control over highly entrepreneurial branch operations. For most of these smaller players, their ambitions should be outgrowing and outexecuting the large incumbents by a significant percentage. This is particularly true when they compete away from the more developed cities and drive deep into the hundreds of emerging second- and third-tier cities, where brand leadership is still wide open. But we believe few of the smaller companies will be able to achieve this—the operational challenges are enormous, even though they are at a smaller scale, and management talent is even harder to attract for these companies. Therefore, focus is a key success factor for these smaller attackers. Too often we have seen companies fail because they tried to do everything—every channel and every geography—at the same time, without the proper management bench, operations, and IT support in place.

Looking at the development of the past decade, there is no reason not to expect a handful of these smaller players to become large, dominant players over the next 10 years, especially in the rapidly growing markets. Leading players in China and India have built their current strong market position within the last 5–10 years. For example, ICICI–Prudential in India has grown its position only in the past few years. For some of today's smaller life insurers, dominance may come from a niche segment, either in terms of customers, distribution models, or products. But we also anticipate that many of the smaller players will struggle with their existing small and undifferentiated operating models. These players might be able to defend their current market share, and will even enjoy the natural growth of these markets for some years. They will probably still be quite profitable, and many will not see the urgency to change the way they operate and experiment with new initiatives. However, in the dynamic world of Asian life insurance, we see a lost opportunity for them to develop a stronger, more defensible niche and they will eventually come under a lot of pressure from larger and stronger players—they will be the first victims of a consolidation wave.

Well-Established Foreign Multinationals

A handful of foreign multinationals such as AIG, Prudential (UK), ING, and Manulife, already have a sizeable share in a number of Asian markets and generate a significant proportion of their global profit from this region. However large their current market positions, these players still only occupy a small share of the overall Asian market, but their future growth potential remains very significant. Total market share of all foreign players across Asia is 25 percent in 2008, and we see this increasing to 30–35 percent within the next 10 years.

The leading multinational players share a number of characteristics. They all have big positions in the "first generation" of Asian markets that have been open to foreign companies (for example, Hong Kong, Singapore, and Taiwan), while some have been first movers in emerging markets such as Indonesia, the Philippines, and Thailand. They have built most of their operations

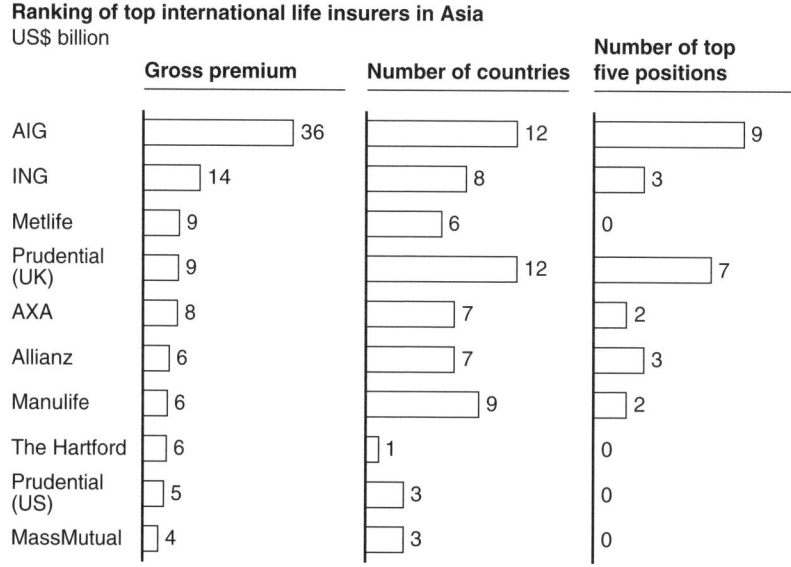

Figure 8.3 Some MNC players have established an extensive footprint in Asia

Source: Regulatory bodies in various countries

organically, with only a handful of acquisitions over the years. All of them have built sizeable Asian management teams which are headquartered in Hong Kong.

Landgrabbing in China and India

The top priority for these multinational leaders is rapid expansion in the large, emerging, landgrab markets, meaning China and India, which promise the strongest potential for growth over the next decades. As matters stand, their current presence in these markets is very small compared to their overall Asia business, mainly because they have been constrained by regulations. However, significant deregulation has started, and, as such, the potential for growth is now mainly constrained by their execution capacity. For example, in India the market is currently open for joint ventures to operate freely, and in China licenses for previously restricted cities are being granted at an accelerated pace. Given the large scale of these countries, the multinationals need to place their bets in a few key geographies as well as move into the vastly underpenetrated hinterland. For instance, ICICI–Prudential, through a bancassurance tie-up with 10 regional rural banks, has access to about 10,000 rural and semi-rural bank branches in five Indian states.

The challenge cannot be overstated. A few decades ago, when the first multinationals entered Asia, they were often the only ones blazing the trail and played a large role in developing the industry. They were seen as the most desired employers by agents and staff, and their brand names carried significant premium to the local companies. Today, the competitive landscape is quite different. Due to the enormous growth prospects in Asia, many more multinationals are frantically entering these markets, even if they have had very little presence in Asia before. In China, there were 23 multinational life joint ventures as of December 2007, and many more are applying for their joint venture license today. In India, there were 18 joint ventures in operation in mid-2008, all competing ferociously across the country. For the few large multinational players who have been providing the main foreign presence in other parts of Asia for decades, the challenge they face in developing their presence in these countries is unprecedented in their history in Asia.

While the challenge is large, these large multinationals do have a significant advantage over their fellow foreign entrants: a strong Asia management bench and long experience of operating in the Asian market environment. Over the past decades, these MNCs have built up a management team that has been successfully operating across many Asian countries. Given their tested operating models and their experience in penetrating high-growth markets, they do have an advantage over less experienced peers, who are mostly betting on a few key hires, or sometimes, counting on their local joint-venture partners to develop their presence.

Capturing Share from Local Incumbents in Mature Markets Such as Japan and South Korea

Apart from landgrabbing in China and India, another growth opportunity for these MNCs is capturing share from the local incumbents in mature markets, especially in Japan and South Korea. In the past, MNCs have not been able to capture a large share of the domestic market in the life insurance business. However, these markets are now at an inflection point for the MNCs—while the local incumbents are fixing their large, legacy sales forces, new channels and products have opened up potential for other players to build market positions in these segments.

The strategy to capture share from the local incumbents is straight-forward. Either these MNCs can outexecute the locals, or they need to develop niche segments. Both of these strategies can work. For example, in many markets the MNCs have an edge in recruiting, training, and infra-structure support since they are leveraging across Asia many of the best practices and tools they have developed. Furthermore, MNCs have been successful in building niche segments, such as The Hartford in variable annuities and AFLAC in medical insurance.

Protecting the Franchise in Established Geographies

The challenge in the more established geographies for the leading MNCs such as Hong Kong, Singapore, and some Southeast Asian markets, such as Thailand, is quite different. In these geographies, the large, foreign MNCs have to defend what they have already built up. In fact, because they were often first movers they have now reached the stage where they need to revitalize their organizations in the face of renewed competition. It is a role reversal—some of these MNC insurers, once seen as attackers and first movers in Asia, are now local incumbents targeted by local upstarts. In recent years, some of these MNC leaders have lost share across some of their strongest markets in Asia to local attackers and other MNC entrants. The MNCs need to ensure that the sales forces in these established countries do not get complacent and live off their accumulated book of business—that they continue to upgrade and attack the market. Product innovation is also important to keep up with developments in the market—these lead-ing MNCs must not lose the competitive edge that made them successful in the first place.

Maximizing Synergies Across Asia

While it is not easy to capture synergies across Asia due to the differ-ing landscapes, languages, and regulations, leading MNCs should use the advantage of their regional network by maximizing synergies across their operations. Historically, many of these companies have taken a very entrepreneurial approach and expanded quickly in each market, often as distinctive business units led by entrepreneurial managers. This business model worked well when the foreign entrant first established itself because it allowed a large degree of flexibility for country managers. But as the Asia headquarters of the leading MNCs built up, these MNCs have now developed into more complex-matrix organizations with myriad functional and geographic lines. In such organizations, some form of standardization and best practice sharing can yield important benefits.

Front-office synergies such as cross-regional training, proprietary selling tools and techniques, and common product development tools can give leading Asian MNCs an advantage over their less regional peers. Synergies across the back office are much harder to achieve, but when done properly, can yield substantial benefits. While not all processes can be operated centrally in the regional headquarters or back-office processing units, in critical areas such as underwriting, investment management, and risk management, building a strong central function can both lower cost and increase the quality of risk control in the various operating units. It is important to note though, that due to the huge differences between the various countries in Asia, capturing back-office synergies for the leading MNCs is only at an early stage. During this process, it is also common to hear lots of complaints from country managements on the inflexibility and bureaucracy from such an approach. At this stage, it is unproven to what extent these back-office synergies will give these MNCs a true cost and operational efficiency advantage over the local players.

Lastly, one of the most important advantages of these leading MNCs is their strong management team and their understanding of the opportunities in Asia. For example, leading MNCs in the region are much quicker to decide on mergers and acquisitions (M&A) opportunities, as well as capturing growing niches in certain markets compared to their less experienced peers. This strength in management is difficult to quantify—in fact, for some it may appear as a bloated regional management structure. However, when compared with other MNCs who have little local management presence in Asia, it is clear that the leading MNCs have built a much better starting position to capture the growth opportunities in these markets.

Emerging Foreign Multinationals

Almost every international insurance company has looked at opportunities in Asia and by now, most have some sort of presence. By the beginning of 2008, of the top 30, listed, non-Asian insurers in the world,[5] 25 had established some form of life insurance operation in one or more Asian countries. Allstate, Great-West, Power, Loews, and Lincoln National are the only five insurers out of the top 30 not to have any Asian presence.

However, up till now, there are only a handful of MNCs that have established a significant presence across multiple Asian countries. Most of the newer MNC players have only ramped up their presence in the region over the last five years and have achieved no more than small market shares in a very limited number of Asian markets. The operating environment for these MNCs is very different from that found by their more established peers who arrived in Asia 10–20 years earlier. Today, competition is far more intense and the opportunity to be a first mover no longer exists. Newcomers need to arrive in the region with considerable capital and patience because breaking even will take at least 6–8 years when the strategy is to build captive agent distribution. And they need to devote substantial management attention—in fact, for many it seems disproportionate attention—to markets that show little immediate prospect of contributing in a meaningful way to profits at the group level.

This raises a number of difficult, and possibly unanswerable, questions. How should they think about Asia as a market, given their currently small position and the challenges in establishing a meaningful franchise? Which market should they place their bets on—the mature or the more developing—each with their very different risk-return profiles? How long will it take before the Asian business becomes a meaningful part of the total group value and returns some cash to start contributing significantly to the bottom line of the group? Should they "test the waters" or lay down a substantial investment? How will they set about building relationships in the region and should they attempt to go it alone or seek partners? Are there suitable acquisitions that can be viable shortcuts? How and where to build a regional headquarters to manage the Asian portfolio? Lastly, are the markets in China and India "too difficult to enter" or "too large to ignore?"

Is it too late to enter Asia? Have we already missed the boat? These questions are often asked by those foreign insurers who are not yet in the region or who have only a small presence in the market. The answer depends on the time frame. If one adopts a long-term horizon, the answer clearly is no. There is no doubt that there are still going to be substantial changes in the market dynamics in virtually all of these Asian countries, and the market landscape in 10 years time will look very different from the one that can be seen today. Many Asian markets, in particular China and India, are still at an early stage of their development curve. Penetration is still low and the growth story of the last 5–10 years could easily continue for another couple of decades. With this perspective, entering Asia now is still plausible, despite the market being much more competitive than before.

Even in the most mature market in Asia, Japan, there are plenty of examples of new players entering the market at the right time, with the right product, and taking market share despite a highly competitive and closed market. These examples include AFLAC's cancer insurance in the 1980s and The Hartford's variable annuities in the early 2000s. These players entered in a specific niche, and had a high level of commitment to their entry efforts. These results are highly encouraging, and demonstrate the point that, even in Japan, there are plenty of success stories.

Choosing an appropriate partner is often a critical part of the strategy. The regulations in China and India dictate that foreign companies need to have a local joint venture partner. In other countries this is not a necessity but could be a powerful entry model. The key success factors for joint ventures are the same as elsewhere: there needs to be a good understanding of each partner's intentions; concrete areas of added value or contribution between the partners; and the development of a shared culture within the joint venture. In circumstances where the partnership is created out of regulatory necessity only, it is critical to have an understanding of what happens when regulatory limitations are lifted.

Not surprisingly, there are many examples of joint-venture failures. One American insurer's joint-venture foray in South Korea proves a good example. Due to differences and miscommunications between the MNC and the local partner, this joint venture led ultimately to financial problems as well as lawsuits for the parent companies. The company made a US$60 million loss in 2001 and in the same year sold its stake to a domestic competitor. A more recent example can be found in India. In 2005, Australia's AMP exited the Indian market by selling its stake to Reliance Capital, citing a strategic decision to focus on its wealth-management business in

Australia and New Zealand. Its local joint-venture partner, Chennai-based Sanmar Group, sold its stake to Reliance as well.

Apart from joint ventures, acquisitions could be part of the entry strategy. Generally, there are not that many available targets in Asia, but there have been success cases. In its early years in Asia, AIG acquired Nanshan in Taiwan while Prudential (UK) bought Chinfon as it entered the same market. More recently MassMutual bought Protective Life in Hong Kong, while Aviva partnered with Woori, a South Korean financial group, to buy LIG Life in South Korea. Manulife, AIG, and AXA all acquired existing firms when entering the Japan market. A few of these acquisitions worked especially well—in most of these cases the MNC buyers actively changed the operating model of the acquired business. For example, Manulife's premium income grew sixfold within four years after its acquisition by using its variable annuity expertise from the US market and building a strong channel relationship with the Tokyo-Mitsubishi bank. At the same time, as with all acquisitions, there are many more cases where the acquisition failed as culture clashes took time to digest. For example, AXA's premiums declined by 25 percent within the first four years of buying Nippon Dantai in Japan.

Going forward, acquisitions are not likely to play a big role in MNC entry into the region, since there are not that many acquisition targets. There are many reasons for this. First, all the pan-Asian franchises are owned by large MNCs who have voiced no intention of scaling back their Asia operations (with the exception of AIG who will likely sell a part or all of its Asian operations after its bailout from the US government). Second, many local Asian insurers are family-owned (especially in Taiwan and South Korea), and they often see the insurance company as a family jewel in a larger, diversified group of businesses. Third, even if acquisition targets are available, they are usually not in the fastest-growing markets since no one wants to trade away their growth story. Furthermore, prices for these scarce opportunities have been high and are likely to remain so. Therefore, while acquisitions will happen, this will remain an opportunistic strategy for MNCs seeking expansion in Asia. Nonetheless, events such as the 2008 financial crisis may create unique opportunities for aggressive acquirers to buy assets that would not normally be available during normal market conditions.

Asia will continue to be a highly attractive marketplace in the next decade. Notwithstanding the certain volatility that comes with these markets, growth prospects are very strong—in particular, compared to the Western markets in Europe and North America. Forty percent of global premium growth in the next five years will be generated in Asia. Also, margins continue to be very attractive and generally much higher than in more mature international markets. This offers plenty of opportunities for local companies and foreign players alike. At the same time, the life insurance industry in Asia is at an inflection point. Competition is getting much tougher, many new players have entered the arena, and the recipes for success are changing dramatically. In this chapter, we have outlined what it takes for life insurers to become, or remain, a winner in Asia in the next decade. We are convinced that in 10 years the competitive landscape will look quite different from now. We will see some familiar names in the list of top performers, but also some unknown or new ones. For sure, the prize of winning in Asia will only go to those who have a clear strategy of how to outperform competitors in the region, and the execution ability to implement that plan. For those who are prepared, the next decade in Asia will bring another enormous opportunity for growth and value creation.

Appendix

Reference Sources

Association of Vietnam Insurers
Australian Prudential Regulation Authority
Bank Negara Malaysia
China Insurance Regulatory Commission
Economist Intelligence Unit
Financial Supervisory Service, South Korea
Global Insight
Insurance Bureau, Ministry of Finance, Indonesia
Insurance Commission, Philippines
Insurance Regulatory and Development Authority, India
Insurance Research Institute, Japan
Life Insurance Association of Japan
Monetary Authority of Singapore
Department of Insurance, Ministry of Commerce, Thailand
Office of the Commissioner of Insurance, Hong Kong
Plan for Life, Australia
Swiss Re Sigma
Taiwan Insurance Institute

Statistical Table

Table A.1

	Unit	Australia	China	Hong Kong	India	Indonesia	Japan	Malaysia	Philippines	Singapore	South Korea	Taiwan	Thailand	Vietnam
Macroeconomic data in 2007														
Gross domestic product (GDP) 2007	US$ bn	960	3,416	207	1,193	421	4,603	194	161	169	963	388	252	72
GDP per capita 2007	US$	44,091	2,586	29,858	1,018	1,819	36,031	7,301	1,830	38,065	19,673	16,974	3,911	819
Purchasing power parity (PPP) GDP per capita	US$	37,757	8,217	43,376	5,264	4,885	33,325	15,313	4,922	41,345	19,116	28,525	11,144	4,018
Institutional assets under management	US$ bn	0	n/a	174	16	n/a	3,765	18	0	n/a	326	137	10	n/a
Personal financial assets (PFA)	US$ bn	0	1,508	314	285	70	12,482	194	0	299	939	741	132	0
Foreign reserve	US$ bn	62	1,166	133	196	40	914	91	25	150	244	267	73	13
Foreign debt	US$ bn	825	346,008	72,503	152,887	128,468	n/a	55,983	77,534	26,872	190,918	91,688	66,240	20,919
Socioeconomic data in 2007														
Population	millions	21	1,314	7	1,120	225	128	26	84	4	49	23	65	85
Number of households	thousands	7,723	379,760	2,226	209,886	59,650	49,390	5,678	17,480	1,039	17,550	7,260	17,500	25,600
Median household income	US$	49,420	2,930	39,080	2,600	2,420	45,770	10,100	2,410	60,990	25,630	25,180	4,680	1,230
% households earning >US$10k pa	percent	93%	3%	87%	5%	6%	100%	50%	5%	99%	95%	98%	17%	1%
Urbanization	% of population	89%	41%	100%	29%	49%	66%	68%	63%	100%	65%	n/a	33%	27%
% of population older than 65 in 2005	percent	13%	8%	12%	5%	5%	20%	5%	4%	8%	9%	n/a	7%	5%
% of population older than 65 in 2025	percent	n/a	15%	26%	10%	10%	28%	11%	9%	26%	20%	n/a	15%	10%
Life insurance data in 2007														
Gross written premiums (GWP) 2007	US$ bn	36	68	20	52	5	325	7	2	13	85	50	6	1
Life insurance penetration	percent	4%	2%	10%	4%	1%	7%	3%	1%	7%	9%	13%	2%	1%
Life insurance density	US$ bn	40	162	31	123	13	325	10	4	18	108	68	10	2
Life insurance assets	US$ bn	219	318	64	217	n/a	2,137	31	9	73	318	265	24	n/a
Investment-linked%	percent	76%	8%	39%	66%	31%	n/a	49%	74%	42%	23%	37%	n/a	0%
Bancassurance%	percent	n/a	34%	38%	9%	25%	n/a	n/a	n/a	19%	40%	34%	28%	n/a
Number of life insurers		32	53	66	17	46	41	16	36	13	22	31	24	7
Number of foreign life insurers		n/a	24	82	18	16	17	13	8	10	8	16	12	7
Foreign share of GWP 2007	percent	27%	6%	71%	18%	56%	18%	55%	74%	59%	19%	38%	65%	65%
Year foreign entry allowed		1980s	1992	n/a	2000	1975	1954	1924	1895	1931	1986	1987	1938	1999

Methodology

All figures have been converted to US$ at the following fixed exchange rates:

Exchange rate of local currency per US$, as of December 31, 2007

Country	Exchange rate per US$
China	7.3041
Hong Kong	7.798099968
Taiwan	32.4345
South Korea	936.1499973
Singapore	1.439999826
India	39.34749857
Japan	111.9449944
Vietnam	16015.84391
Philippines	41.27993944
Thailand	33.685
Malaysia	3.30749811
Indonesia	9392.997338
Australia	1.139299965

- Data for India and Japan occurs on financial year basis, unless otherwise noted: April 1–March 31.
- The total industry figures for South Korea are on the basis of the calendar year: January 1–December 31. All other figures are on the basis of the financial year cycle: April 1–March 31.

Notes

Chapter 1—Life Insurance in Asia: Winning in the Next Decade

1 All references to "Asia ex-Japan" in this book exclude Australia and the rest of Oceania, as well as Japan. References to "12 Asian markets" include all geographies in this book except Australia.
2 All historical monetary figures are calculated on a constant exchange rate basis to cancel out the effect of currency fluctuations.
3 Economist Intelligence Unit (EIU) projections.

Chapter 2—Emerging Themes in Asia

1 A ratio that measures a company's overall after-tax profitability from underwriting and investment activity, often compared to Return on Equity. It is calculated by taking the sum of after-tax net income and unrealized capital gains and dividing it by the mean of prior and current year-end policyholder surplus. Policyholder surplus is defined as the sum of paid-in capital, paid-in and contributed surplus, and net earned surplus, including voluntary contingency reserves.
2 Mortality coverage defined as sum assumed of whole and term life products, which tends to be pure protection.
3 Economist Intelligence Unit.
4 Annual household income less than US$3,500.
5 McKinsey Global Institute.
6 http://aspe.hhs.gov/poverty/figures-fed-reg.shtml.
7 AIG Form 10-k—The remaining 33 percent is derived from Japan and other geographies (Europe, Latin America, the Middle East, and Africa), with Japan taking the bulk of that premium.
8 "Prudential plc says Asia's share of profit rising," September 28, 2007, Reuters News.
9 AIG, Berkshire Hathaway, ING, Allianz, AXA, State Farm, Generali, Manulife, Metlife, and Aviva; China Life was ranked fourth in the world, but excluded in this analysis.
10 McKinsey consumer survey, 2007.
11 *Joongang Daily*, ADB, IMF.
12 Example deposit product with the yield = 2.5 percent, medium accessibility, free ATM withdrawal with charge for transfer.
13 Now defunct.

Chapter 3—China and India: Yes, Size Does Matter

1 Gareth Powell, "China's race to build roads, railways and airports," *Economic Review,* February 20, 2008.

2 Calum MacLeod, "China in a flurry of airport construction," *USA Today,* October 3, 2006.

3 "Airports in China, India struggle to cope with air travel boom," *Platts Commodity News,* September 4, 2007.

4 McKinsey estimates, based on data from various local regulatory bodies, and Global Insight.

5 Economist Intelligence Unit.

6 McKinsey Global Institute China Urbanization Initiative. Includes cities and towns with a population of over 500,000.

7 Economist Intelligence Unit. Household saving sate is (personal disposable income – private consumption)/personal disposable income.

8 *International Directory of Company Histories,* (1994), Volume 65.

9 All references to "foreign players" in China include both joint ventures with a foreign partner and wholly foreign-owned entities.

10 Hospitals in China are categorized as either Class I (township and county level), Class II (100–500 beds), or Class III (over 500 beds).

11 2006 Insurance Information Institute rankings of global Fortune 500 companies; revenues include life and non-life premium and annuity income, investment income, and capital gains or losses, but exclude deposits; also includes consolidated subsidiaries and excludes excise taxes.

12 Financial Year April 2007-March 2008.

13 Proprietary McKinsey market research.

14 Insurance Regulatory Development Agency.

15 Census of India; *Yearbook of China's Cities 2007;* China INFOBANK.

16 Including former Eastern European bloc (Russia, Ukraine, Romania, Belarus, Poland, Serbia, Czech Republic, Bulgaria).

17 McKinsey Global Institute; urban centers defined as cities and towns with a population of over 500,000.

18 Defined as upper aspirant and lower aspirant (annual income between US$1,400–5,500).

19 Andrew Grant and Diana Farrell. "Addressing China's Looming Talent Shortage," McKinsey Global Institute, October, 2005.

20 First year premium per agent per month.

21 Economist Intelligence Unit; based on a per annum household income of US$10,000.

22 "Future eyes 'mallassurance,'" *Business Standard,* May 21, 2008.

Chapter 4—Japan: New Tricks in an Old Market

1 Includes private and postal insurance, but not *kyosai.*

2 April 06–March 07 figures; includes private and postal insurance, but not *kyosai.*

3 Private and postal insurance, but not *kyosai.*

4 *Cooperative Insurance in Japan 2007 Factbook,* (Japan Cooperative Insurance Association Incorporated, 2007), p. 1.

5 Individual whole-life, term-life, and endowment products.

6 Refers to non-Japan Post Insurance, non-*kyosai* business only.

7 Japan Post Insurance generated US$87 billion worth of life insurance gross premium in 2006, and is the single-largest insurer in Japan.

8 Whole-life, term-life, and endowment products, excluding Japan Post Isurance.

9 2006 Insurance Information Institute rankings of global Fortune 500 companies; revenues include life and non-life premium and annuity income, investment income, and capital gains or losses, but exclude deposits; also includes consolidated subsidiaries and excludes excise taxes.

10 As of December 2006: listed companies by market capitalization; private companies by McKinsey's valuation of the world's largest unlisted companies—Japanese insurers were valued at 0 percent perpetual growth on 2005–06 average return on equity (ROE).

11 "Ongoing Change in Japan's Life Insurance Industry," *JETRO, Japan Economic Monthly*, (August, 2005), http://www.jetro.go.jp/en/market/report/pdf/2005_48_m.pdf.

12 Sayuri Shiraishi, "Life Insurance Company Failures and Policyholder Protection," *JCER Researcher Report*, 59, (June, 2005), http://www.jcer.or.jp/eng/pdf/kenrep050421e.pdf.

13 *Statistics of Life Insurance Business in Japan*, 2006.

14 Based on financial year results; newsletter on Pension and Investments.

15 "Big Life Insurers To Skip Dividends On Group Annuities," *The Nihon Keizai Shimbun*, May 6, 2002.

16 United Nations Population Database.

17 "Don't Grow Old," *The Economist*, December 18, 2003.

18 Japan Post Annual Report.

Chapter 5—Asian Tigers: Maturing Markets Still Going Strong

1 Economist Intelligence Unit.

2 Mortality sum assured = sum assured from term-life, whole-life, and group-life insurance; excludes linked, endowments, and annuities.

3 http://www.tdctrade.com/imn/02012404/insurance02.htm.

4 Direct insurers refer to insurance firms that are engaged in primary insurance business, as opposed to reinsurance or captive insurance.

Chapter 6—Southeast Asia: Back on a Growth Trajectory

1 World Bank. Ranking is based on various factors including: starting a business, dealing with licenses, employing workers, registering property, getting credit, protecting investors, paying taxes, trading across borders, enforcing contracts, and closing a business.

Chapter 7—Australia: Light at the End of the Tunnel?

1 "World Insurance in 2007: Emerging markets leading the way," *Plan for Life*, Swiss Re Sigma, No. 3, 2008.
   Note: All values converted from Australian dollars on December 31, 2007 at an exchange rate of AUD 1 = USD 0.8777.

2 APRA Life Office Market Report, December 2007.

3 AXA 2007 Protection Report.

4 AMP 2007 AMP Superannuation Adequacy Index Report, released January 2008.

5 CommInsure Life Insurance Survey, 2004.

6 ANZ 2005 Financial Literacy report.

7 Plan for Life, 2007, Life Insurance Industry Report and Australian Retail and Wholesale Investments Market Share and Dynamics report.

Chapter 8—The Next Decade: What it Takes to Win in Asia

1 Financial year statistics for South Korea, Financial Supervisory Services.

2 Derek Thompson, "Green Isn't Gold for MBAs," *Businessweek*, January 15, 2008.

3 Market value as of December 2006; listed companies by market capitalization; private companies by McKinsey's valuation of the world's largest unlisted companies—Japanese insurers were valued at 0 percent perpetual growth on 2005–06 average return on equity (ROE).

4 Private insurance + Japan Post Insurance.

5 Includes both life-only and multi-line insurers. Australia's AMP also included.

Index